FOLLOWING CHRIST

*God's Word:
Basic Truths and
Guiding Principles*

Be a light! Matthew 5:14-16

Jan Bloch

Jan Cameron Bloch

Following Christ
Gods Word: Basic Truths and Guiding Principles
All Rights Reserved.
Copyright © 2024 Jan Cameron Bloch
v13.0

The opinions expressed in this manuscript are solely the opinions of the author and do not represent the opinions or thoughts of the publisher. The author has represented and warranted full ownership and/or legal right to publish all the materials in this book.

This book may not be reproduced, transmitted, or stored in whole or in part by any means, including graphic, electronic, or mechanical without the express written consent of the publisher except in the case of brief quotations embodied in critical articles and reviews.

Outskirts Press, Inc.
http://www.outskirtspress.com

Paperback ISBN: 978-1-9772-4703-2
Hardback ISBN: 978-1-9772-4709-4

Cover Design © 2024 Jessica Hoft. All rights reserved - used with permission.

Outskirts Press and the "OP" logo are trademarks belonging to Outskirts Press, Inc.

PRINTED IN THE UNITED STATES OF AMERICA

TO: _____

FROM: _____

DATE: _____

MESSAGE: _____
_____
_____
_____

Cover Design by Jessica Hoft

Jessica loves the Lord and is grateful for opportunities to bring honor and glory to God. Jessica and her husband Daron are the proud parents of two boys. They reside in Columbia, SC where Jessica teaches elementary students in the gifted education program.

To Andrew, Julianna, Justin, Lacy, Lizzy, and beloved family past and present for believing and living with faith in Jesus as the cornerstone of life. May your lives touch thousands of others for our Lord. To my future family, whoever you are, wherever you live, I am eager to welcome you into our family and for you to be a part of our lives.

Preface

Life can be a frustrating existence when it is limited to worldly perspectives, advice, and vision. Traveling through each day, the decisions you make will impact tomorrow's happenings. The Holy Bible is the accurate Word of God, given to you so you may have a relationship with him. It is designed to show you the way to salvation. By the grace of God, he will enable you to cope with and conquer your life's trials on earth and give you peace knowing you will be with God through eternity.

This book is an easy-to-read guide to the fundamental truths and principles of *The Holy Bible*, our Lord's guide to salvation and living life on earth. The narratives will provide an overview of the doctrines of the Christian faith and explain how to intertwine faith in daily life experiences. With the help of God, this insight will allow the reader to discover how to make a habit of everyday practices, in both thoughts and actions, which are pleasing to the Lord. To follow the guidance of Jesus Christ is the most crucial decision made each day.

"Pollster George Gallup contends that fewer than ten percent of evangelical Christians could be called deeply committed. Most of those who profess Christianity don't know basic teachings and don't act differently because of their Christian experience."[1] The Word of God offers a path to a life of purpose and peace, confidence and boldness. This book is about how to find the path God has designed for you, and how to make choices that bring honor to God. As you read these pages, ask God to teach and direct you. If you feel powerless, God's promise of hope is available to you, and his power will bring victory over darkness.

The book is divided into four sections: Understanding Your Faith, Living Your Faith, Developing Godly Character, and Developing Healthy Relationships. The topics within each section succinctly identify an essential principle of faith, followed by a brief narrative of how you can apply that principle. Intermittently, themes will be reinforced by poems or lyrics to hymns. The challenges of life will remain. However, the decision to proclaim Jesus as Lord, accept his grace and forgiveness, and follow his guidance, will provide clarity to your life. Thus, you are equipped with a lens through which to view the world with an eternal perspective, and divine purpose.

If you are reading this book on your own or with others, you will gain a greater understanding if you read a topic and allow yourself time to absorb the content before moving to the next issue. As you progress through the book, make a list of the specific areas in which you would like to grow: faith practices, character, relationships. Pray for God to work in your life and help you make these changes. Study scriptures - this material is not a substitute for studying the Holy Bible. Tell a trusted friend of your goals and ask if they might become an accountability partner. And finally, ask forgiveness of those you have wronged. As you move to make different choices in the days ahead, remember change takes time and is a process. May God bless you as you journey to discover a genuine faith and belief system that will lead to a life of grace, peace, hope, and love given to you by your Lord and Savior, Jesus Christ.

A Note from the Author

This book began as a compilation of easily read and understood letters written to my two teenage children. The initial letters have been revised; however, the manuscripts still focus on understanding the value of faith, character, and relationships and how this information impacts one's life and choices. The materials may provide valuable tools for communicating and identifying the important concepts necessary for developing a solid faith in our Lord Jesus Christ and living a purposeful life. Although initially intended for teenagers, the content is helpful for all people confronted with important daily decisions and who want to feel the wonder of a life committed to God. I hope that this book will allow the reader to discover a genuine faith and belief system, gain knowledge about how to simply live life in a more pleasing way to God, and find God's love, salvation, peace, contentment, and purpose. May God guide you on this journey as you allow him to make your life a blessing.

"Finally, beloved, whatever is true, whatever is honorable, whatever is just, whatever is pure, whatever is pleasing, whatever is commendable, if there is any excellence and if there is anything worthy of praise, think about these things." Philippians 4:8

Acknowledgments

My loving thanks to:

God has chosen my path, provided godly mentors, and has been faithful to his promise. Thank you for the wisdom and creativity to write this book. And thank you for salvation through Jesus Christ's death and resurrection.

Doug Bloch, a faithful follower of Christ, a wonderful husband, good friend, and companion, who has shown me great love and support through the completion of this project and every other challenge;

My dear children, Andrew Cameron, Julianna, and Justin Williamson, for their patience and willingness to hang in there as we faced the many joys and challenges of developing a healthy family;

My grandchildren, Lacy and Lizzy Williamson, and the beloved ones I am yet to know. Thank you for the special bond of love, appreciation, fun, and joy;

My faithful niece Jessica Hoft has given support for this journey with encouragement, suggestions, custom cover design, and editing skills;

My dear nieces Annie Hymer, CJ Merrill, Jessica Hoft, and their families as they influence others and me to continually strive to live according to God's Word;

My extended family, Mike, Jane, Trevor, and Trenton Roebke, for the priceless gift of love and friendship shown to my family and me.

To my late parents, Joe and Hester Cain, for telling me the story of Jesus and for the values, love, and commitment they instilled;

To my late sisters, Jo Roebke and Jean Campbell Vogt, for their unconditional love and acceptance throughout my childhood;

To my friends in God's Lunch Bunch for the insightful instruction, commitment to scripture, and unfailing dedication to our Lord;

To my dear friend and author representative, Deni Sinteral-Scott, who has been supportive of my project and has offered kind instruction, encouragement, and patience;

To Dr. Steve Fortosis for his scholarship and editing skills. He has been generous in thinking about the message of this book and clearly communicated how others could utilize the text and benefit.

Finally, thank you to everyone who purchases and reads this book.

Table of Contents

Preface i
A Note from the Author iii
Acknowledgments iv

Understanding Your Faith 1
What is Faith? 3
The Bible Is -The Doctrine of Faith and God's Law 5
Who is God? 8
The Apostles' Creed – I Believe 13
Jesus Fulfilled Old Testament Prophecies 16
Jesus Birth Foretold in the Scriptures 20
Blessed Christmas – Jesus' Birth 22
Names of Christ 26
Jesus – A Man of Miracles 30
Jesus' Power to Overcome Disease 31
    The Man with Leprosy 31
    Jesus Heals a Paralytic 32
    Jesus Heals the Sick 32
Jesus' Power to Overcome Nature 34
    Jesus Calms a Storm 34
    Jesus Feeds Five Thousand 35
    Jesus Walks on Water 35
Jesus' Power to Overcome Demons 36
    Jesus Drives out an Evil Spirit 36

      Healing the Boy with an Evil Spirit 37
      Following Jesus' Crucifixion and Resurrection,
      He Appears to Mary Magdalene 37
Jesus' Power to Overcome Death 39
      Jesus Raises a Widow's Son 39
      A Dead Girl 40
      Jesus' Death, Appearances after
      Death, and His Resurrection 40
The Life Jesus Lived Daily 41
Jesus – A Man of Emotion 44
Jesus – A Man of Prayer 46
The Lord's Prayer 50
The Beatitudes 53
Jesus is the Light 56
Jesus' Death, Resurrection, and Ascension into Heaven 59
Jesus' Gift - Eternal Life for the Believer 62
Holy Spirit 66
Fruits of the Spirit 70
Spiritual Gifts 72
Heaven 75
Hell - Sin and Its Consequences - Judgment 79
Salvation 83
Repentance 86
Grace 88
Baptism 91
Holy Communion 93
A Look Ahead: Humbly Share God's Love 97
Marriage – A Covenant with God 102
The Cost of Discipleship –The Great Commission 105
Christ Saves You and Me 109
The Church 111
Hymns of Praise 114
Related Scriptures 117

Living Your Faith 121
What Would Jesus Do? 123
Hope, Joy, Peace, and Love 125
Jesus' Passion 129
A Heart for God 131
Your Calling - Simplified 134
Purpose in Life 138
God's Children – Chosen and Called 141
Christian Qualities 144
Breath Prayers 147
My Best Friend 150
Spiritual Growth - Habits of Faith 153
Trust God - He Is There For You 155
Live For Today 158
Discover Genuine Freedom 161
Don't Worry What Others Think 164
The Gift of Time - You Cannot Do It All 167
Lessons from the Mountain -1- 169
Lessons from the Mountain -2- 172
Jesus' Lesson about Revenge 174
Living on Earth - Why Is It So Difficult? 177
Trials for God – Bearing a Cross 180
Service Requirements 184
Hardened Hearts 186
Prayer 188
Right with God 191
Learn by Doing - Start Today 194
The Christian Frame of Mind 196
Related Scriptures 200

Developing Godly Character 203
The Gift of God's Armor – Understand and Use It 205
Defining Yourself – Self-worth 208
Your Own Unique Character 211

Seek Wisdom 213
Know and Honor Boundaries 217
Courage – Integrity 221
Responsibility 224
Responsibility to God 226
Time Used Wisely 229
Heartaches – Pain and Confusion 232
Spiritual Obedience 235
Wisdom and Wealth - A Spiritual Guide -1- 237
Wisdom and Wealth – A Spiritual Guide -2- 240
Sense of Humor 243
Anger – Give It to God 247
Forgiveness: Let Go of Grudges/Bitterness 252
Asking For Forgiveness 255
Power of the Tongue – Choose Your Words Wisely 258
Self-Talk – The Voice in Your Head 260
What Attracts Others to You? 265
Healthy Habits 268
Extend Hospitality – Greetings and Farewells 271
Allow People to Be Human – Love or Respect Them Regardless . 275
Christian Responsibilities to the Community 277
Hope – Reliance upon God 279
Related Scriptures 281

Developing Healthy Relationships 285
Love, Marriage, and Family 287
Friendship – A Precious Gift 290
May the Lord Bless and Keep You 293
Date with a Purpose 295
Stages in Relationships 299
How Serious Is Your Relationship 302
Choose a Godly Mate 305
Unacceptable Behaviors in a Partner 308
Prepare Yourself for Marriage 312

Effective Communication - Levels 317
Effective Communication – Set the Stage 320
Family Communication – Plan Ahead.. 323
Build Opportunities to Communicate 326
Difficulties from Your Past – Trust God, Love Yourself, and Heal .. 328
Husbands, Wives and Children – Powerful Choices.................... 334
Love In Action –God's Perfect Example... 339
Honor One Another 343
Bring Out the Best in Your Partner... 345
Love Life – Sex in Marriage... 349
Family Matters... 352
Broken Families... 356
Family Tradition 360
Some Traditions Need to be Broken 362
Families Grow and Change... 365
Praying Together 367
Related Scriptures.. 370

Afterword 372
Bibliography 376
Endnotes.. 380
About the Author 384

Understanding Your Faith

WHAT DOES IT mean to be a follower of Jesus Christ, a Christian? The answer lies in understanding and believing the fundamental doctrine of the Christian faith. This section, written in a concise, simple manner will enable the reader to develop that understanding. It is intended for those who have little or no knowledge of the Christian faith, or as reflection for long-time followers of Christ. The beliefs stated within this section are the basis for the remainder of these writings.

THROUGH SCRIPTURE, WE learn that God wishes to be in a relationship with each of us. He also desires to share the rich benefits of his love and the gift of everlasting life. Peter tells us in his book 2 Peter 1:4, "Thus he has given us, through these things, his precious and very great promises, so that through them you may escape from the corruption that is in the world ... and may become participants of the divine nature." I pray that God may use this text as a stepping stone for your walk with Him.

"I look to the mountains;
where will my help come from?
My help will come from the Lord,
who made heaven and earth.
He will not let you fall;
your protector is always awake.

The protector of Israel
never dozes of sleeps.
The Lord will guard you;
he is by your side to protect you.
The sun will not hurt you during the day,
nor the moon during the night.

The Lord will protect your from all danger;
he will keep you safe.
He will protect you as you come and go
now and forever.

Psalm 121:1-8 (GNB)

What is Faith?

"Choose this day whom you will serve."
Joshua 24:15

"A PART OF being human is to have some sort of belief system. Everyone has a theology, a world view, or a particular way of looking at the world."[2] Your beliefs will guide the choices you make throughout your life. Behaviors, character, relationships, time, money, and other life choices will be guided by your beliefs. For example, a significant decision within your beliefs is the answer to the question, is there a God?

You must choose what you believe. The first choice is to decide if you believe God exists. If you believe God does exist, you must then select the "god" you wish to honor. The basis of this writing is the belief that God does exist, and the one true God is the Triune God: the Father, the Son, and the Holy Ghost. Those who believe in the Triune God are called "Christians" or "Followers of Christ."

Faith is a privilege offered by God; it is not the result of a person's effort. The apostle John tells us in John 15:16-17, "You did not choose me, but I chose you. And I appointed you to go and bear fruit." The development of faith occurs in a progression or a process. First, you must be receptive and willing to listen to the message. The second step in the process is to agree the information is valid. The third and final step is for you to act on the belief and the message. Faith, as a Christian, will continue to grow as the Holy Spirit's presence will allow greater understanding and a greater surrender to the will of God.

The journey toward the conviction that Jesus is the Son of God requires that you think about him, learn about him, and study his Word until you decide that Jesus Christ is indeed the Son of God. You must believe that what Jesus says is accurate and that his Word is holy, perfect, and righteous! This conviction of mind and heart will allow you to make choices and act with assurance of God's Word. You will electively strive to follow his direction and guidance, entering into a more purposeful and rewarding life by believing in Jesus. Have faith in our Lord!

"Although you have not seen him; and even though you do not see him now, you believe in him and rejoice with an indescribable and glorious joy." 1 Peter 1:8

The Bible Is - The Doctrine of Faith and God's Law

> "All scripture is inspired by God."
>
> 2 Timothy 3:16

THE BIBLE IS the doctrine for the beliefs of the Christian faith. The Bible contains both the Old and New Testaments. The Old Testament writings were before Jesus' life, and the New Testament writings occurred after Jesus' time on earth. According to the late Edward Koehler, a long time professor at Concordia College, "God gave His Word to man for a very definite purpose, namely: a) to save man from sin and damnation through faith in Christ, b) to educate and train His children in holiness of life, c) to magnify His glory."[3] The Apostle John tells us in his gospel the purpose of the Bible. "But these are written so that you may come to believe that Jesus is the Messiah, the Son of God, and that through believing you may have life in his name" (John 20:30).

The Gospels are the first four books of the New Testament. Within the Gospels, we learn about the life, death, and resurrection of Jesus and what it means to followers of Christ. The church believes that the Holy Ghost directed men to write the content of the Bible, both Old and New Testaments. Therefore, it is believed by the church that the Bible is written exactly as God intended.

The Bible shows humanity how to have everlasting life. The Word of God has the power to create change in a person. We may receive counsel, education, and training to achieve a more righteous life through God's Word. Through the Holy Spirit, the Word of God will touch your heart. God's Law is explicitly given through the Ten Commandments recorded in Exodus 20-23 and through Jesus' Sermon on the Mount, Matthew 5-7. Throughout the Bible, the Law is illustrated in stories and writings.

You must accept God into your life to have the answers to the heart's deep questions and to feel the warmth and love of a genuine relationship with Him. When you know and love the Living God, he will be an excellent, active, and vital part of your world.

The Bible can be difficult to understand. Therefore, it may be helpful to study with other Christians and to use a Bible commentary to explain the meaning of the scripture.

"You search the Scriptures because in them you have eternal life." John 5:39

Thy Word, Almighty Lord

Thy Word, Almighty Lord,
Where'er it enters in,
Is sharper than a two-edged sword,
To slay the man of sin.

Thy word is power and life;
It bids confusion cease,
And changes envy, hatred, strife,
To love, and joy, and peace.

Then let our hearts obey
The gospel's glorious sound;
And all its fruits, from day to day,
Be in us and abound.

James Montgomery

Who is God?

> "I am the way and the truth and the life."
> John 14:6

Who is God? "Some people try to grasp a picture of God by taking the best version of themselves, projecting that to the nth degree, and factoring in all the goodness they can imagine. That is a picture that falls painfully short of who God is. God is not the best version of what we can think of. He is far more than that, above and beyond all that you can ask or think."[4]

GOD IS ONE divinity. The Bible tells us of the gift of the Triune God, the Trinity – God is one but not alone. The three distinct essences of God are the Father, the Son, and the Holy Spirit. God is the creator of the heavens and the earth. He is sovereign (unlimited, absolute power). God is wise, just, and righteous.

God's Son is Jesus Christ, one with God but came to earth to save the sinner. Jesus' fulfillment of Old Testament prophecies gives evidence that Jesus is the Son of God. Jesus' walk on earth was righteous but he willingly suffered a shameful and painful death on the cross to allow forgiveness of our sins. His resurrection shows he has overcome the power of death, and he offers us the opportunity to join him in heaven. His life, death and resurrection give us the gift of eternal life.

WHO IS GOD?

Studying Jesus' life, you discover he was sometimes lonely, rejected, misunderstood, or weary. When you have those feelings, you can go to Jesus; Jesus has been there. Jesus understands, he cares, and he will give you grace and mercy.

The Holy Spirit is a gift from God to aid us in our journey to serve our Lord. Guidance of the Holy Spirit is essential for understanding the scriptures; he opens our hearts and minds to understanding. The Holy Spirit lives within us and gives the individual personal qualities and skills necessary to fulfill the work of our Lord. The more the individual honestly seeks God, the more they will feel the gifts of the Holy Spirit.

Belief in God means a belief in the Holy Trinity: the Father, the Son, and the Holy Spirit. The concept of one God in three distinct persons is a mystery, but you must believe and be content with the message in the Word of God. God's Word is true!

Additionally, four terms are frequently used to identify attributes of our Lord. These terms are omniscience, omnipotence, omnibenevolence, and omnipresence. The meaning of each of these terms is the significant factor, not the word itself. Each expression clearly defines the authority and power of our Lord. Therefore, let's look at each term independently, discovering its meaning and the scriptural basis for its appropriate usage in describing the authority and power of God.

Omniscient – unlimited understanding and insight, knowing everything.

> "Great is our Lord, and abundant in power; his understanding is beyond measure." Psalm 147:5
>
> "Your Father knows what you need before you ask him." Matthew 6:8

Omnipotence – unlimited power or influence.

"I create both light and darkness; I bring both blessing and disaster. I, the Lord, do all these things." Isaiah 45:7

"For mortals it is impossible, but for God all things are possible." Matthew 19:26

"What is the immeasurable greatness of his power for us who believe." Ephesians 1:19

Omnibenevolence – perfect unlimited goodness.

"The Lord is gracious and merciful, slow to anger and abounding in steadfast love, the Lord is good to all, and his compassion is over all that he has made." Psalm 145:8-9

"For God so loved the world, that he gave his only Son, so that everyone who believes in him may not perish but may have eternal life." John 3:16

Omnipresence – present everywhere at the same time.

"When you pass through the waters, I will be with you; and through the rivers, they shall not overwhelm you; when you walk through fire you shall not be burned, and the flame shall not consume you. For I am the Lord your God." Isaiah 43:2-3

"The eyes of the Lord are in every place, keeping watch on the evil and the good." Proverbs 15:3

"Where can I go from your Spirit? Or where can I flee from your presence?" Psalm 139:7

What do these terms tell you? To begin, there is nothing happening that God does not already know is occurring. There is nothing for him to learn, he knows thoughts, deeds, everything before it even happens. In addition to knowing all, God has the power and kindness beyond our understanding. Therefore, when problems arise, there is confidence that a loving powerful God cares about you and will give you guidance and power to overcome the issue. Also, remember always that God loved you so much that he sent his Son, Jesus, to die so you could have eternal life. Finally, there is great comfort in knowing that God is everywhere. He has been to the places you are going, so you can feel safe traveling there, and he is with you at all times, so you are never alone. God knows our needs and he promises to meet those needs for those who trust in him.

"God has sent the Spirit of his Son into our hearts." Galatians 4:6

"Draw near to me, hear this! From the beginning, I have not spoken in secret, from the time it came to be I have been there. And now the Lord God has sent me and his spirit." Isaiah 48:16

Standing on the Promises

Standing on the promises of Christ, my King,
Through eternal ages let his praises ring;
Glory in the highest, I will shout and sing,
Standing on the promises of God.

Standing on the promises that cannot fail.
When the howling storms of doubt and fear assail,
By the living Word of God I shall prevail,
Standing on the promises of God.

Standing on the promises I cannot fall,
Listening every moment to the Spirit's call,
Resting in my Savior as my all in all,
Standing on the promises of God.

Russell K. Carter

The Apostles' Creed – I Believe

"In the beginning, God created the heavens and the earth."
Genesis 1:1

"God sent His Son, born of a woman, born under the law,
in order to redeem those who were under the law,
so that we might receive adoption as children."
Galatians 4:4-5

"No one can say 'Jesus is Lord,' except by the Holy Spirit."
1 Corinthians 12:3

"Christ loved the church and gave Himself up for her."
Ephesians 5:25

THIS CREED IS a concise way to identify the beliefs in the Christian faith. The Apostles' Creed, written by early church leaders around 140 A.D., is used by many Christian denominations and is frequently recited at worship services. It identifies the deity of one divine God and that the essence of God is three distinct beings. The meaning of the Apostles' Creed is explained with great clarity by Martin Luther in his Catechism.[5]

> I believe in God, the Father Almighty, maker of heaven and earth.

> *What does this mean?* I believe God has made me and all creatures; that He has given me my body and soul, eyes, ears, and all my members, my reason and all my senses, and still takes care of them.
>
> He also gives me clothing and shoes, food and drink, house and home, wife and children, land, animals, and all I have. He richly and daily provides me with all that I need to support this body and life.
>
> He defends me against all danger and guards and protects me from all evil.
>
> All this He does only out of fatherly, divine goodness and mercy, without any merit or worthiness in me. For all this, it is my duty to thank and praise, serve and obey Him.
>
> This is most certainly true.

And in Jesus Christ, His only Son, our Lord, who was conceived by the Holy Spirit, born of the Virgin Mary, suffered under Pontius Pilate, was crucified, died and was buried. He descended into hell. The third day, He rose again from the dead. He ascended into heaven and sits at the right hand of God, the Father Almighty. From thence He will come to judge the living and the dead.

> *What does this mean?* I believe in Jesus Christ, true God, begotten of the Father from eternity, and also true man, born of the Virgin Mary, is my Lord,
>
> who has redeemed me, a lost and condemned person, purchased and won me from all sins, from death, and from the power of the devil; not with gold or silver, but with His holy precious blood and with His innocent suffering and death,
>
> that I may be His own and live under Him in His kingdom and serveHim in everlasting righteousness,

THE APOSTLES' CREED – I BELIEVE

innocence, and blessedness,
    just as He is risen from the dead, lives, and reigns to all eternity.
    This is most certainly true.

I believe in the Holy Spirit, the holy Christian church, the communion of saints, the forgiveness of sins, the resurrection of the body, and the life everlasting. Amen

What does this mean? I believe that I cannot by my own reason or strength believe in Jesus Christ, my Lord, or come to Him; but the Holy Spirit has called me by the Gospel, enlightened me with His gifts, sanctified and kept me in the true faith.
    In the same way He calls, gathers, enlightens, and sanctifies the whole Christian church on earth, and keeps it with Jesus Christ in the one true faith.
    In this Christian church He daily and richly forgives all my sins and the sins of all believers.
    On the Last Day, He will raise me and all the dead, and give eternal life to me and all believers in Christ.
    This is most certainly true.

Jesus Fulfilled Old Testament Prophecies

> "Because he poured out himself to death,
> and was numbered with the transgressors;
> yet he bore the sin of many,
> and made intercession for the transgressors."
>
> Isaiah 53:12 (Old Testament Scripture)

> "For while we were still weak,
> at the right time Christ died for the ungodly.
> But God proves his love for us in that while we were sinners
> Christ died for us."
>
> Romans 5:6, 8 (New Testament Scripture)

EDWARD KOEHLER CLARIFIES for us, "The Old Testament was written at different times during the period approximately from 1500 to 400 B.C. Its principle theme is: Salvation promised in the Messiah."[6] Koehler continues, "The New Testament was written during the second half of the first century after Christ. Its principal theme is: Salvation accomplished by Christ."[7]

Prophets of the Old Testament shared insight regarding many events that would occur later in history, such as wars, the rebuilding of the Jewish temple in Jerusalem, and the plight of the Jewish people. In

JESUS FULFILLED OLD TESTAMENT PROPHECIES

addition, Old Testament prophets declared over 300 prophesies about the life of the Messiah. These godly men share about Jesus' birth, genealogy, life, death, and resurrection. Although written hundreds of years before Jesus' walk on earth, the Old Testament scriptures tell believers what to look for in the coming Messiah.

The testaments are full of scriptures detailing prophecies and their fulfillment. It is important to note, however, that Jesus said he came to fulfill the prophecy. Jesus tells us, "Do not think that I have come to abolish the law or the prophets; I have come not to abolish but to fulfill" (Matthew 5:17). The words of the prophets from the Old Testament told the Jewish people of a coming Savior. The fulfillment of those prophecies shows that Christ was indeed that Savior and that his coming was a part of God's plan from the beginning of creation. Below are a few examples of prophecies that Jesus indeed fulfilled.

A commonly known prophecy refers to Jesus' birthplace, the town of Bethlehem. The Old Testament book of Micah 5:2 reads, "But you, O Bethlehem…from you shall come forth for me one who is to rule Israel, whose origin is from of old, from ancient days." In the New Testament, the scriptures of both Matthew 2:1 and Luke 2:4-6 confirm this prophecy. Matthew 2:1 reads, "In the time of King Herod, after Jesus was born in Bethlehem of Judea."

Jesus' genealogy is prophesied in a number of Old Testament books. One example is from Genesis 12:3, which tells us about Abraham, "…in you, all the families of the earth shall be blessed." In the scriptures of 2 Samuel, we learn of a second example, God's covenant with David, which states in part:

> "When your days are fulfilled, and you lie down with your ancestors, I will raise up your offspring after you, who shall come forth from your body, and I will establish his kingdom.

> He shall build a house for my name, and I will establish the throne of his kingdom forever." 2 Samuel 7:12-13

The genealogy of Christ as recorded in the New Testament supports the statements of prophecy in the Old Testament. The following New Testament scriptures record Jesus' genealogy.

> Beginning with Abraham moving forward to Jesus - Matthew 1:1
>
> Starting with Jesus moving backward to Adam - Luke 3:23

The fulfillment of prophecies is primarily found in the first four books of the New Testament, often referred to as the Gospels. Jesus' life on earth repeatedly fits the signs of the coming Messiah outlined in the Old Testament. The fulfillment of the prophecies also shows the power, knowledge, and provision that our Lord possesses. In addition, the completion validates and gives credibility to the deity of our Lord Jesus Christ. Below is a short list of additional examples of Old Testament prophecies fulfilled in the New Testament.

Prophecy Old Testament	Fulfillment New Testament
The Birth of Jesus	
Virgin birth – Isaiah 7:14	Matthew 1:22-23
The Holy Family's flight to Egypt – Hosea 11:1	Matthew 2:14-15
The child's deity – Isaiah 9:6	Matthew 1:23
Jesus' Ministry	
Preaching, healing, teaching –	
Isaiah 9:1-2	Matthew 4:12-17
Isaiah 53:4	Matthew 8:14-17
Psalm 78:2	Matthew 13:34-35

JESUS FULFILLED OLD TESTAMENT PROPHECIES

The Suffering Servant
- The brutalities Jesus would endure - Isaiah 52:13-14 — Matthew 26:67-68
- Despised and rejected – Isaiah 53:3 — Matthew 27: 30-31
- Bore our sins – Isaiah 53:4-5 — Matthew 8:17

The Passion Week (The week before Jesus was crucified.)
- Jesus' rides a donkey - Zechariah 9:9 — Matthew 21:1-5
- Betrayal of Judas - Psalm 41:9 — John 13:18
- Dividing of Jesus' clothes – Psalm 22:18 — John 19:23-24
- Resurrection – Isaiah 53:9-11 — Mark 16:6

"Long ago God spoke to our ancestors in many and various ways by the prophets, but in these last days he has spoken to us by His Son." Hebrews 1:1-2

Jesus Birth Foretold in the Scriptures

> "So the Master is going to give you a sign anyway.
> Watch for this:
> A girl who is presently a virgin will get pregnant.
> She'll bear a son and name him Immanuel (God-With-Us)."
>
> Isaiah 7:14 (MSG)

IN THE OLD Testament book named after him, the prophet Isaiah foretold Jesus' coming. Isaiah is believed to have written these words approximately 700 years before Christ lived (701 BC). Jesus' birth being foretold is important, as we are reminded that Jesus' coming to earth was not an accident but had long been planned as an intentional gift to us. The following scriptures are foretelling Christ's coming as written by Isaiah. I encourage you to look up the scripture in your Bible!

JESUS BIRTH FORETOLD IN THE SCRIPTURES

"For a child has been born for us, a son is given to us;
authority rests upon his shoulders;
and he is named Wonderful Counselor, Mighty God,
Everlasting Father, Prince of Peace.
His authority shall grow continually,
and there shall be endless peace
for the throne of David and his kingdom.
He will establish and uphold it with justice
and with righteousness from this time onward and forevermore.
The zeal of the Lord of hosts will do this."

Isaiah 9:6-7

Blessed Christmas – Jesus' Birth

"An angel of the Lord appeared to him in a dream and said,
'Joseph, son of David, do not be afraid
to take Mary home as your wife,
For the child conceived in her is from the Holy Spirit.
She will bear a son, and you are to name him Jesus,
and he will save his people from their sins.'"

Matthew 1:20-21

"In those days a decree went out from Emperor Augustus that all the world should be registered…Joseph also went from the town of Nazareth in Galilee to Judea, to the city of David called Bethlehem, because he was descended from the house and the family of David. He went to be registered with Mary, to whom he was engaged and who was expecting a child. While they were there, the time came for her to deliver the child. And she gave birth to her firstborn son and wrapped him in bands of cloth, and laid him in a manger because there was no place for them in the inn." Luke 2:1-7

MATTHEW 1:18-25 AND Luke 2:1-7 record the birth of our Lord Jesus. In reading these passages, we can better understand Jesus' birth and His humble beginning on earth. Consider the following factors of His birth.

BLESSED CHRISTMAS – JESUS' BIRTH

- Jesus was born in a stable, not a hospital or a home.
- A cattle trough was used for his cradle, not a bed with a comfortable mattress.
- He was wrapped in swaddling clothes (strips of cloth), not a cute new outfit.
- Mary was unattended except for Joseph's support, with no nurses or doctors.
- Other than Jesus' parents, the first to see Him was the animals.
- Joseph had trusted God and stayed with Mary.

Christmas is the celebration of the birth of our dear Lord and Savior Jesus Christ. Jesus walked on this earth over two thousand years ago and is still remembered and honored today. So, why celebrate Jesus' birthday? What made Him so special? It can be explained quite simply.

- Jesus is God who chose to be born as a vulnerable human child in the most humble conditions. (He was born in a stable with no medical help, and as a human, he experienced physical pain and human emotion.)
- He lived the simple life of a carpenter and owned nothing.
- He loved and obeyed His Father in heaven.
- He ministered to people the last three years of His life, only three years! During that time, he performed many miracles showing his love and compassion for humanity, and his power over demons, death, nature (storms, etc.), and disease. His ministry still speaks to people today!
- He loved us so much that He allowed himself to be painfully crucified on the cross to forgive our sins.
- Death did not have power over Jesus. He was resurrected on the third day and ascended into heaven. He invites us to spend eternity with Him in heaven.

During the Christmas season ponder how precious and important the

FOLLOWING CHRIST

gift of the Christ Child is to us! Thank God for this most cherished gift given to you and me! May every Christmas be esteemed as you celebrate the true gift of the Christ Child.

"Jesus went throughout Galilee, teaching in their synagogues and proclaiming the good news of the kingdom and curing every disease and every sickness." Matthew 4:23-24

"My Father, if it is possible, let this cup pass from me; yet not what I want but what you want." Matthew 26:39

"While he was blessing them, he withdrew from them and was carried up into heaven." Luke 24:51

O Holy Night

O holy night, the stars are brightly shining,
It is the night of the dear Savior's birth.
Long lay the world in sin and error pining,
'Till He appeared and the soul felt its worth.
A thrill of hope – the weary world rejoices,
For yonder breaks a new and glorious morn.

Fall on your knees! O hear the angel voices!
O night divine! O night when Christ was born.
O night, O holy night, O night divine!

John S. Dwight

Names of Christ

> "The angel said to her, 'Do not be afraid, Mary,
> for you have found favor with God.
> And now, you will conceive in your womb and bear a son,
> and you will name him Jesus.'"
>
> Luke 1:30-31

WHILE ON EARTH, Jesus was called many names. Especially in that day, a name often revealed something about the birth or character of the person. There are hundreds of different names for Jesus in the Bible. Below is a brief listing:

My Beloved Son – Jesus is the beloved Son of God. (Matthew 17:5)

Redeemer –To redeem is to free someone by paying the price with no obligation for repayment. Jesus paid a great price for us by his death on the cross, thus allowing us forgiveness of sin and everlasting life. (Mark 10:45, Titus 2:14)

Savior – A Savior is the one who saves another individual from difficulty or danger. Jesus suffered, died, and was resurrected to save humanity from an eternity in hell. (Ephesians 5:34; Titus 1:4, 3:6; 2 Peter 2:20)

Messiah – Is defined as a person who brings hope for a solution to a cause. Jesus took away the power of sin and death. He opens the door to heaven and everlasting life. (John 4:25-26)

The Lamb of God – In the Old Testament, animals (often lambs or birds) were sacrificed to God to repair the relationship with God broken by sin. Jesus' death and bloodshed on the cross allow us forgiveness from our sins, and removes the need to sacrifice animals. (John 1:29, 36)

The Light of the World – Jesus helps mankind to understand the nature of God. You will have light in your path; you will not walk in darkness. (John 8:12, 3:19-21; 12:46)

Emmanuel (Immanuel) – This name means God with us. (Matthew 1:23)

A Refuge from the Storm / My Rock and My Fortress – Jesus is a spiritual rock! He brings strength in times of need, distress, and the storms of life. (Isaiah 25:4; Psalm 31:2; Psalm 31:3)

Blessed – Revered, honored, and worshiped are terms often used to define blessed. In addition, it means to give divine care and protection, bringing pleasure or contentment. (Psalm 72:17; 21:6)

The Lord or Prince of Peace – This is a name of honor for our Lord Jesus, who teaches and models a life of peace. (II Thessalonians: 3:16; Isaiah 9:6)

The King of: Kings, Jews, Nations, and over all the Earth – A king is a man who holds a position of authority over given territories. Jesus is referred to as a king but this often created trouble for him with those in position to rule (the kings). Jesus' kingdom is that of heaven, and it is not of this earth. (Zechariah 14:4, 5, 9, 16; Revelations 19:16; Matthew 2:2; John 19:19)

FOLLOWING CHRIST

The Way – It is only through faith in Jesus Christ that you may have everlasting life. Jesus is the Way. (John 14:6)

The True God – Scripture acknowledges that Jesus is the True God. (1 John 5:20)

As you consider these names of our Lord, remember that each one tells of the gift he has given us, bought with his flesh and blood. What a wonderful Savior and friend in Jesus!

"Blessed be the name of God from age to age, for wisdom and power are his." Daniel 2:20

"Blessed be his glorious name forever; may his glory fill the whole earth." Psalm 72:19

Jesus Our Brother, Kind and Good

Jesus our brother, kind and good,
Was humbly born in a stable rude,
And the friendly beasts around him stood,
Jesus our brother, kind and good.

Traditional English Carol

Man of Sorrows

Man of sorrows what a name
For the Son of God, who came
Ruined sinner to reclaim:
Hallelujah, what a Savior!

Bearing shame and scoffing rude,
In my place condemned he stood,
Sealed my pardon with his blood:
Hallelujah, what a Savior!

Guilty, helpless, lost were we;
Blameless Lamb of God was he,
Sacrificed to set us free:
Hallelujah, what a Savior!

He was lifted up to die;
"It is finished" was his cry;
Now in heaven exalted high:
Hallelujah, what a Savior!

When he comes, our glorious King,
All his ransomed home to bring,
Then anew this song we'll sing:
Hallelujah, what a Savior!

P. P. Bliss

Jesus – A Man of Miracles

> "He does great things and unsearchable,
> marvelous things without number."
>
> Job 5:9

JESUS PERFORMED MANY miracles. Jesus' miracles were not meant to create a magic show but to show evidence of the Lord's power, power even more significant than that of Satan's. The miracles also show that Jesus has compassion and understanding of human suffering. Looking at the examples of his miracles gives us great insight into the character of Jesus. He did not want the miracles to overshadow his message, so he frequently told the witnesses not to share what they had seen. Jesus' purpose was to spread the Word of God, which is the message of repentance and salvation.

Jesus' Power to Overcome Disease

"Wherever he went, into villages or cities or farms, they laid the sick in the marketplaces, and begged him that they might touch even the fringe of his cloak, and all who touched it were healed."

Mark 6:56

JESUS DEMONSTRATES HIS power over illness/disease as he continues to minister to the outcasts of society. To experience the wonders of God, one must ask for something specific and have faith in God's gifts of wisdom and grace.

The Man with Leprosy

"A leper came to him begging him, kneeling he said to him, 'If you choose, you can make me clean.' Moved with pity, Jesus stretched out his hand and touched him, and said to him, 'I do choose. Be made clean!' Immediately the leprosy left him, and he was made clean."
Mark 1:40-42

Jesus Heals a Paralytic

"'So that you know the Son of Man has authority on earth to forgive sins' – he said to the one paralyzed – 'I say to you, stand up and take your bed and go to your home.' Immediately he stood up before them, took what he had been lying on, and went to his home, glorifying God." Luke 5:24-25

Jesus Heals the Sick

"Now Simon's mother-in-law was in bed with a fever and they told him about her at once. He came and took her by the hand and lifted her up. Then the fever left her and she began to serve them." Mark 1:30-31

It is essential to understand that Jesus came to heal from the effects of sin. He did not come to earth primarily for physical healing. Physical healing was only one aspect of his ministry. He came that we might live in righteousness and die to sin. By his death on the cross we have been healed spiritually, and given the promise of eternal life in heaven with him.

Beneath the Cross of Jesus

Beneath the cross of Jesus
I fain would take my stand,
the shadow of a mighty Rock
within a weary land;
a home within the wilderness,
a rest upon the way,
From the burning of the noontide heat
and the burden of the day.

Elizabeth C. Clephane

Jesus' Power to Overcome Nature

> """Seeing a fig tree by the side of the road,
> he went to it and found nothing at all on it but leaves.
> Then he said of it, 'May no fruit ever come from you again!'
> And the fig tree withered at once."
> Matthew 21:19

JESUS DEMONSTRATES HIS power over storms and other limits of nature. Storms can be in the form of passion, sorrow, depression, etc. However, Jesus can help us handle the hardships of life if we have faith and give Him the opportunity. He will provide you shelter from life's storms.

Jesus Calms a Storm

"One day he got into a boat with his disciples, and he said to them, 'Let us go across to the other side of the lake.' So they put out...A windstorm swept down on the lake, and the boat was filling with water, and they were in danger. They went to him and woke him up, shouting, 'Master, Master, we are perishing!' And he woke up and rebuked the wind and the raging waves; they ceased, and there was a calm." Luke 8:22-24

Jesus Feeds Five Thousand

"Taking the five loaves and the two fish, he looked up to heaven, and blessed and broke the loaves and gave them to his disciples to set before the people; and he divided the two fish among them all. And all ate and were filled, and they took up twelve baskets full of broken pieces and of the fish. Those who had eaten the loaves numbered five thousand men." Mark 6:41-44

Jesus Walks on Water

"But when they saw him walking on the sea, they thought it was a ghost, and cried out; for they all saw him and were terrified. But immediately he spoke with them and said, 'Take heart, it is I, do not be afraid.'" Mark 6:49-50

Jesus' Power to Overcome Demons

"God added to his testimony by signs and wonders
and various miracles,
and by gifts of the Holy Spirit,
distributed according to his will."

Hebrews 2:4

GOD WANTS TO help us restore order to a disordered life. When Christ lived, exorcists performed elaborate ceremonies in an attempt to free individuals of demons. Jesus demonstrates authority over satanic forces by quiet words of command. The following scripture, once again, shows Jesus' compassion for human suffering.

Jesus Drives out an Evil Spirit

"In the synagogue, there was a man who had the spirit of an unclean demon, and he cried out with a loud voice, 'Let us alone! What have you to do with us, Jesus of Nazareth? Have you come to destroy us? I know who you are, the Holy One of God.' But Jesus rebuked him, saying, 'Be silent, and come out of him!' When the demon had thrown him down before them, he came out of him without having done him any harm." Luke 4:33-35

Healing the Boy with an Evil Spirit

"Just then a man from the crowd shouted, 'Teacher, I beg you to look at my son; he is my only child. Suddenly a spirit seizes him and all at once he shrieks. It convulses him until he foams at the mouth; it mauls him and will scarcely leave him…' Jesus answered, '…Bring your son here.' While he was coming, the demon dashed him to the ground in convulsions. But Jesus rebuked the unclean spirit, healed the boy and gave him back to his father." Luke 9:38-42

Following Jesus' Crucifixion and Resurrection, He Appears to Mary Magdalene

"Now after he arose early on the first day of the week, he appeared first to Mary Magdalene, from whom he had cast out seven demons." Mark 16:9

Christ Jesus Hath the Power

Christ Jesus hath the power,
The power to renew,
The power to cleanse your heart from sin,
And make you wholly true.
Christ Jesus hath the power
For evermore to keep;
Oh none can pluck you from His hand,
Or rob Him of His Sheep.

James M. Gray

Jesus' Power to Overcome Death

> "When the perishable body puts on imperishability,
> and this mortal body puts on immortality,
> then the saying that is written will be fulfilled:
> 'Death has been swallowed up in victory.
> Where, O death, is your victory?
> Where, O death, is your sting?'"
> 1Corinthians 15:54-55

BE AWARE OF Jesus' power. He speaks and life returns. The scripture also shows the deep emotion Jesus felt.

Jesus Raises a Widow's Son

"As he approached the gate of the town a man who had died was being carried out. He was his mother's only son, and she was a widow; and with her was a large crowd from the town. When the Lord saw her, he had compassion for her and said to her, 'Do not weep.' Then he came forward and touched the bier, and the bearers stood still. And he said, 'Young man, I say to you, rise!' The dead man sat up and began to speak and Jesus gave him to his mother." Luke 7:12-16

A Dead Girl

"Just then, there came a man named Jairus, a leader of the synagogue. He fell at Jesus feet and begged him to come to his house, for he had an only daughter, about twelve years old, who was dying..." (Luke 8:41-42). "While he (Jesus) was still speaking, someone came from the leader's house to say, 'Your daughter is dead; do not trouble the teacher any longer.' When Jesus heard this, he replied, 'Do not fear. Only believe, and she will be saved.' When he came to the house, he did not allow anyone to enter with him except Peter, John, and James, and the child's father and mother. They were all weeping and wailing for her; but he said, 'Do not weep; for she is not dead but sleeping.' And they laughed at him knowing that she was dead. But he took her by the hand and called out, 'Child, get up!' Her spirit returned, and she got up at once" (Luke 8:49-55).

Jesus' Death, Appearances after Death, and His Resurrection

Jesus' own death and resurrection gives evidence to his power. These facts will be reviewed later in this section however you should read about them in scripture. The discovery of the empty tomb is found in each of the gospels: Mathew 28:1-10, Mark 16:1-11, Luke 24:1-12, and John 20:1-18. Following his death, Jesus' appeared to others on several occasions. Some of these appearances are recorded in Mark 16:12, Luke 24:13-35, Luke 24:36-49, John 20:19-29, and Matthew 28:16-20.

Just as Jesus performed miracles during His ministry, God is performing miracles in our world today. Keep a watchful eye on the lives of those who love God. When you see the hand of God, take time to give thanks and, following Jesus' example, give the glory to God for his wonderful goodness!

The Life Jesus Lived Daily

"I beg you to lead a life worthy of the calling to which you have
been called, with all humility and gentleness, with patience,
bearing with one another in love, making every effort
to maintain the unity of the Spirit in the bond of peace."

Ephesians 4:1-3

WHEN YOU CONSIDER the life of Christ, it is common to recall the great moments. We think of miracles, parables (stories), or significant events such as death on the cross or Christ's resurrection. Each of those is significant and worthy of our praise. However, looking at Christ's life allows us insight into his personhood and character. As a person, a human, Jesus would grow weary and hungry after a long day; he needed rest and nourishment as we do. He walked wherever he went, and he did not have worldly possessions. Yet, he awakened each morning and went forth to build relationships and teach about the path to salvation.

The scriptures tell us of many of Jesus' trials. When Jesus began his ministry, he quickly had adversaries from the Jewish leaders who wanted him killed. Matthew 16:21 tells us, "Jesus began to show his disciples that he must go to Jerusalem and undergo great suffering at the hand of the elders and chief priests and scribes, and be killed, and on the third day be raised." John also writes of accusations against Jesus, "The Jews said to him, 'Now we know that you have a demon"

(John 8:52). Jesus, however, kept his focus on God's purposes and continued moving onward to accomplish his task for God.

Christ filled his life with God's purpose, prayer, love, and service when he encountered difficulties. William Barclay, renowned biblical scholar and well known for his writing of the Daily Study Bible series, tells us,

> "…no man could have lived that life of love and pity, compassion and forgiveness, service and help in the life of the everyday unless he had been in God and God in him. It is not by working miracles that we can prove that we belong to Christ, but by living a Christ-like life every moment of every day. It is in the ordinary things of life that we show that we belong to him."[8]

In life, we, too, face many trials. Challenges and difficulties can destroy the hope, joy, and love that bring beauty into our existence. In your everyday decisions, make your life a model of your Lord Jesus. Let people know, through your actions, that you belong to Him. The Holy Spirit will guide your walk with God and empower you with strength and vitality to meet the challenges.

"Let the same mind be in you that was in Jesus Christ." Philippians 2:5

Turn Your Eyes upon Jesus

O soul, are you weary and troubled?
No light in the darkness you see?
There's light for a look at the Savior,
And life more abundant and free!

(Refrain)
Turn your eyes upon Jesus,
Look full in His wonderful face,
And the things of earth will grow strangely dim,
In the light of His glory and grace.

His Word shall not fail you – He promised;
Believe Him, and all will be well;
Then go to a world that is dying,
His perfect salvation to tell!

Helen H. Lemmel

Jesus – A Man of Emotion

"Jesus, looking at him, loved him."
Mark 10:21

JESUS' WALK ON earth demonstrated that he felt emotions similar to our feelings, and he understood the complications of life. Below are a few of the many scriptures that reveal Jesus' experiences with emotion.

Angry yet Grieved
"He looked around at them with anger; and was grieved at their hardness of heart." Mark 3:5

Tired and Weary
"But he was in the stern, asleep on the cushion; and they woke him up." Mark 4:38

Amazed
"And he was amazed at their unbelief." Mark 6:6

Anguish
"In his anguish he prayed more earnestly." Luke 22:44

Sighs
"And he sighed deeply in his spirit." Mark 8:12

Compassion
"When he saw the crowds, he had compassion on them."
Matthew 9:36

Love
"I reprove and discipline those whom I love." Revelation 3:19

Examples of Jesus' emotions may draw you closer to him as you realize he truly understands the challenges of human beings on earth. Jesus not only understands, but he has lived through difficult trials. Throughout his life, his words, actions and deeds show him to be a man of compassion and caring. How fortunate you are that we have a God who willingly came to this earth to experience human life and to suffer a dreadfully painful death on the cross that you might have a better, more whole and glorious life with him in heaven.

Jesus Loves Me

Jesus loves me, this I know,
For the Bible tells me so.
Little ones to him belong;
They are weak, but he is strong.

(Refrain)
Yes, Jesus loves me!
Yes, Jesus loves me!
Yes, Jesus loves me!
The Bible tells me so.

Anna Bartlett Warner

Jesus – A Man of Prayer

"But he would withdraw to deserted places and pray."
Luke 5:16

CHRIST, A MAN of prayer, is a perfect example of a life lived in relationship with God, his Father. Christ prayed to God for guidance, strength, courage, and thanksgiving. Below are examples of times Christ went to his father in prayer.

Baptism
"Now when all the people were baptized, and when Jesus also had been baptized and was praying, the heaven was opened, and the Holy Spirit descended upon him in bodily form like a dove."
Luke 3:21-22

Choosing Disciples
"Now during those days he went out to the mountain to pray, and he spent the night in prayer to God." Luke 6:12

Transfiguration
"And while he was praying the appearance of his face changed, and his clothes became dazzling white." Luke 9:29

For Peter
"I have prayed for you, that your own faith may not fail; and you, when once you have turned back, strengthen your brothers."
Luke 22:32

Garden of Gethsemane
"In his anguish he prayed more earnestly." Luke 22:44

Time of Death
"Then Jesus, crying with a loud voice, said, 'Father, into your hands I commend my spirit.' Having said this, he breathed his last."
Luke 23:46

Renewal
"After saying farewell to them, he went up on the mountain to pray." Mark 6:46

Prayer offers many blessings, and is a key in establishing a relationship with God. Prayer is a means to honor God, and to seek his help. Jesus Christ was a man of prayer. Let's briefly look at each of these areas.

> Prayer builds a relationship with God – Relationships must share time to grow and flourish. Through prayer, you learn about God and yourself as you share special and difficult times with him. God cares; he will laugh or cry with you. Through prayer, God will help you see his purpose for your life and guide your choices.

> Prayer honors God. Offer thanksgiving to God for the many blessings he provides. Tell God you love him; acknowledge he is powerful and that you need his help.

FOLLOWING CHRIST

<u>Prayer is an avenue through which you may talk to God about your desires</u>. He wants you to have a life of purpose and contentment. Remember, God has given you examples of godly qualities and character. Consider asking for God's help in the development of those qualities and characteristics: contentment, compassion, strength, peace, understanding, wisdom, etc. You will see beautiful results if you believe and honor your God.

Why pray? Jesus prayed to his Father on many occasions for various reasons. God loves you, too. God wants you to come to him in prayer! He is your friend. So, spend some time with Him!

Sweet Hour of Prayer

Sweet hour of prayer, sweet hour of prayer,
That calls me from a world of care,
And bids me at my Father's throne
Make all my wants and wishes known.
In seasons of distress and grief,
My soul has often found relief,
And oft' escaped the tempter's snare
By they return, sweet hour of prayer!

Sweet hour of prayer, sweet hour of prayer,
Thy wings shall my petition bear,
To Him whose truth and faithfulness
Engage the waiting soul to bless;
And since He bids me seek His face,
Believe His word and trust His grace,
I'll cast on Him my every care,
And wait for thee, sweet hour of prayer.

W. W. Walford

The Lord's Prayer

"Jesus was praying in a certain place,
and when he finished, one of this disciples said to him,
'Lord, teach us to pray…'"

Luke 11:1

The Lord's Prayer

"Our Father who art in heaven, hallowed be Thy name.
Thy kingdom come.
Thy will be done, on earth as it is in heaven.
Give us this day our daily bread.
And forgive us our debts,
as we also have forgiven our debtors.
And do not lead us into temptation,
but deliver us from evil.
For Thine is the kingdom, and the power,
and the glory, forever. Amen"

Matthew 6:9-15 (NASB)

ONE OF JESUS' disciples asked him to teach them to pray. In response to the request, Jesus shared the words of a prayer we now call "The Lord's Prayer." Jesus provided this prayer to teach us—a perfect prayer that we might use as a guide. As you look closely at the Lord's Prayer, there is much to be learned.

THE LORD'S PRAYER

The first lesson Jesus teaches is that prayer begins with an acknowledgment of God and his many divine qualities. Jesus begins the prayer addressing God as "Our Father." He is speaking to his Father as a Son. Notably, Jesus reminds us that we, too, can claim God as our Father. Not in the same sense of a human, sinful father of earth, but a Holy God in heaven. The prayer continues to give praise, glory, and reverence to God. This is our first lesson: Give glory, adoration, and honor to God, your Father.

The second lesson Jesus teaches is that after you have recognized God's power and glory, you may bring him personal requests. The praise and credit you give God help you understand the need for his guidance and love. The adoration also helps you to recognize that you willingly put your trust in him. The second part of the prayer is to trust God by sharing your need for daily food, shelter, etc. The majesty of God may also remind you that you are a sinner. Ask that he forgive your sins and help you as you forgive others. In addition, as a sinner, you are easily tempted to sin. Pray that God will help you meet and overcome those tests and challenges. The trials and temptations will come, but God will stand with you and see you through to victory. Jesus identifies three personal requests: 1) provisions for the day in the manner or strength, wisdom, nourishment, etc., 2) forgiveness of sin and the willingness to forgive others, and 3) for God's help that you may withstand evil and the temptations that are certain to arise.

The third and final lesson is a return to offering praise to God. It is a beautiful and perfect ending to the prayer as it expresses respect, admiration, and praise to the everlasting God. The term "Amen" means "so be it." This closing utterance signifies certainty and assurance that God will hear and answer your prayer according to his will.

The Lord's Prayer is not intended to be our only manner of talking to God. As you may recall from the previous reading, *Jesus – A Man of Prayer*, Jesus talks to God in a variety of circumstances. Prayer may be sung or spoken, but it may also be the thoughts, meditations, and desires of the heart. In talking to God, Solomon requests, "Let the words of my mouth and the meditation of my heart be acceptable to you, O Lord, my rock and my redeemer" (Psalm 19:14). Therefore, always pray that your words, meditations, and your heart are acceptable to God.

"Your Father knows what you need before you ask him. 'Pray then in this way:'" Matthew 6:8-9

The Beatitudes

> "When Jesus saw the crowds, he went up the mountain;
> and after he sat down, his disciples came to him.
> Then he began to speak, and taught them."
>
> Matthew 5:1-2

THE BEATITUDES (BE-AT-I-TUDES) are from Jesus' sermon that is often called "Sermon on the Mount." The Beatitudes are at the heart of Jesus' teachings which he was sharing with his newly chosen disciples. These teachings were designed to give the disciples insight as to how they should live life, how to be more like Jesus. Too often, we rely on individuals well-studied in the discipline of faith and diminish the significance of those with a heart for God. A follower of Jesus has a desire to be truly righteous, not just religious. We too should strive to be more like Jesus, attentive to his teaching yet always nurturing a welcoming heart for Christ.

The word Beatitudes comes from the Latin meaning "happy" or "blessed." Each of the Beatitudes begins with the term, "Blessed" which is often defined as divine favor from God. The divine favor may be protection or a valued quality or attribute. Blessed is more than feeling emotionally secure. It is a deep sense of well-being and confidence in God's compassion and omnipotence over his creation. Below is a listing of each of the Beatitudes (Matthew 5:3-10) and a brief narrative detailing to whom the scripture is addressed.

FOLLOWING CHRIST

"Blessed are the poor in spirit, for theirs' is the kingdom of heaven."

Reference: Those who rely on God's power, not their own.

"Blessed are those who mourn, for they will be comforted."

Reference: Those who are saddened by the condition of the world; the rejection of Christ's teachings, and their sin.

"Blessed are the meek, for they will inherit the earth."

Reference: Those who take on Christ's spirit of gentleness and humbleness.

"Blessed are those who hunger and thirst for righteousness, for they will be filled."

Reference: Those who seek honesty, integrity, justice, and high moral standing; those who are willing to sacrifice for those ideals.

"Blessed are the merciful, for they will be shown mercy."

Reference: Those who show compassion and help others. Punishment is not their goal.

"Blessed are the pure in heart, for they will see God."

Reference: Those who have a clear conscience, whose motives and thoughts are pure; who have no ulterior motive for their excellent works.

"Blessed are the peacemakers, for they will be called sons of God."

Reference: Those who actively intervene to make peace, those willing to get involved to settle disagreements.

"Blessed are those who are persecuted because of righteousness for theirs is the kingdom of heaven."

Reference: Those who suffer for doing the right thing.

Jesus was a great teacher. His lessons in the Beatitudes describe the qualities of a perfect disciple for Jesus. His message is still relevant for learning and practice today. In teachings such as the Beatitudes the focus is on the path to discovering blessedness. The underlying theme is to love one another.

Prayer of St. Francis

Lord, make me an instrument of your peace;
Where there is hatred, let me sow love;
Where there is injury, pardon;
Where there is doubt, faith;
Where there is despair, hope;
Where there is darkness, light;
And where there is sadness, joy.
Oh Divine Master,
Grant that I may not so much seek
To be consoled as to console;
To be understood, as to understand;
To be loved, as to love;
For it is in giving that we receive,
It is in pardoning that we are pardoned,
And it is in dying that we are born
To eternal life.
Amen

Jesus is the Light

> "I am the light of the world,
> whoever follows me will never walk in darkness,
> but will have the light of life."
>
> John 8:12

JESUS IS THE light. William Barclay gives insight to the Book of John as he adds clarity to the concept of lightness and darkness. "To John, the Christless life was life in the dark. The darkness stands for life without Christ, and especially for that which has turned its back on Christ."[9]

Jesus' light touches the spirit, mind, and heart of humanity with wisdom. Jesus' light enables believers to know real life on earth and live a full, rich purposeful life. Jesus' light removes doubt and uncertainty, making way for peace and joy. Light provides a guiding principle, created by God, to allow wisdom to impact decisions. The light will enable you to see the mistruths offered by our world and avoid the evil pitfalls. Barclay tells us that Jesus' light delivers people from shadows. Greater clarity of these concepts is below:[10]

- There is the shadow of fear. Sometimes you are afraid to look forward. Sometimes, especially when you see what happens to others, you are afraid of the chances and the changes of life.

- There are shadows of doubts and uncertainties. Sometimes the way ahead is far from being clear and you feel like you are groping among the shadows with nothing firm to cling to.
- There are the shadows of sorrow. Sooner or later the sun sets at midday and the lights go out.
- Those who walk with Jesus are delivered from fear; they are liberated from doubt; they have joy that no one takes from them.

The apostle John tells you in the book of John 1:5, "The light shines in the darkness and the darkness did not overcome it." Jesus' light gives insight and spiritual clarity to servants of God. Floyd Filson, an American scholar and past professor at McCormick Theological Seminary, writes, "Darkness is not mere absence of spiritual light; it is the realm of active hostility to God, to the Light and to believers in Jesus."[11] The darkness is hostile, and it actively opposes the workings of the Light of Jesus. However, John reminds you, Jesus' Light will prevail; it is not overcome by darkness. If you believe in Jesus as your Lord and Savior, His light will stay in you.

Darkness refers to the evils in the world. Sinful and evil acts, ignorance, or life without Christ bring darkness. "It is believed that there were two great opposing powers in the universe, the god of the light and the god of the darkness...This whole universe was a battleground in the eternal, cosmic conflict between the light and the dark; and all that mattered in life was the side a person chose."[12]

How can you see God's light? Look around! God's light is in everything!

"Jesus cried aloud, 'I have come as light into the world, so that everyone who believes in me should not remain in the darkness.'"
John 12:44-46

Joyful, Joyful, We Adore Thee

Joyful, joyful, we adore You,
God of glory, Lord of love;
Hearts unfold like flow'rs before You,
Opening to the sun above.
Melt the clouds of sin and sadness;
Drive the dark of doubt away;
Giver of immortal gladness,
Fill us with the light of day!

Always giving and forgiving,
Ever blessing, ever blest,
Well-spring of the joy of living,
Ocean-depth of happy rest!
Loving Father, Christ our Brother,
Let Your light upon us shine;
Teach us how to love each other,
Lift us to the joy divine.

Henry Van Dyke

Jesus' Death, Resurrection, and Ascension into Heaven

> "The Messiah died for our sins,
> exactly as Scripture tells it;
> that he was buried;
> that he was raised from the dead on the third day,
> again exactly as scripture says."
>
> 1 Corinthians 15:3-4 (MSG)

THE DEITY OF Christ as the Supreme Being, the almighty God, is fundamental to the Christian faith. Jesus is the true God and also a real human being. Because of the sinful nature of humanity, we must die. However, Jesus lived a sinless life, and he did not have to die. Jesus chose to die for our sins; his death was a voluntary act.

Christ was beaten, bloodied, facing agony and shame, as he bore our guilt and was nailed to the cross. Jesus suffered in our place. Yet, by a genuine faith in Christ, our sins are forgiven. Christ has redeemed us from the bondage of sin. The Christian observance of Jesus' crucifixion and death is known as Good Friday, always the Friday before Easter. This occasion is marked with penitence. Each of the gospels, Matthew 27:45-61, Mark 15:33-47, Luke 23:44-56, and John 19:25-42, describe the death of Jesus.

FOLLOWING CHRIST

After his crucifixion, death, and burial, three days later, Jesus rose from the grave. Christ' resurrection is told in each of the four gospels immediately following the passages describing his death. Jesus' resurrection from the dead is essential to the Christian gospel as it clearly shows the truth of Jesus' message and his power to overcome death. Jesus' triumph over death is celebrated by the Christian observance of Easter, and is considered the most sacred Sunday of the year.

In addition, it is essential to understand that following his resurrection, Christ physically left the earth and ascended into heaven forty days later. Christ's ascension into heaven was witnessed by eleven of his apostles, and is recorded in the gospels of Mark 16:19, and Luke 50-53. Without Christ's death, resurrection, and ascension into heaven our faith would be meaningless.

The sins of all humanity are forgiven and we may be reconciled with God. Praise be to God, because of Christ's willingness to follow His Father's will, this is true. Furthermore, Christ's ascension into heaven gives confidence to believers that they may rest in the assurance that they will be resurrected from the dead and given eternal life with Christ in heaven.

John in his book 16:7-16 records Jesus' telling the disciples he is going away and the coming of the Holy Spirit, the Spirit of truth, to be their helper. Ten days after Jesus ascended into heaven, the Holy Spirit descended on the church, just as Jesus had foretold. Christians celebrate this event as the Day of Pentecost. Additional information will be given about the Holy Spirit in subsequent writings.

"Christ, who through the eternal Spirit offered himself without blemish to God." Hebrews 9:14

JESUS' DEATH, RESURRECTION, AND ASCENSION INTO HEAVEN

"Remember how he told you, while he was still in Galilee, that the Son of Man must be handed over to sinners, and be crucified, and on the third day rise again." Luke 24:6-7

The Old Rugged Cross

On a hill far away stood an old rugged cross,
The emblem of suffering and shame;
And I love that old cross where the dearest and best
For a world of lost sinners was slain.

(Refrain)
So I'll cherish the old rugged cross,
Till my trophies at last I lay down;
I will cling to the old rugged cross,
And exchange it some day for a crown.

O that old rugged cross, so despised by the world,
Has a wondrous attraction for me;
For the dear Lamb of God left his glory above
To bear it to dark Calvary.

To that old rugged cross I will ever be true,
Its' shame and reproach gladly bear;
Then he'll call me some day to my home faraway,
Where his glory forever I'll share.

George Bennard

Jesus' Gift - Eternal Life for the Believer

"For the wages of sin is death,
but the free gift of God is eternal life in Christ Jesus our Lord."
Romans 6:23

AS THE SCRIPTURE tells you, the gift of salvation, eternal life, is a gift from God. "For by grace you have been saved through faith, and this is not our own doing; it is the gift of God" (Ephesians 2:8-9). Billy Graham Jr., a Southern Baptist minister and an American evangelist, tells you, "To us it's free, but it cost God the life of His Son. The reason is because on the cross Jesus Christ became the final sacrifice for our sins. He paid for our salvation with His blood."[13]

God offers you the gift of salvation, but as John 3:16 tells you, "For God so loved the world that he gave his only Son so that everyone who believes in him may not perish but have eternal life." The second part of John's message reveals that you must believe to receive the gift. It is important to note: "While those who follow Jesus will seek to live according to His ways, salvation is not based on anything we do, but is accepted by faith alone based on God's grace."[14]

The greatest gift ever is that of eternal life. The only way to receive this wonderful gift is through Jesus Christ, who died on the cross to forgive your sins. To receive the gift, however, you must ask. God will welcome you just as you are. God wants you on his team, and you do not have to be anything but yourself. When you ask God for forgiveness and to come into your heart, then and only then will he open your eyes so that you may learn and begin understanding his purpose for your life. "Others may lead us to friendship with Christ, but we must claim and enjoy the friendship ourselves."[15]

In addition to the gift of salvation (eternal life), you receive blessings as you travel on this earth, waiting for your reward of heaven. This journey on earth is difficult, and Jesus' gifts indeed lighten the load. Below, William Barclay shares specifics as to what Christ does for men and women:[16]

- He opens their eyes. When Christ comes into people's lives, he enables them to see things they never saw before.
- He turns them from the darkness to the light. Before people meet Christ, it is as if they were facing the wrong way; after meeting Christ, they are walking toward the light, and the way is clear.
- He transfers them from the power of Satan to the power of God. Once evil had control over people, but now God's triumphant power enables them to live in victorious goodness.
- He gives them forgiveness of sins and a share with the sanctified. For the past, the penalty of sin is broken; for the future, life is re-created and purified.

Jesus' power and direction in your life will enable you to look at yourself and accept yourself and your true character. Jesus values each person and will show you the value he sees in you. Jesus sees your heart, the evil, the hurt, the pain. He also sees the greatness and the potential within you. Knowing and loving you, He wants purpose for you. Jesus wants to fill your spirit with the inner-peace that comes when one listens and follows God's counsel. Jesus takes away your shame. We have all sinned and feel sadness, guilt, and embarrassment resulting from our poor choices. Jesus wants to wash away the stain. He will allow you to use your life as a means to reach others.

In closing, the apostle Paul tells you in his letter to the Romans "confess with your lips that Jesus is Lord and believe in your heart that God raised him from the dead, you will be saved" (Romans 10:9). The Lord has given you the gift of salvation. To receive the gift, you must believe Jesus Christ is your savior and accept his wonderful gift of everlasting life. God will be with you!

"For God so loved the world that he gave his only Son, so that everyone who believes in him may not perish but have eternal life." John 3:16

JESUS' GIFT - ETERNAL LIFE FOR THE BELIEVER

Low in the Grave He Lay

Low in the grave he lay, Jesus my Savior,
Waiting the coming day, Jesus my Lord!

(Refrain)
Up from the grave he arose;
With a mighty triumph o'er his foes;
He arose a victor from the dark domain,
And he lives forever, with his saints to reign.
He arose! He arose! Hallelujah! Christ arose!

Vainly they watch his bed, Jesus my Savior,
Vainly they seal the dead, Jesus my Lord.

Death cannot keep its prey, Jesus my Savior;
He tore the bars away, Jesus my Lord!

Robert Lowry

Holy Spirit

> "Do you not know that you are God's temple
> and that God's Spirit dwells in you?
> God's temple is holy, and you are that temple."
>
> 1 Corinthians 3:16-17

OUR LORD IS one God, but three separate persons; the Father, the Son, and the Holy Ghost (often referred to as the Holy Spirit). Jesus appeared to the disciples after his death on the cross and his resurrection. The book of John recorded Jesus' conversation with the disciples, "Jesus said to them again, 'Peace be with you. As the Father has sent me, so I send you.' When he had said this, he breathed on them and said to them, 'Receive the Holy Spirit.'" (John 20:21-22)

The Holy Spirit is a gift from God to aid you in your journey to serve our Lord. Guidance of the Holy Spirit is essential to the understanding of scripture. William Barclay describes the power of the Holy Spirit as,

> "The Christian courage to meet the dangerous situation, the Christian power to cope with life more than adequately, the Christian eloquence when eloquence is needed, and the Christian joy which is independent of circumstances are all attributed to the work of the Spirit. The degree to which we can possess the Spirit is conditioned by the kind of people we

are." Barclay continues, "Anyone who is honestly trying to do the will of God will experience more and more of the wonder of the Spirit."[17]

In Paul's Letter to the Romans, he tells you, "Likewise the Spirit helps us in our weakness; for we do not know how to pray as we ought, but that very Spirit intercedes with sighs too deep for words. And God, who searches the heart, knows what is the mind of the Spirit, because the Spirit intercedes for the saints according to the will of God" (Romans 8:26-27). Sarah Frazer, author of several Bible study resources, and a missionary in Honduras explains six ways the Holy Spirit intercedes in our prayers. Below is the listing of intercessions with brief excerpts describing each of the appeals.[18]

1. The Holy Spirit prays for us in a power we don't own. When you fall asleep, and are too weak or just emotionally exhausted, the Spirit of God steps in and gives you the strength you need to continue in prayer.
2. The Holy Spirit prays for us with the wisdom we lack. Sometimes our lives seem completely chaotic and we don't even know what to pray.
3. The Holy Spirit prays for us in mercy we could never fathom. Although Satan would like to feed us lies like "You don't belong here…God doesn't love you…and you are unworthy…" The Spirit stands in the gap and says mercy and grace live here.
4. The Holy Spirit prays for us with a connection we can't possess. Being a part of the Trinity he possesses a connection beyond what we can imagine. Nothing can separate us from the Father because the Spirit is that bond.
5. The Holy Spirit prays for us with God's will in mind. Sometimes I am so tired and I can't pray. It's in these times that I need to lean on the Holy Spirit.
6. The Holy Spirit prays for us with love we can't contain. The

> Spirit will always love us and nothing can separate us from His love. It is with this love the Spirit speaks to the Father on our behalf.

As the scripture tells us, the Holy Spirit will dwell in you if you ask. "When you believe and receive Jesus, God moves into you in the person of the Holy Spirit, guiding your mind, heart, and will."[19] A heart-warming, comforting reality is that the Holy Spirit will pray with you; you do not pray alone. The Holy Spirit will also empower you with the fruits of the Spirit and spiritual gifts to guide and help you in service to the Lord. A description of the empowerment of the Holy Spirit will be reviewed next.

"I will ask the Father, and he will give you another Advocate, to be with you forever. This is the Spirit of truth, whom the world cannot receive, because it neither sees him nor knows him. You know him, because he abides with you, and he will be in you." John 14:16-17

He Leadeth Me

He leadeth me! O blessed thought!
O words with heavenly comfort fraught!
Whate'er I do, where'er I be,
Still 'tis God's hand that leadeth me.

(Refrain)
He leadeth me, He leadeth me,
By His own hand He leadeth me:
His faithful follower I would be,
For by His hand He leadeth me.

Sometimes 'mid scenes of deepest gloom,
Sometimes where Eden's flowers bloom,
By waters still, o'er troubled sea,
Still 'tis His hand that leadeth me!

And when my task on earth is done,
When, by Thy grace, the victory's won,
E'en death's cold wave I will not flee,
Since God through Jordan leadeth me.

Joseph Gilmore

Fruits of the Spirit

"The fruit of the Spirit is love, joy, peace, patience,
kindness, generosity, faithfulness, gentleness and self-control.
There is no law against such things."
Galatians 5:22-23

THE FRUITS OF the Spirit are qualities that develop in followers of Christ as they study, learn, believe God's Word, and begin to act on the will of God. The fruits of the Spirit empower your service to God and enrich the quality of your life. **The fruits are love, joy, peace, patience, kindness, generosity, faithfulness, gentleness, and self-control.** As the Spirit works within your life, the fruits will begin to grow and take a more powerful place in your interactions with others and your reactions to life's challenges. If you have received the Holy Spirit, you will know.

When the Holy Spirit is with you, you will experience life with a new awareness and attitude as suggested below:

    Seek and experience inner peace

    Develop greater understanding and acceptance of others

    Know you are loved and not alone

    Discover healing of spirit

Experience hope

Desire to learn

Develop confidence in the power of what you believe

Feel gladness and sincerity of heart

Christians understand that the grace of Christ and the Holy Spirit are what allow the believer to be morally firm, exhibiting integrity and truth. Only the presence of the Holy Spirit and Christ's mercy will enable you to make a difference for God. "Anyone who is honestly trying to do the will of God will experience more and more of the wonder of the Spirit."[20] May God's gift of the Holy Spirit bear these fruits in you!

Spiritual Gifts

"Serve one another
with whatever gift each of you has received."
1 Peter 4:10

IF YOU ARE willing and desire to serve God, He will supply you with spiritual gifts that are more than our natural physical and mental abilities to do His work. Spiritual gifts are given to you by the Holy Spirit to help you do the work of God. As you work to complete daily tasks and begin to view them as a service to God, you may start to recognize and sense the presence of these gifts in your actions and service.

Spiritual gifts are a present given to all believers. Paul writes in his letter to the Corinthians, "Now there are varieties of gifts, but the same Spirit; and there are varieties of services, but the same Lord; and there are varieties of activities, but it is the same God who activates all of them in everyone" (1 Corinthians 12:4-6). When God speaks and asks for your service, you can rest assured, he will provide the gifts of the Spirit to allow you to do his work with grace and faith. Christians should always listen for God to speak to them, as he may speak through many venues. God may show you a need to serve through the eyes of another's heartache, a spiritual leader, friend, colleague, parent, or the reading and study of the Bible. If you are attentive to God's will, he will allow you to discover his need for your service.

Remember, when God calls you to his service, he will provide. God has many requests for service on earth, and will contact you. "To each is given the manifestation of the Spirit for the common good. To one is given through the Spirit the utterance of wisdom, and to another the utterance of knowledge according to the same Spirit, to another faith by the same Spirit, to another gifts of healing by the one Spirit, to another the working of miracles, to another prophecy, to another the discernment of spirits, to another various kinds of tongues, to another the interpretation of tongues" (1 Corinthians 12:7-10). Teaching, witnessing, offering service, charity, leadership, mercy, encouragement, cheerfulness, or sharing biblical knowledge, may be your calling. The responsibility may initially create discomfort, but you may find peace in knowing that you are an instrument of God and he will provide. Like many skills and talents in life, spiritual gifts take time to grow and develop into maturity.

Be patient as you mature in your faith and the use of your spiritual gifts. Remember the goal, God's will be done. It is essential to know that God designed your spiritual gift to be used in tandem with the skills of other followers of Christ. God uses spiritual gifts to support the advancement of His church, His kingdom, and His glory.

"The gifts he gave were that some would be apostles, some prophets, some evangelists, some pastors, and teachers, to equip the saints for the work of ministry, for building up the body of Christ, until all of us come to the unity of the faith and of the knowledge of the Son of God." Ephesians 4:11-13

"But the wisdom from above is first pure, then peaceable, gentle, reasonable, full of mercy and good fruits, unwavering, without hypocrisy." James 3:17

Come, Holy Spirit, Heavenly Dove

Come, Holy Spirit, heavenly Dove,
With all Thy quick'ning powers;
Kindle a flame of sacred love
In these cold hearts of ours.

O raise our thoughts from things below,
From vanities and toys,
Then shall we with fresh courage
To reach eternal joys.

Awake our soul to joyful songs;
Let pure devotion rise,
Till praise employs our thankful tongues,
And doubt forever dies.

Come, Holy Spirit, heavenly Dove,
With all thy quick'ning powers;
Come, shed abroad a Savior's love,
and that shall kindle ours.

Isaac Watts

Heaven

Rejoice and be glad, for your reward is great in heaven."
Matthew 5:12

GOD TELLS OF the existence of heaven through the scriptures. Matthew 25:34 tells the believer, "Come, you who are blessed by my Father, inherit the kingdom prepared for you from the foundation of the world." Matthew continues in verse 46 as he tells us, "The righteous will go into eternal life." Jesus ascended into heaven with the promise we may join him there.

It is difficult for the human mind to imagine the wonder and bliss of heaven. Even if your mind creates the most beautiful vision, it will fall short of the magnitude of the heavens. Let's look at the facts. To have a greater understanding, the Bible is an excellent source to which we can turn.

The greatest gift of heaven is that God is there. God's presence is often overlooked by picturing loved ones and streets of gold. It is stated in scripture that Jesus is with God. In his letter to the Philippians, the apostle Paul writes, "Our citizenship is in heaven, and it is from there that we are expecting a Savior, the Lord Jesus Christ" (Philippians 3:20). Luke tells you in his gospel, "From now on the Son of Man will be seated at the right hand of the power of God" (Luke 22:69).

FOLLOWING CHRIST

In addition to being in the presence of God, the Bible shares further insight into heaven.

"To convey to us some faint idea of the surpassing splendor, glory, and joy of heaven, the Bible indeed employs terms and illustrations taken from this earthly life."[21] The Bible shares the following details of heaven:

- "eat and drink at my table...sit on thrones." Luke 22:30
- "In my Father's house there are many dwelling places." John 14:2
- The apostle John wrote the Book of Revelation and in his book he tells us the following of the holy city:
  » "radiance like a very rare jewel" 21:11
  » "...the city is pure gold...the foundations of the wall of the city are adorned with every jewel..." 21:18-19
  » "The city has no need of sun or moon to shine on it for the glory of God is its light, and its lamp is the Lamb." 21:23
  » "Outside are the dogs and sorcerers and fornicators and murderers and idolaters, and everyone who loves and practices falsehood." 22:15
- "So it is with the resurrection of the dead. What is sown is perishable, what is raised is imperishable. It is sown in dishonor, it is raised in glory, it is sown in weakness, it is raised in honor. It is sown a physical body, it is raised a spiritual body." 1 Corinthians 15:42-44
- Where is heaven? The Bible does not give direct reference to the location. Rather Jesus tells us how to get to heaven. "I am the way, and the truth and the life. No one comes to the Father except through me." John 14:6
- The Old Testament Book of Psalms also tells us of heaven. "You show me the path of life. In your presence there is fullness of joy; in your right hand are pleasures forever more." Psalm 16:11

It seems the focus of our world is on earthly happenings and temporal constraints. As a result, few people spend time considering the lovely aspects of heaven as promised by our Lord. However, with your mindset on heaven, the perspective of this world may change. Below is a list of considerations regarding how life and focus may change when we consider the rewards of heaven as our goal rather than worldly trappings.

- Choices and thoughts will begin to look to the Lord rather than the world.
- Attitudes will be more focused on owning and using possessions wisely, following biblical principles.
- The focus and purpose will be to demonstrate the way to eternal life for others. Guide people to the good news Christ offers.
- Through pain and suffering, miracles happen. "So you have pain now, but I will see you again, and your hearts will rejoice, and no one will take your joy from you." John 16:22
- Enjoy small moments and remember the pleasures of heaven, a good meal, great party, faithful friends, good book, refreshing walk, loyal dog; they will become beautiful memories.
- Use your time on earth for grooming your soul for heaven. Fix your heart on heaven. Be ready when God calls.
- Remember, you belong in another land, heaven. You are a stranger in this world, just passing through.

The values of this earthly life teach you the road to happiness is through money, possessions, influential careers, perfect family, retirement, leisure time, and credentials. These teachings are untrue and may bring sadness and grief. As a follower of Jesus Christ, you have become a citizen and an heir to heaven. Therefore, while on earth, your behaviors and attitudes should be a reflection and testimony to your God. Live your life with love and truth.

FOLLOWING CHRIST

"So if you have been raised with Christ, seek the things that are above, where Christ is seated at the right hand of God. Set your minds on things that are above, not on things that are on earth, for you have died, and your life is hidden with Christ in God. When Christ who is your life is revealed, then you also will be revealed with him in glory."
Colossians 3:1-4

I Can't Feel at Home Anymore

This world is not my home I'm just a passing through,
My treasures are laid up somewhere beyond the blue;
The angels beckon me from Heaven's open door,
And I can't feel at home in this world anymore.

(Refrain)
Oh Lord you know I have no friend like you,
If Heaven's not my home, oh Lord, what would I do?
The angels beckon me from Heaven's open door,
And I can't feel at home in this world anymore.

I have a loving Savior up in glory-land,
I don't expect to stop until with Him I stand,
He's waiting now for me in Heaven's open door,
And I can't feel at home in this world anymore.

A. P. Carter

Hell - Sin and Its Consequences - Judgment

> "For out of the heart come evil intentions,
> murder, adultery, fornication, theft, false witness, slander."
>
> Matthew 15:19

THE SCRIPTURES SPEAK clearly about heaven and hell. After death, the human soul may reside in either of these places. It is essential to know that both heaven and hell exist and that there is life after death.

The scripture identifies heaven as a place of reward and hell as a place of punishment resulting from sin. Since all humanity is sinful, Jesus' willingness to die on the cross to forgive our sins results in the gift of salvation. That is the essential message! Salvation is the deliverance from the power of sin. If you are interested in learning more about these places, there are many good resources available. However, this writing will not further explain specifics.

Sin may be defined as an offense or immoral act against religious or divine law, or a transgression against God's law. Sin may be speaking, thinking, or acting with words or deeds not pleasing to God. The nature of sin is to put your selfish desires before the will of God. One of the primary reasons people struggle in their relationship with God is because we prefer our own opinions and desires. We are self-centered, not God-centered. We often fail to glorify, worship, or thank God. According to William Barclay,[22]

> We all have been in a situation when we know what is wrong and that is the last thing we want to do. Yet, somehow, that is exactly what we do. Our will is pulling us in different directions. We have the ability to see good, and the inability to do it. The ability to recognize evil (wrong) and the inability to not do it is a source of frustration to humans. Somehow, we hate sin, yet we also love it. It is a choice but often difficult to avoid the evil impulse within. We will never be as good as we would like to be. Only when we know Christ can we do what we know we ought to do.

There are consequences to sin. God loves each of us and does not ignore those who choose to disobey him. God holds people accountable and allows repercussions of choices to follow. The Christian faith teaches that Jesus will judge each individual according to their beliefs and actions, and will determine if one's soul goes to heaven or hell.

You stand alone when you go before Jesus in judgment. Neither parents, nor friends, co-workers, or possessions will be with you at the time of judgment. If you have lived your life with Christ, he will support you at judgment; he will be by your side. You will account for your services to God, sharing how your service has benefitted his will for you, his people, and his kingdom. You will bare your heart and soul before the Lord.

In Romans 8:34, Paul reminds us that Jesus died, rose from the grave, sits at the right hand of God, and intercedes for us. Jesus is there to be our advocate, not to condemn. Moses tells us in the Book of Deuteronomy 32:36, "The Lord will vindicate his people and have compassion on his servants." William Barclay tells us, "Paul has seen Christ not as the judge but as the lover of human souls."[23]

HELL - SIN AND ITS CONSEQUENCES - JUDGMENT

Judgment will come for each of us as sin is a part of our world and has separated us from our God. Jesus Christ has come to restore our relationship with God. Live by God's Word. It is true and right. If we live in Christ, God doesn't see our imperfections of sin. God will show mercy and grace for those whose hearts show God's love through prayer, presence, service, gifts, and witness to our Lord. Go to God in prayer and ask for his help! Trust God's ways and follow his guides.

God is just. His judgment will come to all people, and all will be held accountable for how they have lived and loved. Through Jesus Christ, we can escape the hold of evil and sin. The Holy Spirit will help us to make better choices. Christ will offer forgiveness when we fall short. Ask for God's guidance; He loves you!

"…on the day when, according to my gospel, God, through Jesus Christ, will judge the secret thoughts of all." Romans 2:16

"He does not deal with us according to our sins, nor repay us according to our iniquities. For as the heavens are high above the earth, so great is his steadfast love toward those who fear him."
Psalm 103:10-11

FOLLOWING CHRIST

Have You Counted the Cost?

There's a line that is drawn by rejecting our Lord,
Where the call of His Spirit is lost,
And you hurry along with the pleasure-mad throng –
Have you counted, have you counted the cost?

(Refrain)
Have you counted the cost, if your soul should be lost
Though you gain the whole world for your own?
Even now it may be that the line you have crossed,
Have you counted, have you counted the cost?

You may barter and hope for eternity's morn,
For a moment of joy at the most,
For the glitter of sin and the things it will win –
Have you counted, have you counted the cost?

While the door of His mercy is open to you,
Ere the depth of His love you exhaust,
Won't you come and be healed, won't you whisper I yield –
I have counted, I have counted the cost.

J. Hodge

Salvation

"There is salvation in no one else,
for there is no other name under heaven given among mortals
by which we must be saved."

Acts 4:12

SALVATION IS A gift from God that we receive through the life, death, and resurrection of Jesus Christ. Salvation is God's deliverance from the power and consequences of our sins - death and eternal damnation. This gift is of tremendous significance! Our Lord Jesus Christ offers salvation, and because of his death on the cross and resurrection, we might share everlasting life in heaven with him. Jesus Christ's death on the cross to pay for our sins is the grace of salvation.

The Bible offers us many scriptures to introduce Jesus' saving grace. Matthew writes, "She will bear a son, and you are to name him Jesus, for he will save his people from their sins" (Matthew 1:21). Paul writes to Timothy, "The saying is sure and worthy of full acceptance, that Christ Jesus came into the world to save sinners" (1Timothy1:15). John tells us of Jesus' words regarding salvation, "I am the way, the truth, and the life. No one comes to the Father except through me" (John 14:6).

The deliverance described above is indeed the critical aspect of salvation. However, Jesus' gracious gift of salvation also touches our everyday lives as we live on this earth. It will keep Christian believers safe in the present time and throughout eternity. According to William Barclay, Christ came to offer salvation for everlasting life but also much more.[24]

> <u>Salvation for physical illness</u> (Matthew 9:21; Luke 8:36). It is not a completely other-worldly thing. It is aimed at rescuing an individual in body and in the soul.
>
> <u>Salvation from danger</u> (Matthew 8:25, 14:30). It is not that it gives people a life free from perils and dangers, but it gives them security of soul no matter what is happening.
>
> <u>Salvation from life's infection</u> (Acts 2:40). Those who have Christian salvation have a kind of divine antiseptic which keeps them from infection by the evil of the world.
>
> <u>Salvation from lostness</u> (Matthew 18:11, Luke 19:10). It is to seek and save the lost that Jesus came. The unsaved man or woman is on the wrong road. The saved man or woman has been put on the right way.
>
> <u>Salvation from sin</u> (Matthew 1:21). Men and women are like slaves in bondage to a master from whom they cannot escape. Christian salvation liberates them from the tyranny of sin.
>
> <u>Salvation from the wrath (anger) of God</u> (Romans 5:9). There is in this world a moral law and in the Christian faith an inevitable element of judgment. Without the salvation which Jesus Christ brings, we can only stand condemned.

God loves you. God allows you the freedom of choice, but you stand condemned when you do not accept God as your Lord and choose not to follow his guidance. Only by the gracious gift of salvation offered to believers of Jesus Christ are you forgiven. Praise God for his gift of salvation.

"Here is the Lamb of God who takes away the sin of the world!"
John 1:29

To God Be the Glory

To God be the glory, great things He hath done;
So loved He the world that He gave us His Son.
Who yielded His life an atonement for sin,
And opened the lifegate that all may go in.

O perfect redemption, the purchase of blood
To ev'ry believer the Promise of God;
The vilest offender who truly believes,
That moment from Jesus a pardon receives.

Great things He hath taught us, great things He hath done,
And great our rejoicing thro' Jesus the Son;
But purer, and higher, and greater will be
Our wonder, our vict'ry when Jesus we see.

Praise the Lord, praise the Lord, let the earth hear His Voice!
Praise the Lord, praise the Lord, let the people rejoice!
O come to the Father thro' Jesus the Son,
And give Him the glory, great things He hath done.

Fanny J. Crosby

Repentance

> "Just so, I tell you, there is joy in the presence of the angels of God over one sinner who repents."
>
> Luke 15:10

REPENTANCE IS AN act of the heart. To repent, you must experience contrition, a heartfelt sorrow, regarding the sinful deed. The sinful nature of people and the act of sin brings fear and distance between you and God. Unrepented sin can bring damnation and hell. However, the follower of Christ knows that with a sorrowful and contrite heart, there is forgiveness. Jesus' death on the cross and his resurrection give hope for the forgiveness of sins and everlasting life. Therefore, when you come to God with penitence, seeking his forgiveness, the relationship with him can be healed.

When sin happens and you are repentant, knowing Jesus' death on the cross was for your forgiveness of sin, you no longer need to feel the guilt and shame; nor will you feel distanced from God. The fruit of repentance is considered the good works that follow your forgiveness. Because of the Lord's forgiveness, your grateful heart seeks to serve him, thankful for his ever-loving kindness, grace, and mercy. Your sins are forgiven. Praise God.

"For godly grief produces a repentance that leads to salvation and brings no regret, but worldly grief produces death."
2 Corinthians 7:10

"If we confess our sins, he who is faithful and just will forgive us our sins and cleanse us from all unrighteousness." 1 John 1:9

"For the wages of sin is death, but the free gift of God is eternal life in Christ Jesus our Lord." Romans 6:23

"For the Lord your God is gracious and merciful, and will not turn away his face from you, if you return to him." 2 Chronicles 30:9

Grace

> "For God so loved the world that he gave his only Son,
> so that everyone who believes in him may not perish
> but may have eternal life."
>
> John 3:16

GRACE IS A gift from God that is free, unearned and undeserved. According to Edward Koehler, "The grace of God by which we are saved is that merciful, affectionate disposition, that good will of God toward men according to which He forgives sins to those who are worthy of eternal death. It is the unmerited love of God toward men."[25] It is not about what you have done for God or your worthiness. It is only about what God has done for you. God loved you so much that he gave his Son so that your sins would be forgiven and you could have everlasting life.

> "God is like a human father; he promises to love his children no matter what they do. True, he will love some of us with a love that makes him glad, and he will love some of us with a love that makes him sad; but in either case it is a love which will never let us go. It is dependent not on our merit but only on God's own generous heart."[26]

As much as you might try to be righteous, you are human, and we humans fall very short! You may desire to do what is right, but you make choices that conflict with God's will unceasingly. Yet, when you follow Christ, he will stand with you and help you. When you fall, he will forgive you and give you the strength to get up and try again. God wants a life of peace and fulfillment for you, and he loves you, even though you are not worthy. That is an essential component of grace.

Grace is unearned and undeserved. As humans, we fall into a cycle of sin, and because of God's grace, he offers forgiveness. The following points outline the cycle.

- There are Laws, God's Laws. God's Law offers guidance regarding how to live a righteous life.
- There is choice. Given free choice, we choose to believe God's Word and seek his will and forgiveness, or we willingly break the Laws and await punishment. Choose to believe God's Word and seek his will in your life. Act accordingly.
- There are transgressions. Despite our best efforts, humans sin.
- There is God's wrath. God gives us the Laws to help and, even when we choose otherwise, we are unable to keep the Law. God is mad.
- There is repentance. We must go to the Lord and ask forgiveness for our sins. Without repentance and forgiveness, we await condemnation.
- There is GOD'S GRACE. We are saved through Jesus Christ's death on the cross. God does not condemn but gives incredible, undeserved grace.

God should be angry with you as he considers your consequences, but God is full of grace and love. God wants a relationship with you in which you love him and make efforts to do his will. He knows you will be less than perfect. Nevertheless, God will bless your relationship with him and, by his grace, bring you to a more purposeful, and trusting life in him. Give thanks to God for his grace, mercy, and forgiveness.

"There is no one righteous, not even one." Romans 3:10

Just as I Am

Just as I am without one plea,
But that Thy blood was shed for me,
And that Thou bid'st me come to Thee,
O Lamb of God, I come! I come!

Just as I am though tossed about
With many a conflict, many a doubt;
Fightings within, and fears without,
O Lamb of God, I come, I come!

Just as I am, Thou wilt receive,
Wilt welcome, pardon, cleanse, relieve;
Because Thy promise I believe,
O Lamb of God, I come, I come!

Just as I am, Thy love unknown
Has broken every barrier down;
Now, to be Thine, yea, Thine alone,
O Lamb of God, I come, I come!

Charlotte Elliott

Baptism

> "The one who believes and is baptized will be saved;
> but the one who does not believe will be condemned."
>
> Mark 16:16

BAPTISM IS A beautiful happening and should be celebrated! The Lord has called believers to be baptized. Matthew 28:19 says, "Go therefore and make disciples of all nations, baptizing them in the name of the Father and of the Son and of the Holy Spirit." Baptism brings us into a relationship with the Triune God: the Father, the Son, and the Holy Spirit.

Baptism is another of God's great blessings. You and I are all sinners and fall very short of what God would ask of us. Nevertheless, our Lord still loves you, and baptism allows you the forgiveness of sins which opens the door for life everlasting and eternal salvation (heaven). As you may note in the scripture cited above, Mark 16:16, there are two conditions for the promise of salvation: 1) believe in God and 2) be baptized.

It is the command of God, not the water, which cleanses us as we are baptized in the name of the Father, the Son, and the Holy Spirit. The blessings given by God are what make this a special happening. "But when the goodness and loving kindness of God our Savior appeared, he saved us, not because of any works of righteousness that we had

FOLLOWING CHRIST

done, but according to his mercy, through the water of rebirth and renewal by the Holy Spirit" (Titus 3:5).

Baptism allows the Holy Spirit to enter into your being to help you understand and act on God's message and his purpose for your life. Human nature is mean-spirited, and the Holy Spirit in your life will help you understand your less desirable, sinful ways and therefore strive to live a more righteous and pure life for Christ. Thus, the more you seek the Holy Spirit, the more the Holy Spirit will enrich your life.

"I baptize you with water for repentance, but ...He will baptize you with the Holy Spirit and fire." Matthew 3:11

Holy Communion

> "While they were eating, Jesus took a loaf of bread,
> and after blessing it he broke it,
> gave it to the disciples, and said,
> 'Take, eat; this is my body.'
> Then he took a cup,
> and after giving thanks
> he gave it to them, saying,
> 'Drink from it, all of you;
> for this is my blood of the covenant,
> which is poured out for many for the forgiveness of sins.'"
>
> Matthew 26: 26-28

HOLY COMMUNION IS known by many names. It is called the Lord's Supper, the Breaking of Bread, The Sacrament of the Alter, or the Eucharist to name a few. Jesus instituted this divine practice at the last supper with his disciples. In a communion service, the bread and wine are consecrated (made sacred, devoted to God) and shared in the spiritual act of receiving the body and blood (the presence) of Christ. Communion is a spiritual benefit to Christians. It must be a service of reverence and solemnity. As humans, we cannot fully understand this sacrament. However, Jesus tells us in Luke 22:19 to do this in remembrance of him.

Following are six purposes of communion. First, as we were told in

Luke and 1 Corinthians 11:25, "Do this as often as you drink it, in remembrance of me." This statement in scripture is a command, not a choice. Thus, we are to partake in communion often as a way to remember the life, purpose, and deity of our Lord Jesus. Secondly, the act of communion is to give us a peaceful conscience, comfort, and joy as we recall the spiritual blessing of the forgiveness of sins and salvation provided by our Lord Jesus' death on the cross. Thirdly, the reassurance of God's grace and love rekindles our spirits to have a heart for God. 1 John 4:19 expresses our renewed feelings toward our Lord, "We love, because he first loved us." Fourth, as we approach the Lord's Table, it is essential to realize that we are sinners just as our brother, each of us in need of forgiveness. Despite our differences and shortcomings, we are to love one another. Fifth, as our faith is strengthened, we have the assurance that God is with us and gives patience and strength to face life's challenges and bear our crosses. Finally, Holy Communion strengthens our certainty of eternal salvation through Jesus Christ our Lord.

Christ shed his blood and gave his body and life to forgive our sins. The observance of Holy Communion is a sacrament that strengthens faith and helps instill the desire to seek God's will in your life. The act of going to the Lord's Table is humbling as you confess that you believe the Word of God to be accurate and that Christ indeed has died for the forgiveness of your sins and to give life everlasting.

Prior to taking communion, it is essential to take time for self-evaluation. 1 Corinthians 11:28 tells us, "Examine yourselves, and only then eat of the bread and drink of the cup." Self-examination involves introspection and soul-searching. Below are thoughts to consider as you proceed with self-reflection.

1. Ask yourself if you truly believe that Christ died to forgive your sins and offers you everlasting life. Additionally, although we do not understand the actual, tangible, physical action of the

HOLY COMMUNION

elements, we believe it is indeed the body and blood of our Lord Jesus.

2. You must repent of your sins and be sincerely sorry.
3. You must believe that your sins are forgiven.
4. In addition to examining your relationship with God, it is critical to make every effort to resolve conflicts you may have with other humans. Anger and bitterness open the heart to the devil. "If it is possible, so far as it depends on you, live peaceably with all" (Romans 12:18).
5. Ask yourself if you genuinely desire to live a life more pleasing to God. If this is your desire, you must understand that this sacrament will strengthen your faith and that God will help you on this journey.

The Lord's Supper is a sacred sacrament. Prepare yourself. Do not join in communion when you are complacent or not serious about the observance. The Lord's Supper is not just another everyday meal.

Christian denominations have varying views regarding the sacraments of Baptism and Holy Communion. The specific doctrines, the procedural practices, or the nature of the elements of body and blood for communion may differ. This writing will not elaborate on these variations. However, as you grow in your faith, it is very appropriate to ask a leader or pastor in the church to clarify the beliefs of the particular denomination.

The Sacrament of Holy Communion fortifies our faith. The challenges in life can cause us to doubt or lose sight of God's goodness and his purpose for our lives. Communion can help us resist the temptations of life and overcome evil. Spend time in prayer asking the Holy Spirit to prepare your heart so you may worship the Lord in a worthy manner.

FOLLOWING CHRIST

Fairest Lord Jesus

Fairest Lord Jesus,
Ruler of all nature,
O thou of God and man the Son,
Thee will I cherish,
Thee will I honor,
Thou, my soul's glory, joy, and crown.

Fair is the sunshine,
Fairer still the moonlight,
And all the twinkling starry host:
Jesus shines brighter,
Jesus shines purer
Than all the angels heaven can boast.

Beautiful Savior!
Lord of all the nations!
Son of God and Son of Man!
Glory and honor,
Praise, adoration,
Now and forevermore be thine.

Unknown

A Look Ahead: Humbly Share God's Love

AS I BEGIN to address the topic of marriage and related content later in this book, it is essential to realize that society's views do not always align with Biblical principles. These topics may create controversy. Knowing best how to handle differences of opinion may be challenging, discernment may be a struggle. It is essential to remind ourselves that Christianity is not simply about acting right, it is about the heart. Therefore, it is necessary to review three themes in scripture: 1) Love one another, 2) Jesus did not come to condemn but to save the lost, and 3) Pray for the wisdom of speech. It is also necessary to identify God's command for each of us. The passages below remind Christians of the responses they should consider as they interact with people of differing viewpoints. The reader should note that the repetition of these themes in the New Testament emphasizes their importance and value.

Love One Another

"This is my commandment, that you love
one another as I have loved you."

John 15:127

You will find similar passages in Matthew 22:37-39,
John 13:34-35, John 15:17, and 1 John 4:7.

Jesus Did Not Come to Condemn but to Save

"If anyone hears my message and does not obey it,
I will not judge him.
I came not to judge the world but to save it."

John 12:47 (GNB)

"The Son of Man came to seek out and save the lost."

Luke 19:10

You will find similar passages in John 3:17 and Matthew 7:1-2.

Pray for Wisdom of Speech – Open Doors

"Be gracious in your speech. The goal is to bring out the best in others in a conversation, not put them down, not cut them out."

Colossians 4:5-6 (MSG)

"A wise, mature person is known for his understanding.
The more pleasant the words, the more persuasive he is."

Proverbs 12:21 (GNB)

Later in this book, you will discover that Christ commissions all Christians to share the gospel with the world (Matthew 28:16-20).

A LOOK AHEAD: HUMBLY SHARE GOD'S LOVE

We are not required to fix anything, only to share the story of Jesus and to extend love to others, allowing Jesus' love to flow through us. Therefore, consider the Apostle Paul's message to the Corinthians regarding barriers to sharing the good news of Christ.

> "Endure anything rather than put an obstacle
> in the way of the gospel of Christ."
> Corinthians 9:12

> "To those outside the law, I became as one outside the law (though
> I am not free from God's law but am under Christ's law) so that I
> might win those outside the law."
> Corinthians 9:21

Paul tells us that we must always attempt to follow God's law, but we should also strive to remove barriers and distractions from the goal of sharing the gospel. People need to hear the good news of Christ as well as see his touch on our lives. The gospel is the focus. Do all things for the sake of the gospel.

God commands that we share the gospel of Jesus Christ. We must also humbly share God's love, lift others in prayer, and ask the Holy Spirit for guidance. The topic of marriage and the many blessing offered by this union has become a contentious subject in today's society. We should show God's love (not condemnation) through our words and deeds, pray for wisdom, and that we may always speak the truth in love. Live in a manner that shows others the love of God and what Christians believe and support rather than what we oppose. Share the gospel. All people need our loving God. Trust God to touch individual lives through his Holy Spirit. The path to personal peace and salvation is through a deep enduring friendship with our loving God. That is the message we lovingly need to share. That is the message those lost in this world need to hear.

"But God does care
when you use your freedom carelessly
in a way that leads a fellow believer still vulnerable
to those old associations
to be thrown off track."

1 Corinthians 8:9 (MSG)

I Will Sing the Wondrous Story

I will sing the wondrous story
Of the Christ who died for me.
How He left His home in glory
For the cross of Calvary.
I was lost, but Jesus found me,
Found the sheep that went astray,
Threw His loving arms around me,
Drew me back into His way.

I was bruised, but Jesus healed me;
Fain was I from many a fall;
Sight was gone, and fears possessed me,
But He freed me from them all.
Days of darkness still come o'er me,
Sorrow's paths I often tread,
But the Savior still is with me;
By His hand I'm safely led.

He will keep me till the river
Rolls its waters at my feet;
Then He'll bear me safely over,
Where the loved ones I shall meet.
Yes, I'll sing the wondrous story
Of the Christ who died for me,
Sing it with the saints in glory
Gathered by the crystal sea.

Francis H. Rowley

Marriage – A Covenant with God

"For this reason a man will leave his father and his mother and be joined to his wife, and the two will become one flesh."

Ephesians 5:31

MARRIAGE IS A covenant, holy and sacred. The term covenant, when referenced with theology is an agreement that brings about a committed relationship between God and his people. The terms holy and sacred are similar in meaning and are defined as something dedicated to or representative of God. The marriage covenant is an agreement with God regarding the commitment of the relationship. Thus, God is a part of the promise in a covenant. At the time of creation, God intended that marriage be a three-part union, God, Man, and Woman. In summary, the covenant is a two-part promise 1) God, husband, and wife committing to share life, 2) this union will strive to bring glory and honor to God. According to Edward Koehler, "Matrimony is called 'a mystery' not because it confers the grace of perfecting the natural love and sanctifying those who are joined in marriage, but because the right relation between husband and wife portrays the spiritual relation between Christ and His Church."[27]

In society, a completed process is necessary to have a legal marriage. This process often includes a license, sometimes physical tests or exams, an authorized person to perform the service, an exchange of vows, and a certificate to make the marriage official. Although God wishes for each of us to honor the laws of the land, in the eyes of God these civil requirements are not necessary to be married. According to Koehler, "It is not the minister, priest, or judge that actually unites a man and a woman in marriage; but before the public wedding, the parties themselves unite and bind themselves in wedlock by their free and mutual consent and agreement to be husband and wife; it is by their own consent and agreement that God joins them together."[28]

The primary importance of the marriage is to make known that the relationship is a promise with God and should bring honor to God. Therefore, all thoughts and actions should keep the Lord and the marriage relationship top priority. Thus, the order of precedence in the covenant of marriage should be God first, marriage second, and the individual third.

Scriptures are clear about the relationship between husband and wife and God's intentions for marriage. This writing will not give details of those differences, yet you can find additional information in the following books within the Bible. In his letter to the Ephesians, chapter 5, the apostle Paul compares the marriage relationship between a husband and a wife to the relationship of Jesus Christ and the church. Solomon gives you a description of a godly woman in his book Proverbs 31:10. The Song of Solomon, also written by Solomon, details the sexual desires of a man and woman. If you are interested in further study, the above scriptures are an excellent place to start.

God designed the marriage covenant to be a lifetime commitment. In marriage, both partners leave their families and promise to share their lives and futures in love, honor, and faithfulness to one another. "What God has joined together, let no one separate" (Matthew: 19:6).

A marriage covenant includes God in the partnership. Marriage in society occurs for a variety of reasons. Some marry for family interests, others for personal happiness, romantic fulfillment, or a person may simply be in love with "being in love." Unfortunately, these reasons are risky and dangerous, often resulting in pain and distress for many people. Psalm 127:1 tells us, "Unless the Lord builds the house, those who build it labor in vain." Do not expect your spouse to do for you only what God can do. That expectation puts tremendous pressure on your spouse and is impossible for any human to provide. Only two spiritually healthy people who love God can make a healthy marriage.

The Bible gives clarity about the covenant of marriage and the responsibilities of the husband and wife. A wedding is a binding promise between you, your spouse and God. God is a vital part of your marriage; include him. Pray to create a marriage that brings glory and honor to him. Pray for his wisdom and grace as you face daily challenges. Service to the Lord in the covenant of marriage will increase joy and contentment in your relationship.

"Let marriage be held in honor by all." Hebrews 13:4

The Cost of Discipleship – The Great Commission

> "Whoever does not carry the cross and follow me cannot be my disciple."
>
> Luke 14:27

> "Whoever does not take up the cross and follow me is not worthy of me."
>
> Matthew 10:38

THE CROSS IN ancient days was a sign of shame, pain, suffering, and agony. Many people were crucified in public, and crosses were laid along the roadside to help maintain civil order. Jesus made the comments above when he was on the road to Jerusalem. He knew the pain and suffering of the cross awaited him.

To "carry the cross" means a Christian may have to sacrifice personal dreams, desires, and ambitions. It requires a daily willingness to end selfishness and accept potential reproach for honoring Christ. A Christian may not receive power and glory on earth. The reward is in heaven. The teachings of Jesus deepen the sense of love, loyalty, and relationships. However, followers of Christ must be willing to stand with Jesus if there is conflict. "He must be ready for a loyalty which would sacrifice the dearest things in life and for a suffering which

FOLLOWING CHRIST

would be like the agony of a man upon a cross."[29] A Christian must look to what God wants and needs and follow God's lead. Then, God will provide whatever is required for his service.

The cost of discipleship is about following God's commands. After Jesus' death on the cross, and his resurrection, he appeared to his disciples on a mountain in Galilee. At that time, Jesus gave his last instructions to the disciples before he ascended into heaven. This instruction is known as the Great Commission and is recorded in Matthew 28:18-20, and Mark 16:14-18.

> "All authority in heaven and on earth has been given to me. Go therefore and make disciples of all nations, baptizing them in the name of the Father and the Son and of the Holy Spirit, and teaching them to obey everything that I have commanded you. And remember, I am with you always, to the end of the age." Matthew 28:18-20

Jesus tells the disciples that he has been given all authority in heaven and on earth, which means he can make decisions and enforce compliance. He then instructs them to go to the world, tell people about God, and baptize them in the name of the Father, the Son, and the Holy Spirit. Jesus further instructs them to teach people about the commands of God and the necessity of each individual to follow the will of God. With this commission, Jesus promises the disciples that he will be with them always. To fulfil the commission, you choose to follow Christ and are willing to sacrifice and pay the cost of discipleship. You must be willing to put him above everything else.

The decision you make to follow Christ is to offer him your everything. Jesus directs his disciples (Jesus' followers) to go to all nations. Each individual must listen to God's message to know what that means personally. For you, it may mean to be of service to your neighbors and community and that God desires you to stay in your present location.

THE COST OF DISCIPLESHIP – THE GREAT COMMISSION

The service God calls you to may mean to travel to new communities, new lands. God will prepare you with wisdom and appropriate tools to carry out his work wherever you are planted. The vital aspect of your service is that in all you do, in word and deed, your behaviors should point to the fact that you are a "Child of God."

Many of the previous writings tell of a life of inner-peace, hope, joy, and love that Christ offers to his followers. This message is true and accurate. However, the power of these qualities is from within the believer. Life on earth is difficult and troublesome. Although God does not promise to remove the struggles, he offers to show you the way to peace and victory through the complex challenges and trials of life. There will be a cost to your discipleship, and because of God's promises, you may have confidence that you are not alone. He is with you, and together, you will be victorious.

The kingdom of God comes at a cost. You must count that cost and willingly trust God. "If we are daunted by the high demands of Christ, let us remember that we are not left to fulfill them alone. He who called us to the steep road will walk with us every step of the way and be there at the end to meet us."[30] The message of the cost of discipleship is difficult and sobering. Salvation is free, but it is costly to walk with God.

"For he has graciously granted you the privilege not only in believing in Christ but of suffering for him as well..." Philippians 1:29

Blessed Assurance

Blessed assurance, Jesus is mine!
O what a foretaste of glory divine!
Heir of salvation, purchase of God,
Born of His Spirit, washed in His blood.

Perfect submission, perfect delight!
Visions of rapture now burst on my sight;
Angels descending bring from above
Echoes of mercy, whispers of love.

Perfect submission, all is at rest!
I in my Savior am happy and blest,
Watching and waiting, looking above,
Filled with his goodness, lost in His love.

This is my story, this is my song,
Praising my Savior all the day long;
This is my story, this is my song,
Praising my Savior all the day long.

Fanny J. Crosby

Christ Saves You and Me

> "For we ourselves were once foolish, disobedient, led astray,
> slaves to various passions and pleasure, passing our days
> in malice and envy, despicable, hating one another.
> But when the goodness and loving kindness
> of God our Savior appeared, he saved us,
> not because of any works of righteousness that we had done,
> but according to his mercy."
>
> Titus 3:3-5

TO CHRISTIANS, IT is considered a joyous happening when people choose to turn from the ways of the world to follow the path of our Lord. The term for this happening is often referred to as a **"conversion"** or being **"saved."** A conversion is an act of the Holy Spirit; it is an act of grace. When a person experiences "conversion," it is a particular time in their life; it may be a dramatic experience or come slowly over time. However the occasion occurs, dramatic or subtle, two components are necessary. First, the individual must recognize and believe that Jesus is our Lord and Savior, and secondly, the individual must make a conscious choice to follow and obey Jesus.

He chose you before you were born, and he has great plans for you. He wants you to come to him and honestly ask him to show you the way. When you humbly ask God for strength, guidance, and comfort,

FOLLOWING CHRIST

God will answer your prayer, show you the way and provide for your needs.

"Give thanks to the Lord, because he is good; his love is eternal." 1 Chronicles 16:34

"Blessed be the God and Father of our Lord Jesus Christ! By his great mercy he has given us a new birth into a living hope through the resurrection of Jesus Christ from the dead, and into an inheritance that is imperishable, undefiled, and unfading kept in heaven for you." 1 Peter 1:3-4

"Look at what's happened! This is our God! We waited for him and he showed up and saved us!" Isaiah 25:9 (MSG)

"Be anxious for nothing, but in everything by prayer and supplication with thanksgiving let your requests be made known to God. And the peace of God, which surpasses all comprehension, shall guard your hearts and your minds in Christ Jesus." Philippians 4:6-7 (NASB)

The Church

> "For where two or three are gathered in my name,
> I am there among them."
>
> Matthew 18:8

> "You are citizens with the saints
> and also members of the household of God,
> built upon the foundation of the apostles and prophets,
> with Christ Jesus himself as the cornerstone.
> In him the whole structure is joined together
> and grows into a holy temple in the Lord;
> in whom you also are built together spiritually
> into a dwelling place for God."
>
> Ephesians 2:19-22

THE LORD CALLS on his followers to join in worship, fellowship and service. For the Christian, this place of worship is known as the church. Various religions call the place of worship by different names: Buddhist worship in Temples, Jewish in Synagogues, Catholics in Cathedrals, and Mormons in Chapels or Meetinghouses. However, to the Christian, the term church is more than just a building to worship with other Christians. The church includes any individual who is in a close personal relationship with Christ. Faith as a Christian requires trust in God's Word, the forgiveness of sins, and salvation through Jesus Christ.

The local church provides Christians in close proximity to establish a ministry. Through this ministry, they strengthen one another in faith as they join together and encourage discipline, praise, and honor to the Lord through regular worship services, special celebrations of faith, teaching, and service to God and others. The church is an excellent source of education and preaching as it serves the mission of bringing humans to faith in Jesus Christ. It is essential that Christians become and remain a part of a local church.

The universal church is a congregation of people throughout the world who genuinely believe in the Gospel of Christ. A common bond of faith, hope, service, and mutual love intimately connects anyone who believes and loves Christ. A true Christian believer is a member of the universal church regardless of the denomination to which they belong. Universal church fellowship and belonging is not determined by formal membership to a local church or by distance.

Unfortunately, local churches often have active participants who are unbelievers and hypocrites. Some people do not enjoy attending a local church because of the false Christians present. However, God calls us to be a part of his church. Therefore, we should pray for unbelievers, and through our words, actions, and deeds, seek the Holy Spirits' presence in their lives so they too may become children of God.

"So we, who are many, are one body in Christ, and individually we are members one of another." Romans 12:5

"Keep watch over yourselves and over all the flock, on which the Holy Spirit has made you overseers, to shepherd the church of God that he obtained with the blood of his own Son." Acts 20:28

The Church's One Foundation

The Church's one foundation is Jesus Christ, her Lord;
She is his new creation by water and the Word.
From Heav'n he came and sought her to be his holy bride;
With his own blood he bought her, and for her life he died.

The Church shall never perish. Her dear Lord to defend,
To guide, sustain, and cherish, is with her to the end.
Tho' there be those that hate her and strive to see her fail,
Against both foe and traitor she ever shall prevail.

Yet she on earth hath union with God the Three in One,
And mystic sweet communion with those whose rest is won.
O happy ones and holy! Lord, give us grace that we,
Like them the meek and lowly, on high may dwell with Thee.

S. J. Stone

Hymns of Praise

> "I rely on your constant love;
> I will be glad, because you will rescue me.
> I will sing to you, O Lord,
> Because you have been good to me."
>
> Psalm 13:5-6 (GNB)

A HYMN IS a song of prayer, worship or praise to the Lord. The better, more powerful hymn is one in which the words and the message are taken directly from God's Word, the Bible. The words, or lyrics, provide the hymn's strength, dignity, simplicity, and reverence. The message must be God-centered.

The lyrics of hymns are often poems set to music. The accompanying music is essential; however, the message within the lyrics is the significant component of a hymn. This powerful message and beautiful music allow the hymn to spiritually touch the participants as they hear, learn, and respond to God's message. Messages of hope, truth, grace, forgiveness, redemption, and love are only a few of the restorative aspect of hymns.

Hymns that are true to the gospel are not based on feelings. Instead, they provide a deeply sincere and lovely message to add vitality to a growing spiritual life. Hymns are a beautiful addition to Christian worship.

It is essential to note that Matthew 26:30 tells us of Jesus singing before going to the Mount of Olive. After the Last Supper with his disciples, they sang a hymn. Knowing what trials were before him as he faced crucifiction, Jesus chose to sing. In a time of great distress, Jesus sang.

Throughout this book, various themes are reinforced by poems. Several of the poems are lyrics to hymns. I hope you have the opportunity to hear some of these beautiful hymns set to music. For your convenience, the end of this book includes an Index of Hymns.

"You made me so happy, God. I saw your work and I shouted for joy."
Psalm 92:4 (MSG)

"Teach and instruct one another with all wisdom. Sing psalms, hymns, and sacred songs; sing to God with thanksgiving in your hearts."
Colossians 3:16 (GNB)

"About midnight Paul and Silas were praying and singing hymns to God, and the other prisoners were listening to them."
Acts: 16:25 (GNB)

"Sing to the Lord, and praise him! Proclaim every day the good news that he has saved us." Psalm 96:2 (GNB)

Praise Him! Praise Him!

Praise Him! Praise Him!
Jesus our blessed Redeemer!
Sing, O earth, His wonderful love proclaim!
Hail Him! Hail Him! Highest archangels in glory;
Strength and honor give to His holy Name!
Like a shepherd, Jesus will guard his children,
In his arms he carries them all day long.

(Refrain)
Praise Him! Praise Him!
Tell of His excellent greatness.
Praise Him! Praise Him!
Ever in joyful song.

Praise Him! Praise Him!
Jesus our blessed redeemer!
For our sins, he suffered, and bled, and died.
He our rock, our hope of eternal salvation.
Hail Him! Hail Him! Jesus, the crucified.
Sound His praises! Jesus who bore our sorrows,
Love unbounded, wonderful, deep and strong.

Fanny J. Crosby

Related Scriptures

"Faith is the assurance of things hoped for, the conviction of things not seen." Hebrew 11:1

"The Lord is near to all who call on him, to all who call on him in truth." Psalm 145:18

"Your word is a lamp to my feet and a light to my path." Psalms 119:105

"The words that I have spoken to you are spirit and life." John 6:63

"Jesus spoke to them saying, 'I am the light of the world. Whoever follows me will never walk in darkness but will have the light of life'." John 8:12

"Ask, and it will be given to you; search, and you will find; knock, and the door will be opened for you. For everyone who asks receives, and everyone who searches finds, and for everyone who knocks, the door will be opened." Matthew 7:7-8

"When you search for me, you will find me, if you seek me with all your heart." Jeremiah 29:13

"God causes everything to work together for the good of those who love God and are called according to his purpose for them." Romans 8:28

"We have gifts that differ according to the grace given to us: prophecy, in proportion to faith; ministry, in ministering; the teacher, in teaching; the exhorter, in exhortation; the giver, in generosity; the leader, in diligence; the compassionate, in cheerfulness." Romans 12:6-8

"God has not given us a spirit of fear, but of power, and of love, and of a sound mind." II Timothy 1:7

"If any of you lacks wisdom he should ask God, who gives generously to all without finding fault, and it will be given to him." James 1:5

"I am convinced that nothing can ever separate us from His love. Death can't, and life can't. The angels can't, and the demons can't. Our fear for today, our worries about tomorrow, and even the powers of hell can't keep God's love away." Romans 8:38

"I will trust in God, so why should I be afraid? What can mere mortals do to me?" Psalm 56:11

"All scripture is inspired by God and is useful for teaching, for reproof, for correction, and for training for righteousness, so that everyone who belongs to God may be proficient, equipped for every good work." II Timothy 3:16-17

"Grace to you and peace from God our Father and from the Lord Jesus Christ." Romans 1:7

"Our citizenship is in heaven, and it is from there that we are expecting a Savior, the Lord Jesus Christ." Philippians 3:20

RELATED SCRIPTURES

"Hallelujah! Salvation and glory and power to our God, for his judgments are true and just." Revelation 19:1-2

"For we will all stand before the judgment seat of God."
Romans 14:10

"Indeed, God did not send the Son into the world to condemn the world, but in order that the world might be saved through him."
John 3:17

"Jesus was despised and rejected – a man of sorrows, acquainted with the bitterest grief. We turned our backs on him and looked the other way when he went by. He was despised, and we did not care." (Forgive me, Lord.) Isaiah 53:3

"Anyone, then, who knows the right thing to do and fails to do it, commits sin." James 4:17

"Do not fear those who kill the body but cannot kill the soul; rather fear him who can destroy both soul and body in hell."
Matthew 10: 28

"The mind of a sinful man is death, but the mind controlled by the Spirit is life and peace." Romans 8:6

Living Your Faith

The belief in Jesus Christ as your Lord and Savior is life-changing. As one's life becomes busy and stressed, one often fails to utilize the gifts of our Lord. As you move forward in your walk on earth, you should daily call upon the Lord for strength, guidance, joy, hope, and love. This section brings to life the many ways, both large and small, in which you can connect with God daily. These connections will enrich your life and offer service and obedience to our Lord.

Understanding the beliefs of the Christian faith should serve as a guide to living your life. In addition, the following writings will address behaviors in life and how choices regarding these behaviors can impact your world. The value of prayer, the purpose of life, spiritual growth, and habits of faith, are a few of the topics addressed. When these and other behaviors are identified and practiced, you may feel a greater sense of purpose, inner peace, enhanced joy, and personal fulfillment.

May God Bless You

May God bless you with discomfort at easy answers,
half-truths, and superficial relationships,
so that you may live deep within your heart.
May God bless you with anger at injustice,
oppression, and exploitation of people
so that you may work for justice, freedom, and peace.
May God bless you with tears to shed
for those who suffer from pain, rejections, and starvation
so that you may reach out your hand to comfort them
and to turn their pain into joy.
And my God bless you with enough foolishness
to believe that you can make a difference in this world
so that you can do what others claim cannot be done.
May God bless you with the weirdest blessing possible –
his divine burden.

Unknown

What Would Jesus Do?

> "Give your servant therefore an understanding mind…
> able to discern between good and evil."
> Psalm 119:17

WHAT WOULD JESUS Do? In our society, we wear jewelry and clothing that begs the question, but do we know? Wearing these reminders would suggest that one is interested in living a life pleasing to God, as was Jesus' life. What would Jesus Do? How to live such a life? The answer is complex, but a beginning would be to learn about Jesus, his life and his choices.

To learn about the life of Jesus is an essential step to knowing what He did while on earth. Having a sound mind is a blessing, but without the knowledge of how Jesus led his life, a sound mind alone, will not reason as Jesus might. The general nature of humans is to be selfish and self-serving. Jesus, however, always was serving others and his Lord. At no time do we read in the scriptures when Jesus acted selfishly, especially when he faced crucifixion on the cross for you and me. When one takes time to better understand the reasons behind Jesus' choices in times of trial, temptation, and joy, one's thinking is challenged.

May you come to know the true Son of God and to fall in love with an awesome Jesus! I hope and pray that you and I will make choices that are both aligned closely with what Jesus would do and are pleasing to our Lord. What does it mean to be a follower of Jesus Christ, a Christian? What would Jesus do? He is eager for you to know and follow his example. Ask him to show you the way. He is waiting for you!

"I'm your servant - help me understand what that means, the inner meaning of your instructions." Psalm 119:125 (MSG)

Hope, Joy, Peace, and Love

"May the God of hope fill you
with all joy and peace in believing, so that you may abound in
hope by the power of the Holy Spirit."
Romans 15:13 (NRSV)

EACH NEW DAY is a unique opportunity. As you go forward and face the challenges of the days ahead, may the gifts from our Lord, hope, peace, joy, and love fill your spirit and give you strength and comfort.

Hope – Sometimes, life seems to be an endless road of difficulty. The future may seem hopeless. Yet, God can give you the expectation for a better tomorrow, the belief that good will come. God allows you to know hope in your life because he has a need and a plan for you if you are open to his calling. He has things planned for you that you likely cannot even imagine.

Hope knows that the future holds eternal life for those who believe in Jesus Christ, knowing you will join him in heaven and overcome the power of sin and death. The message of hope is shared when one tells of the birth of God, a Savior on earth, who knows your pain, and who is today in heaven waiting for you to join him.

- "Rejoice in hope, be patient in suffering, and persevere in prayer!" Romans 12:12

- "Hope does not disappoint us, because God's love has been poured into our hearts by the Holy Spirit that has been given to us." Romans 5:5

Joy – The responsibilities and circumstances of life may be overwhelming and can darken one's sense of pleasure. God can return the state of happiness and delight; allowing you to feel well-being and good fortune even in grim circumstances. Seek the positive things in life: time with family and friends, flowers, music, good food, celebrations. Be playful, laugh, smile, and be happy; these are all gifts of God. Knowing Christ is joy.

- "And the ransomed of the Lord shall return, and come to Zion (heaven) with singing; everlasting joy shall be upon their heads, and they shall obtain joy and gladness, and sorrow and sighing shall flee away." Verse of prophecy from Isaiah 35:10.
- "I will sing of your steadfast love, O Lord, forever; with my mouth I will proclaim your faithfulness to all generations. I will declare that your steadfast love is established forever, your faithfulness is as firm as the heavens." Psalm 89:1-2

Peace – Life can be a struggle--broken, disturbed, unordered. It may seem hostile and oppressive. God's love and care allow you to feel freedom from this strife and teach you how to handle a state of tranquility, silence, harmony. God does not take away the tears and suffering, but he is in control and will allow you to feel comfort and peace during trying times. In this world, there will always be pressures, stress. Don't feel overly responsible and try to fix everything. God is in control, pray for his guidance.

- "By the tender mercy of our God…guide our feet into the way of peace." Luke 1:78-79
- "For a child has been born for us, a Son is given to us;

authority rests upon his shoulders; and he is named Wonderful Counselor, Mighty God, Everlasting Father, and Prince of Peace." Isaiah 9:6

Love – Each human has a deep desire and capacity for love. However, being human, you make mistakes and may hurt those you love most. The love of your Lord is a love of devotion and tenderness. He freely accepts you as you are, hoping for you only the best and working with you to become even better. God offers unconditional love to you, even a sinner. When your adorable, sweet puppy destroys your favorite belonging, you forgive your puppy and continue to love unconditionally. God's love is similar to that but so very much more!

- "For God so loved the world that he gave his only Son, so that everyone who believes in him may not perish but may have eternal life." John 3:16
- "Love one another. Just as I have loved you, you also should love one another." John 13:34
- Qualities of Christian Love – Read Romans: 12:9-21
- The Greatest of These is Love – Read 1 Corinthians 13:4-7

God deeply desires to forgive you and allow you to be blessed by his guidance and love. To do your part, you must choose God's will for your life. Take time to pray for the guidance of the Holy Spirit, listen, read, and learn about God. He will show you the way! God loves you and wants to be in a relationship with you. Tell God your joys and your struggles. He wants to help you!

What Wondrous Love Is This

What wondrous love is this, O my soul, O my soul!
What wondrous love is this, O my soul!
What wondrous love is this that caused the Lord of bliss
To bear the dreadful curse for my soul, for my soul.
To bear the dreadful curse for my soul!

When I was sinking down, sinking down, sinking down,
When I was sinking down, sinking down,
When I was sinking down beneath God's righteous frown,
Christ laid aside his crown for my soul, for my soul,
Christ laid aside his crown for my soul.

To God and to the Lamb I will sing, I will sing;
To God and to the Lamb I will sing;
To God and to the Lamb, who is the great I AM,
While millions join the theme, I will sing, I will sing,
While millions join the theme, I will sing.

And when from death I'm free, I'll sing on, I'll sing on;
And when from death I'm free, I'll sing on;
And when from death I'm free, I'll sing his love for me,
And through eternity I'll sing on, I'll sing on,
And through eternity I'll sing on.

Unknown

Jesus' Passion

THE STUDY OF Jesus' life, through scripture, provides an example of how we might best live our own lives. Below are four qualities of life that Jesus practiced daily.

<u>Jesus had a purpose.</u>
"The Word, the Word-made-flesh
that I have spoken and that I am,
that Word and no other is the last word.
I'm not making any of this up on my own.
The Father who sent me gave me orders,
told me what to say and how to say it.
And I know exactly what his command produces:
real and eternal life.
That's all I have to say.
What the Father told me, I tell you."
John 12:49-50 (MSG)

<u>He displayed tenderness and caring.</u>
"This is how much God loved the world:
He gave his Son, his one and only Son.
And this is why: so that no one need be destroyed; by believing in him anyone can have a whole and lasting life. God didn't go to all

the trouble of sending his Son merely to point an accusing finger
telling the world how bad it was.
He came to help, to put the world right again.
Anyone who trusts in him is acquitted."
John 3:16-17 (MSG)

He lived a modest and humble life.
"Think of yourselves the way Christ Jesus thought of himself.
He had equal status with God but didn't think so much of himself
that he had to cling to the advantages of that status no matter what.
Not at all. When the time came,
he set aside the privileges of deity and took on the status of a slave,
became human! Having become human,
he stayed human. It was an incredibly humbling process.
He didn't claim special privileges. Instead, he lived a selfless,
obedient life and then died a selfless, obedient death –
and the worst kind of death at that – a crucifixion."
Philippians 2: 5-8 (MSG)

He spoke courageously for God.
"Then Jesus entered the temple and
drove out all who were selling and buying in the temple,
and he overturned the tables of the money changers
and the seats of those who sold doves.
He said to them, 'It is written,
My house shall be called a house of prayer,
but you are making it a den of robbers.'"
Matthew 21:12-13

YOU SHOULD USE Jesus' example as a guide for your life! Live with purpose; display tenderness and caring for others; live modestly and humbly; and speak out courageously for your God!

A Heart for God

> "Keep your heart with all vigilance,
> for from it flows the springs of life."
>
> Proverbs 4:23

KING SOLOMON TELLS us in the scripture above, that your heart is the basis of knowing God's will. The reference to heart is not that of the organ in your body, but the entirety of your being, mind, emotions, and will. Your heart must be receptive, so that God can communicate with you, and you will understand his will. God speaks to your heart; he speaks to you through his Bible, wise counsel of other people, family, friends, colleagues, the yearning of the heart, etc. God also expects you to use common sense and personally evaluate issues based on his teachings. Therefore, you should guard your heart so you may know and understand God's Word, and be obedient to God. His Word is a guide for you and will make your life on earth more purposeful, and joyful. Having a heart for God allows him to show you the way to everlasting life.

If your heart is hardened and selfish, God's Word and his messages for your life will not be heard. Therefore, it is important to keep your heart open and sensitive to hear God's guidance and direction for you. You must also be watchful of the worldly happenings that may harden your heart. As people age, habits become hard to break, and hearts may become hardened.

FOLLOWING CHRIST

Guard your heart so it will always have a desire to seek your Lord! Train your heart, your entire being, to be ready, receptive and sensitive to God's message. That is the single most important preparation you can do to discover the wonder of your God. A heart turned toward God will allow the words of Matthew to become true and personal for you; "...search, and you will find" (Matthew 7:7).

"My child, be attentive to my words; incline your ear to my sayings. Do not let them escape from your sight; keep them within your heart."
Proverbs 4:20-21

Whispering Hope

Soft as the voice of an angel,
Breathing a lesson unheard,
Hope with a gentle persuasion
Whispers her comforting word:
Wait till the darkness is over,
Wait till the tempest is done,
Hope for the sunshine tomorrow,
After the shower is gone.

(Refrain)
Whispering hope, oh, how welcome thy voice,
Making my heart in its sorrow rejoice.

Hope, as an anchor so steadfast,
Rends the dark veil for the soul,
Whither the Master has entered,
Robbing the grave of its goal;
Come then, oh, come, glad fruition,
Come to my sad weary heart;
Come, O Thou blest hope of glory,
Never, oh, never depart.

Septimus Winner

Your Calling - Simplified

"Lead a life worthy of the calling
to which you have been called,
with all humility and gentleness, with patience,
bearing with one another in love,
making every effort to maintain the unity of the Spirit
in the bond of peace."

Ephesians 4:1-3

"You are chosen...
in order that you may proclaim the mighty acts of him who called
you out of darkness into his marvelous light."

1 Peter 2:9

IT IS COMMON in life for people to have a deep desire to make a difference, impact the world, and do something extraordinary. This desire often sets us on a path to discover our calling, our purpose. For some, this search can be overwhelming and frustrating. However, in Ephesians and 1 Peter, we are told in the simplest terms that God calls us to share the gospel of Jesus Christ with others through our actions, humility, gentleness, patience, love, and unity. Your job is to be an example for others, live life serving God, and be prepared to share the gospel in love.

The idea of sharing God's Word can be daunting; however, the book of John 15:4-5 records Jesus' message to the disciples at their last supper together. A portion of Jesus' message during that meaningful evening was, "Abide in me as I abide in you. Just as the branch cannot bear fruit by itself unless it abides in the vine, neither can you unless you abide in me. I am the vine, you are the branches." Verse 2 tells us that God prunes the vine so that it may bear fruit. As a follower of Christ, God provides experiences in life that challenge you to grow and learn (pruning), thus, creating within you a firm foundation of faith and discipline. Pruning, teaches you to live your life with an awareness of God's will and make choices accordingly, yielding to his teaching and guidance. This foundation empowers you to respond to your Lord's call for service as you become His evidence, His ambassadors, and His credentials. Allow God to be the vine and yourself the branch that will bear fruit for the Lord.

As you face joys and trials daily, you may display trust and obedience to your God as you affirm added strength, enduring hope, and prayer. You are called to witness to others by exhibiting, through your actions, a belief in the Lord's love and faithfulness. However, sharing God's message requires discernment.

Consider the phrase that has been around for centuries, "your actions speak louder than words." This phrase reminds us that a person's actions are often more meaningful than what one says. Faith is not something to debate or argue people into believing. Additionally, condemning or demeaning others are defeating practices that may cause some individuals to close the door as judgments, debates, or heated arguments cause divisiveness. God is the only one who can open one's heart to hear His Word. God will prepare their hearts and minds and open the door. God is continually calling for new believers to come unto him. So lift a prayer for God to soften the hearts and open the minds of specific individuals you know who are nonbelievers.

FOLLOWING CHRIST

Christians should always seek opportunities to share the gospel through thoughtful actions or loving conversations. We should consciously behave and speak in a manner that brings people to Christ, acknowledging that actions may be the very tool God uses to draw others to Him. Your life may be the catalyst for another person to walk through the open door, choosing faith in God and His Word.

We each want to leave a legacy beyond our possessions, jobs, goals, or dreams. If you let God be your friend, companion, guide, and Lord, he will fulfill your calling. He will use your gifts to bring others to Him. Let your faith shine brightly through your actions to the world around you. Your words, thoughts, and deeds should reflect the love of our Lord Jesus Christ. That is your calling!

The hymn, *Great Is Thy Faithfulness*, follows. The lyrics within this poem remind us of the faithfulness, mercy and love of our Lord Jesus. We only need to bring this light to others so they may see and experience the beauty of knowing our Lord and Savior, Jesus Christ. God will take care of the rest.

"Children, let us love, not in word or speech, but in truth and action."
1 John 3:18

"But you are the ones chosen by God…God's instruments to do his work and speak out for him, to tell others of the night-and-day difference he made for you –from nothing to something, from rejected to accepted." 1Peter 2:9 (MSG)

Great Is Thy Faithfulness

Great is thy faithfulness, Oh God my Father,
There is no shadow of turning with thee.
Thou changest not, thy compassions, they fail not;
As thou hast been, thou forever wilt be.

Refrain:
Great is thy faithfulness!
Great is thy faithfulness!
Morning by morning new mercies I see;
All I have needed thy hand hath provided.
Great is thy faithfulness, Lord, unto me!

Pardon for sin and a peace that endureth,
Thine own dear presence to cheer and to guide,
Strength for today and bright hope for tomorrow,
Blessing all mine, with ten thousand beside!

Thomas O. Chisholm

Purpose in Life

> "Go therefore and make disciples of all nations,
> baptizing them in the name of the Father
> and of the Son and of the Holy Spirit,
> and teaching them to obey
> everything I have commanded you."
>
> Matthew 28:19-20

HOWARD THURMAN, A prominent religious figure in the 20th century, states, "Don't ask what the world needs but rather ask, what makes you come alive, because what the world needs is people who come alive." Finding purpose in life should be both rewarding and enjoyable. Sometimes, it feels like a burden or a job. But God does indeed have a plan for your life as scripture states, in Jeremiah 29:11, "I know the plans I have for you, says the Lord, plans for your welfare and not for harm, to give you a future of hope."

There are important ways to enrich your world and support the discovery of your purpose. Remember, God does not work in magic; he often works through his people. Below are considerations that may help you discover your passion and purpose: surround yourself with godly people, consider your values, continue growing and learning.

Surround yourself with godly people and friends who support you, your growth, and your dreams. In return, offer support for them and their growth and goals. This relationship will add enlightenment, joy and confidence to your life.

A second consideration is to know what you value in life. It can be difficult to know your personal values in this world because so many voices can relay so many different messages. Consider the statements of the world sent through television programs, commercials, radio commentaries, music, movies, sports, etc. The values demonstrated by Jesus' choices are not readily visible in the world, yet they are the way to the truth. Your values will guide your choices, thoughts, decisions, and actions. Learn what you value; know what you stand for; acknowledge who you are, a child of God.

As you consider what you value, also consider what you enjoy and where your skills lie. Make a list of things and activities that give you pleasure and that you perform well. See if a pattern develops. You may discover a single area of interest, or you may find you have multiple interests. Either way, you are beginning the journey to discover your purpose. God will show you the way. You may be young in life or an older adult. The journey is different for each individual. In addition, your purpose may evolve to incorporate new faces, challenges, and adventures. Relax and enjoy the journey. God is in control, and he will see you through to a rewarding, joyful victory.

Finally, you must keep learning and growing. Seek opportunities to enjoy life and learn more about yourself and your faith. These junctures of growth may be structured as Bible studies, classes, training, workshops, etc. The opportunities may, however, be unstructured casual events where you meet new people, read books, watch movies, etc. Additionally, you must learn from past mistakes. Unfortunately, mistakes can make you feel judged or small, but keep moving forward. Mistakes often teach life lessons. The Lord understands and will forgive you if you repent. Although sometimes difficult, you must learn to forgive yourself. Rather than dwell on past mistakes, ask yourself what you can learn from this situation. Ask God for forgiveness, forgive yourself, and then move on.

Jessica Roebke Hoft, my dear niece, a gifted education teacher, and a follower of Christ, tells me, "God's plan is not always specific. So, make a choice, and if you don't like it, make a different one."[31] She recommends you do not put pressure on yourself to follow one divinely ordained path; it is difficult enough to follow the general expectations set out in the Bible. Always remember, "You can't mess up God's plan."[32]

What makes you come alive? What do you enjoy? What are your specific gifts, your passions, your struggles? God has great plans for you! As you prayerfully seek to discover these answers, you will find God's purpose in your life. The Holy Spirit will bless your preparation for service and the fulfillment of that service. Life will be spiritually richer and more contented as you serve your God and invest in a cause greater than yourself.

Jesus lived with purpose, enthusiasm and eagerness. He displayed tenderness and caring. He lived a modest and humble life. He spoke courageously for God. We should use His example as a guide for our lives!

God's Children – Chosen and Called

> "I came that they may have life, and have it abundantly."
>
> John 10:10

GOD HAS OFFERED us each the gift to become a "Child of God." God realizes we are sinners and make mistakes, but his love for us is so great that he still wants to have a close relationship. As a child of God, you can enjoy the confidence in his protection from evil and the promise of everlasting life. God's power will also give you the strength to change your life, moving from cowardice to confidence, selfishness to service, or possibly exhaustion to renewal. God knows your needs; he will guide you to a more joyful, fulfilled life.

Below is the listing and excerpts from William Barclay regarding the things for which we are chosen and to which we are called.[33]

- You are chosen for joy. It is true that the Christian is a sinner, but he is a redeemed sinner; and therein lies his joy.
- You are chosen for love. We are sent out into the world to love one another. Sometimes we live as if we were sent into the world to compete with one another, or to dispute with one another, or even to actively fight with one another. But

Christians are sent into the world to live in such a way that we show what is meant by loving our fellow humans.
- Jesus has called you to be His friend. That is a tremendous offer. It means that no longer do we need to gaze longingly at God from afar.
- Jesus called you to be His partner. He has shared His mind with you, and opened His heart to you, and told you of His plans, His aims, and His ambitions. Jesus has given you the honor of making you His partner in His task.
- Jesus chose you to be ambassadors. He did not choose you to live a life retired from the world; He chose you to represent Him in the world. Jesus chose you first. Come unto Him, and then go out to the world.
- Jesus chose you to be advertisements. He chose you to go out and bear fruit, and to bear fruit which will remain, which will stand the test of time. The only way to bring others to the Christian faith is to show them the fruit of the Christian life. Jesus sends us out, not to argue individuals into Christianity… but to attract them into Christianity, to live that the fruits may be so wonderful that others may desire these fruits for themselves.
- Jesus chose you to be a privileged member of the family of God. God is with you and will provide whatever you ask in His name and seeking His will.

When times are difficult, we can find comfort in that we are children of God. In the listing below, you will discover additional gifts God gives his children. After reading this list, pause and ask the Holy Spirit to open your eyes to see the gifts God has prepared for you this day.

- God's guidance will give you greater confidence in your chosen path. You will see things as you have not seen them before and have greater clarity.
- As you experience greater confidence, the seeds of doubt,

despair, frustration, and fear will lessen or leave entirely. Jesus is in control; find rest in his guidance and his purpose for your life. He will help you overcome the clutch of evil and destructive ways and allow his power to work within you for goodness and purpose.
- God loves you and will be with you through all of life. He is your constant companion. He offers you the forgiveness of sin and gives you a future of a purposeful, fulfilled life on earth and everlasting life in heaven.
- Suppose you truly accept God's laws as commands that are designed to make your life better. Your acceptance gives more peace, loveliness, compassion, strength of character, knowledge, etc. You will reap the benefits that companionship with our Lord offers.

To be a child of God is to live to serve him. This change in your nature takes time. It is a process; it doesn't happen by making a one-time commitment; it comes step-by-step over time, as God sees you are ready for the next step. God loves you; his plans are for good. He will lovingly care for you.

Christian Qualities

> "Give your servant, therefore, an understanding mind…
> able to discern between good and evil."
>
> 1 Kings 3:9

RELATIONSHIPS CAN BE one of the most rewarding or the most frustrating gifts on earth. Each human has the power to strengthen or diminish relationships by their choice of behaviors. Most everyone desires a close intimate relationship with another person or persons. Examples often seen on television, in song, or within society are destructive. However, the Holy Bible is a powerful guide and gives many examples of human behaviors that enrich relationships and demonstrate a Christ-like spirit. Keep the following list of behaviors and references close to your heart and fresh in your mind so you may grow in your ability to use them throughout your life.

1. **Love one another**:
   - "Just as I have loved you, you also should love one another." John 13:34
   - "Love one another deeply from the heart." Hebrews 10:24
   - "For this is the message you have heard from the beginning, that we should love one another." 1 John 3:11
   - "Beloved, let us love one another, because love is from God; everyone who loves is born of God and knows God." 1 John 4:7

2. **Be devoted to others:**

    - "Let love be genuine; hate what is evil, hold fast to what is good; love one another with mutual affection; outdo one another in showing honor." Romans 12:9-10
    - "All of you must clothe yourselves with humility in your dealing with one another." 1 Peter 5:5
    - "Be subject to one another out of reverence for Christ." Ephesians 5:21
    - "For you were called to freedom...only do not use your freedom as an opportunity for self-indulgence, but through love become a slave to one another." Galatians 5:13

3. **Spend time with one another:**

    - "Greet one another with a holy kiss." Romans 16:16, 1Corinthians 16:20, 2 Corinthians 13:12
    - "Greet one another with a kiss of love." 1 Peter 5:14
    - "Be hospitable to one another without complaining." 1 Peter 4:9
    - "If we walk in the light as he himself is in the light, we have fellowship with one another." 1 John 1:7

4. **Allow others to be imperfect - don't become irritated with them**:

    - "With all humility and gentleness, with patience, bearing with one another in love, making every effort to maintain the unity of the Spirit in the bond of peace." Ephesians 4:2
    - "Bear with one another and, if anyone has a complaint against another, forgive each other; just as the Lord has forgiven you, so you also must forgive." Colossians 3:13
    - "Welcome one another, therefore, just as Christ has welcomed you, for the glory of God." Romans 15:7
    - "Be at peace with one another." Mark 9:50

5. **Build one another up with words -- be helpful to one another:**

   - "Let us then pursue what makes for peace and for mutual upbuilding." Romans 14:19
   - "Therefore encourage one another and build up each other." 1 Thessalonians 5:11
   - "So then, putting away falsehood, let all of us speak the truth to our neighbors." Ephesians 4:25
   - "I myself feel confident about you...that you yourselves are full of goodness, filled with all knowledge and able to instruct one another." Romans 15:14
   - "Let the word of Christ dwell in you richly; teach and admonish one another." Colossians 3:16
   - "Let no evil talk come out of your mouths, but only what is useful for building up, as there is need, so that your words may give grace to those who hear." Ephesians 4:29

6. **Have a gentle heart toward others in difficulty:**

   - "Encourage one another with these words." 1 Thessalonians 4:18
   - "Be kind to one another, tenderhearted, forgiving one another, as God in Christ has forgiven you." Ephesians 4:32
   - "Have unity of spirit, sympathy, love for one another, a tender heart, and a humble mind." 1 Peter 3:8

The qualities above are essential, but you must also remember another gift from our Lord, **a smiling face**. It is one of the most attractive and contagious images in the world. You have the power to make the life of another person more cheerful with a gentle, caring, infectious spirit. A new friendship may be cultivated and a new soul saved for the Lord if you develop and share with others the qualities noted above. Throw in a cheerful smile, too.

"Keep a smile on your face." Romans 12:8 (MSG)

Breath Prayers

"The prayer of the righteous is powerful and effective."
James 5:16

PRAYER IS YOUR way to talk to God. Breath Prayers are one-sentence statements about something you want to share with God. Breath Prayers are easy to use and comforting. This step-by-step explanation to create Breath Prayers may be helpful to begin this practice, but quickly, you will discover your brief yet personal conversation with God.

Step 1:
Remind yourself that God Loves You!

> "Be still and know that I am God" (Psalm 46:10).
> "The Lord is my shepherd" (Psalm 23:1).

Step 2:
God asks you: "(Insert your name)" what do you need?"

Step 3:
Answer God with what is directly on your heart.

Step 4:
Choose your favorite name for God and call God by name.
(God, Jesus, Lord, Counselor, other)

Step 5:
Combine your chosen name for God and your answer to his question and you have a prayer.

Examples: (Try to limit the statement of prayer to 6-8 words)

- Dear Lord, let me feel your peace.
- God, let me think clearly on this test.
- Lord, this situation is too much for me. Help!
- God, please help me know what to do about (insert your concern).
- God, guide me in your ways.
- Lord, help me show your love to others.
- Open the eyes of my heart, Lord!
- Jesus, give me your strength, comfort, and guidance.

Breath prayers are powerful. God listens, and God will always act in your best interest. Trust in his love, wisdom, and power. Go to him in prayer today and always.

His Eye Is on the Sparrow

Why should I feel discouraged,
Why should the shadows come,
Why should my heart be lonely,
And long for heaven and home;
   When Jesus is my portion?
   My constant friend is he;
   His eye is on the sparrow,
   And I know he watches me;
   His eye is on the sparrow,
   And I know he watches me.

(Refrain)
I sing because I'm happy,
I sing because I'm free;
For his eye is on the sparrow,
And I know he watches me.

Civilla D. Martin

My Best Friend

> "No one has greater love than this,
> To lay down one's life for his friends."
>
> John 15:13

BEST FRIENDS ARE lovely gifts. But, in this entire world, your very best friend can be your Lord, Jesus Christ. Why? There are a few reasons why Jesus can be your best friend…1) He knows you at your best and worst, and he loves you. 2) He shows you how to best live your life and make choices to give your life purpose, fulfillment, joy, and inner peace, and 3) He will never leave you.

Jesus knows you! Wow, he even knows you better than you know yourself. He knows your world, having been with you from the start and seeing your life unfold. He knows the burdens and brokenness that have left scars on your heart, and it saddens him. He knows your skills and shortcomings, your dreams, pain, confusion, tears. The world does not always understand. Commonly, you may sometimes try to hide your inner self (feelings, dreams, hurts), but Jesus knows. You cannot hide from him. That is wonderful. He knows you and loves you as an imperfect and flawed child of God! You can go to him in joy and sadness, and he gets it. He does not judge you harshly. Instead, Jesus wants you to invite him into your world. He wants to help build your life to have purpose, fulfillment, joy, and inner peace. He loves you!

MY BEST FRIEND

Jesus' life on this earth is an example to you as to how our Lord made choices. Jesus has been on this earth and lived the emotional pain, sadness, love, and joy. As you face the challenges of each day, reflect on Jesus' example and know the better choices to make. If the result does not unfold as you might wish, you have the confidence that Jesus is with you, you are not alone, and he will give you strength. He knows humans are not perfect and will mess up, but he wants to help you and see you through. If you open your heart to him, he will show you how to live life with meaning, empowerment, gladness, and harmony. What a gift!

Finally, Jesus will never leave you! This world can be a lonely place. Even among many people, you can feel alone, as if you do not belong. It is a hurtful feeling and can be difficult. But, today, you know that Jesus has not left you alone. He is with you! In times of joy or sadness, Jesus is by your side. You know this. You may talk to him like your friend. He doesn't leave you, and you always feel his love. His love is a great comfort!

Jesus wants to be your friend, but how do you allow Jesus to be that friend? As you have read, you have to open your heart and mind to him. What exactly does that mean? Be active in seeking knowledge about him. You should take time to listen to others who love him, and you should read about him. As you begin to know and better understand Jesus, you will find him. God is your friend. He will be there for you always. May God bless you with the joy of feeling his friendship, touch and love all your days.

Going with Jesus, Walking Together

He is the author of our life
Our comforter and friend.
He's with us now and he will be
Right with us to the end.

(Refrain:)
We're going with Jesus, walking together,
Over the path he has trod,
And up every mountain down every valley,
We walk along with God.

We've heard his word we know it's true,
He came to save the world;
Let's help the people, all the people,
Jesus keeps his word.

O Lamb or God you died for us,
You taught us how to live.
To love each other, help each other,
Just the way you did.

Love's like a candle God sets out,
To light your world and mine.
If each of us would light but one
Just think how it would shine.

Unknown

Spiritual Growth - Habits of Faith

> "I have called you friends,
> because I have made known to you everything
> that I have heard from my Father."
> John 15:15

JESUS INVITES YOU to know him and to know him intimately. Very few people will ask how you're doing spiritually, so ask yourself. Is my walk with God more deliberate today than a year ago? Is my spiritual journey growing or has it slowed or even stopped? Answer honestly, and although it may prove challenging, if necessary, look for ways to adjust your habits. Seek time to read, attend church, study, and pray. As you grow spiritually, your life will be blessed through relationships with other followers of Christ and in the knowledge of your Lord and Savior. Ask God to help you find ways to grow spiritually. The Holy Spirit will be with you and honor that request.

Start small. I encourage you to look for ways that God is moving in your life. He is there! Begin with small steps of seeking Him. Say, "Hello, God!" each day when you wake up, as you dress or eat, while you study or relax, or while you drive in heavy or light traffic. Begin in small ways, and soon you will have developed a habit of seeing God each day, and begin to see more opportunities to be close to him. With this small effort, you will feel his presence and blessings in your life.

It will become a habit as you begin to actively practice speaking to the Lord and listening for his will. This "habit of faith" will give you great peace and joy as you journey through life. God will be there to share with you as a good friend and caring Father. Learn to look to God and lean on his strength. To do so, you must be in the practice of seeking the assistance of our Lord, offering thanks for joyful times, and looking to the Holy Spirit for guidance.

Share your life with your Lord by remembering him throughout your day. Speak with him during times of joy and happiness, offering thanks. Seek his guidance and wisdom in times of pain or trial. Ask for specifics, healing a friendship, a clear mind for an exam, forgiveness from a hurt, playing a good game, etc. The more often you practice including him, the more you will notice he is there for you! His continual presence in your life adds a dimension of great peace and joy!

Practice this "habit of faith" each day as you are in the habit of brushing your teeth each morning. Make your faith a part of your nature so it is automatic to quietly speak to your God in thanksgiving or in search of support and guidance. God is yours, and he will rejoice in your new relationship with him! Try it! Spend some time with God today!

"You are indeed my rock and my fortress; for your name's sake, lead me and guide me." Psalm 31:3

> "God expects but one thing of you,
> And that is that you…
> Let God be God in you."
>
> Meister Eckhart

Trust God - He Is There For You

> "They are not afraid of evil tidings;
> Their hearts are firm, secure in the Lord."
>
> Psalm 112:7

WE ALL TRY to make sense of our world with all of the rules and systems of order. The world says we will be successful if we earn a lot of money, have a big home, drive a nice car, marry a physically attractive person, have a position of power, etc. These rules and systems are in place to maintain order and control. Unfortunately, this system of order also has a tendency to harm and diminish relationships. The world's systems create pain, self-centeredness, and violence. It builds a belief that we are each on our own and somewhat insignificant.

The world's way is not God's way! God wants to have a relationship with us and accepts each of us as we are today. God only asks that we make an effort to learn about and get to know him. He will join us!

To have a personal relationship with God, you must trust him. Know that God loves you! Although you may not always see and understand God's ways, you can trust him. He wants what is best for you. Share with him; get to know him better by spending time learning about his Word and his ways. God will help you discover your authentic self. He will loose the hold of pain, sorrow, and brokenness, that everyone sometimes experiences and show you something extraordinary in its place.

Scripture cites numerous examples of God keeping his promises to the faithful. For example, the Old Testament scripture cites Psalms 119:58, written by David, shepherd boy and king, "I implore your favor with all my heart: be gracious to me according to your promise." In the New Testament, the apostle John writes in his book John 14:23, Jesus' words, "Those who love me will keep my word, and my Father will love them, and we will come to them and make our home with them." The apostle Peter also tells you of God's faithful promise in his letter 2 Peter 1:2, "May grace and peace be yours in abundance in the knowledge of God and of Jesus our Lord."

God is indeed faithful and trustworthy. Even when you do not understand his guidance or perspective, he will be faithful if you trust him. You are not alone, ever! God loves you, he is your friend! Seek his wisdom! Never forget to offer thanks for his friendship! God is good!

"Do not be conformed to this world, but be transformed by the renewing of your minds, so that you may discern what is the will of God – what is good and acceptable and perfect." Romans 12:2

Trust and Obey

When we walk with the Lord
In the light of his word,
What a glory he sheds on our way!
While we do his good will,
He abides with us still,
And with all who will trust and obey.

(Refrain)
Trust and obey, for there's no other way
To be happy in Jesus, but to trust and obey.

But we never can prove
The delights of his love
Until all on the altar we lay;
For the favor he shows, for the joy be bestows,
Are for them who will trust and obey.

John H. Sammis

Live For Today

"Come now you who say,
'Today or tomorrow we will go to such and such.'
Yet you do not even know what tomorrow will bring.
Instead you ought to say,
'If the Lord wishes, we will live and do this or that.'"

James 4:13-15

WM. PAUL YOUNG, in his book, *The Shack*, asks the question, "Do you think humans are designed to live in the past, the present or the future?"[34] Ask yourself the same question. In your mind, do you spend most of your time thinking about yesterday's happenings, experiencing today's events, or are you concerned and planning for tomorrow? Young continues to explain that most of us spend little time enjoying the present. Instead, we spend a good portion in the past, and a great deal of time trying to figure out the future.

The past provides you a good tool for learning. How can you learn from these experiences? What choices and experiences worked well? What might be improved upon? Determine the answers to these questions, and then leave the past behind. It may be healthy to look back occasionally to remember what you learned, but keep moving forward. Do not stay in the past.

Human beings tend to be uncomfortable with the unknown, and the future is unknown. The future can be scary, so human beings spend much time worrying or preparing for future happenings. You have limited or little control of the future. When you have faith and trust in the Lord, you have peace with the unknown because you have the assurance that he will care for you. God does know what the future holds, and God is powerful. Looking to the future can be healthy when you seek ways to create present day actions that will help achieve the goals you and the Lord have determined. Matthew tells you of Jesus' words in Matthew 6:34, "So do not worry about tomorrow, for tomorrow will bring worries of its own. Today's trouble is enough for today."

Faith in God allows you to spend most of your time living in the present. Thus, you have the freedom to enjoy the gifts of here and now, and address the challenges of today. To live in the present, you must learn to believe and understand that God loves you, he is good, and he is all-powerful. When fear takes hold, you do not see God's hand in the situation; step back and look for God. He is there with you and will guide you to a resolution, an open door. He has been there for you from the beginning and is there for you every day, in your past, present, and future! God loves you!

Day by Day

Day by day and with each passing moment,
Strength I find to meet my trials here;
Trusting in my Father's wise bestowment,
I've no cause for worry or for fear.
He whose heart is kind beyond all measure
Gives unto each day what he deems best –
Lovingly, it's part of pain and pleasure,
Mingling toil with peace and rest.

Ev'ry day the Lord himself is near me,
With a special mercy for each hour;
All my cares he gladly bears and cheers me,
He whose name is Counselor and Pow'r.
The protection of his child and treasure
Is a charge that on himself he laid:
"As your days, your strength shall be in measure"-
This the pledge to me he made.

Carolina Sandell

Discover Genuine Freedom

> "Choose this day whom you will serve...
> but as for me and my household,
> we will serve the Lord."
>
> Joshua 24:15

FREEDOM DOES NOT mean that you are allowed to do whatever you want. There are many influences in your life that restrict your freedom including genetic heritage, body build, activity within your brain (mental conversations), family structure, family health, and climate. Additional influences are evident throughout our society: such things as television programs, movies, advertisements, propaganda, and politics are just a few societal factors that impact your freedom. These influences in your life can cause mixed up, confused feelings, a loss of joy and peace! How can you find freedom? How can you be truly free and at peace?

The path to freedom is offered as a choice: The world's way or God's way? The world teaches the way to happiness and freedom is selfishness. Many people have tried this path and have found disillusionment. The perfect job, great wealth, the large fine home, and beautiful clothes did not fulfill their needs as they had been led to believe. Life was shallow and meaningless.

The apostle Paul, in his letter to the Galatians 4:7, shares, "So you are no longer a slave but a child, and if then a child, also an heir through God." Before Christ, you were a slave to the forces of the world, religious rules, and practices of the ungodly, not living by the grace and Spirit of God through Jesus Christ. God sent Jesus into the world to take you from bondage and give the gift of salvation and everlasting life. Christians experience a sense of belonging with God as the Holy Spirit creates this feeling within. Those who believe in Jesus Christ as their Savior develop an intimacy with God and faith in his promises.

God offers true freedom. "Freedom is a process that happens inside a relationship with him. All the stuff you have churnin' around inside will start to work its way out."[35] As you learn to understand the ways of your Lord and start to practice those ways in your life, you will begin to feel the freedom of spirit that will allow you to have a life with meaning. Understanding and choosing God's way will allow you to handle situations with peace, knowing the better choice, and feeling confident with whatever might happen in this mixed up world. The great joy and inner peace you will experience through the grace of God makes the time and effort worthwhile.

Stand Up, Stand Up for Jesus

Stand up, stand up for Jesus,
stand in his strength alone;
The arm of flesh will fail you,
ye dare not trust your own.
Put on the gospel armor,
each piece put on with prayer;
where duty calls or danger,
be never wanting there.

Stand up, stand up for Jesus,
the strife will not be long;
This day the noise of battle,
the next, the victor's song.
To those who vanquish evil
a crown of life shall be;
He with the King of Glory
shall reign eternally.

George Duffield

Don't Worry What Others Think

"In God I trust; I am not afraid.
What can mere mortals do to me?"

Psalm 56:11

THROUGHOUT LIFE'S EXPERIENCES, we often feel the judgment of others. The assessment may create positive or negative feelings. However, the power these judgments hold on you, over time, may cause you to be overly concerned about what others think. The power of what others' think could motivate you to be more considerate or to try harder to gain a common understanding. But, unfortunately, there are times when the fear of others' opinions can be debilitating. If you sense you are overly concerned about what others might think, and you would like to develop greater concern for God's thinking on the matter, there is help. Let's evaluate the nature of judgment from God, and dampen the power of judgement from other people.

> God's judgment: We never know what God is actually thinking, however, the Bible shares insight into his being. We know that God will take our concerns seriously, and he wants to help us (Psalm 46:1-3). God also has the power to provide and help (Isaiah 41:10, Hebrews 13:6). Furthermore, God knows you, and all aspects of your life. He is with you always and cares about you and the situation

in which you are currently living (Psalm 23:1-6, Philippians 4:6-7). God wants to help!

<u>Other people's judgment</u>: First, realize that other people have their own lives to live and have little time to care about you. Their judgments may come from personal experiences, prideful attitudes, shortcomings or hurts. Although their negative opinion of you may be painful, it is likely not really about you. They are focused on themselves.

You cannot control others, however, you can pray for them and for God's help and guidance. Prayer may not immediately ease the pain, but it may help you as you give your challenge to God and allow his wisdom, compassion, and power to strengthen you and resolve the matter.

Practice intentional behaviors. Take time to learn God's ways and look for opportunities to practice them. Make deliberate effort to stop the worry. You did what you thought was right at a given time, therefore allow yourself the freedom from fear. Pray that your choices may always be guided by a genuine attempt to be honorable to God.

Leaning on the Everlasting Arms

What a fellowship, what a joy divine,
Leaning on the everlasting arms;
What a blessedness, what a peace is mine,
Leaning on the everlasting arms.

(Refrain)
Leaning, leaning,
Safe and secure from all alarms;
Leaning, leaning,
Leaning on the everlasting arms.

What have I to dread, what have I to fear,
Leaning on the everlasting arms?
I have blessed peace with my Lord so near,
Leaning on the everlasting arms.

E. A. Hoffman

The Gift of Time - You Cannot Do It All

"Be still and know that I am God."
(Psalm 46:10)

THIS WORLD OFFERS endless tasks to be completed or experienced. Unfortunately, you cannot do it all! It is a fact that there will always be more to do than can be done; work, leisure, travel, friends, family, etc. If you look at Jesus' life, one will see that even he did not attempt to handle everything. Jesus worked hard to minister to the people and teach God's message. He cared deeply for people, but he was tired, maybe even exhausted at the end of a day, yet he remained calm. Why? Jesus ministered to many people, but he did not minister to everyone. Jesus looked to his Father to help him understand his call, his use of time, and his priorities. The world had many needs, and Jesus was not sent to cure or solve them all. He was, however, sent to show us how to obtain a better life in the life to come, in eternity. Jesus' choices during his time on earth were helping people and giving honor, praise, and service to God.

We can use Jesus' life as an example for us. We will never be able to meet all the needs around us or accomplish all that needs to be done, regardless of our intelligence, strength or capabilities. However, we can find time and the ability to do what God is calling us to do. Upon further examination of Christ's life, one will find suggestions for the use of time:

- Cultivate relationships with people of faith and others. Developing relationships with people is time-consuming. Plan time for significant others, family and friends, to create strong connections.
- Plan regular quiet time with God. Discover for yourself some manner in which to learn more about your God. Study His Word. Talk to God in prayer; he wants to hear from you. Throughout the day, take a few minutes to think of God, and include him in your daily activities.
- Honor God in all aspects of your life. Each person has twenty-four hours a day and no more. Prioritize your time to serve the Lord's purposes. Try to live your life so, in the end; the Lord will say, "Well done, good and trustworthy servant!" Matthew 25:21

Give up the frustrations and quit unnecessary tasks; put first things first, prioritize! Just as Jesus allowed God to guide him and his use of time on this earth, we can and should do the same. Life can be full of greater contentment and less stress if we learn to use our time and understand the saying:

> "You are not responsible for everything,
> That's My job.
> Love, God"
>
> Unknown

Lessons from the Mountain -1-

"Take heart, son; your sins are forgiven."
Matthew 9:2

IN PREVIOUS WRITINGS, you have read of the qualities of our Lord Jesus and how we each must strive to live our lives to model these qualities. But as humans, we all continually fall short. In Jesus' Sermon on the Mount (Matthew 5-7), he identifies many behaviors that must be put on each individual's 'Stop Doing' list. Robert (Bob) Casady, my friend, author, and pastor for many years, shares an outline of these behaviors:[36]

- Don't do things to draw attention to yourself!

    "So when you give something to a needy person, do not make a big show of it, as the hypocrites do in the houses of worship and on the streets. When you help a needy person, do it in such a way that even your closest friend will not know about it." Matthew 6:2, 3 (GNB)

- Don't stockpile things down here!

    "Do not store up for yourselves treasures on earth where moth and rust destroy and where thieves break in and steal; but store up for yourselves treasures in heaven...For where your treasure is, there your heart will be also." Matthew 6:19-21

FOLLOWING CHRIST

- Don't think that God isn't concerned about your everyday needs.

    Matthew tells us of Jesus' words in Matthew 6:25, "I tell you, do not worry about your life, what you will eat or what you will drink, or about your body, what you will wear." The most money, the newest toys, the biggest house, or the best grades will not lead to contentment or peace. Only God can give real peace.

- Don't get worked up about what may or may not happen in the future.

    Again, Matthew tells us of Jesus' words; "Do not worry about tomorrow, for tomorrow will bring worries of its own. Today's trouble is enough for today." Matthew 6:34

Pastor Casady summarizes this sermon with the following thought, "How do we pick ourselves up when we sin? We don't. We reach out to God who loves us and desires that we love him. God lifts us up! As we repent (change our thinking) and seek forgiveness, God welcomes us into his loving arms."[37]

'Tis So Sweet to Trust in Jesus

'Tis so sweet to trust in Jesus,
And to take him at his word;
Just to rest upon his promise,
And to know, "Thus saith the Lord!"

(Refrain)
Jesus, Jesus, how I trust him!
How I've proved him o'er and o'er!
Jesus, Jesus, precious Jesus!
O for grace to trust him more!

Louisa M. R. Stead

Lessons from the Mountain -2-

> "When Jesus saw the crowds,
> he went up the mountain; and after he sat down,
> his disciples came to him.
> Then he began to speak and taught them."
>
> Matthew 5:1-2

THE STUDY OF Jesus' teachings from the Sermon on the Mountain continues to look at the scripture from Matthew 5:17-48. In life, you have limited control of your circumstances. However, with God's help, you can work to control your thoughts and how you react to various situations. The following materials are excerpts from a sermon by Pastor Bob Casady:[38]

- Jesus refers to murder in verses 21-22. He explains it is not enough to avoid killing; you must also <u>relinquish anger and hatred.</u>
- Jesus refers to offerings in verses 23-26. He explains it is not enough to offer gifts; you must also <u>have a right relationship with God and others, and must give offerings in joy, love and service to your God.</u>
- Jesus refers to adultery in verses 27-30. He explains it is not enough to avoid sexual relationships with anyone other than your spouse; you must also keep your hearts from lusting and <u>be faithful in all ways to your commitment</u> to your spouse.

LESSONS FROM THE MOUNTAIN -2-

- Jesus refers to divorce in verses 31-32. He explains it is not enough to be legally married; you must also <u>live out your marriage commitments</u>. Live out the promises made in the wedding vows and share unselfish love as God identifies in 1 Corinthian 13.
- Jesus refers to oaths in verses 33-37. He explains that there are times and occasions when it is appropriate to make an oath; you must also <u>avoid casual and irresponsible commitments. Your word should be honorable.</u>
- Jesus refers to revenge in verses 38-47. He explains it is not enough to seek justice; you must <u>extend mercy and show love to others.</u>

Jesus' message on the mountain identifies areas in which humans may struggle. Pray for the guidance of the Holy Spirit as these challenges confront you. Pray as David prayed in Psalm 19:14 "Let the words of my mouth and the meditation of my heart be acceptable to you, O Lord, my rock and my redeemer."

"So then, anyone who hears these words of mine and obeys them is like a wise man who built his house on rock. The rain poured down, the rivers flooded over, and the wind blew hard against the house. But it did not fall, because it was built on rock. But anyone who hears these words of mine and does not obey them is like a foolish man who built his house on sand. The rain poured down, the rivers flooded over, the wind blew hard against that house, and it fell. And what a terrible fall that was!" Matthew 7:24-27

Jesus' Lesson about Revenge

"Love your enemies, do good to those who hate you,
bless those who curse you, pray for those who abuse you.
If anyone strikes you on the cheek, offer the other also."

Luke 6:27-29

AMONG THE FIRST lessons Jesus' taught his disciples, in his Sermon on the Mountain, was concerning the subject of revenge. Jesus' message to offer the other cheek if someone strikes you is recorded in Luke 6:29 and Matthew 5:38. This phrase is to teach us to avoid the need to retaliate for offenses. This passage, however, may be confusing because the Lord gives us the will to face evil boldly.

In today's world, this verse is sometimes interpreted through a lens of modern culture rather than that of Jesus' time, thus creating confusion and misunderstanding. Nowadays, some believe "turning the other cheek" means looking the other way, letting it go, being compliant, or surrendering. This choice may allow exploitation or oppression to go unchallenged or place you or others in danger; it falls short of Jesus' message. Our Lord does not call us to be doormats to evil. Proverbs 28:1, we are told, "Honest people are relaxed and confident, bold as lions (MSG)."

During Jesus' time, listeners clearly understood this lesson because of the practices of society. For example, if a more affluent individual were to strike a person of less privilege, the power of a right-handed strike was more robust than a left-handed strike. Therefore, the lesser privileged person would turn their face to offer the other cheek requiring the oppressor to use their weaker hand if they struck again, lessening their power.

What is meant by this passage, on a personal level, for personal attacks? Jesus' command is to forego retaliation for offenses; do not fight violence with violence. This scripture is not saying let others do whatever they want to you and ignore their behaviors. As Paul tells you in his letter to Romans 12:18-19, "Do everything possible on your part to live in peace with everybody. Never take revenge, my friends, but let God's anger do it. For the scripture says, 'I will take revenge, I will pay back, says the Lord (GNB).'" Paul continues, "Do not let evil defeat you; instead, conquer evil with good (GNB)." You should have standards and uphold them by finding creative nonviolent ways to address the issue. When your respect or dignity is challenged or attacked, you are not to retaliate with revenge. You should pray for your adversaries and love them. God will take care of the judgment. We are to graciously stand up for what we believe. This power comes as the Holy Spirit provides the necessary restraint, wisdom, and patience to seek God's guidance and will. Always remember Jesus' words as he was facing crucifixion, he prayed, "Father, forgive them, for they do not know what they are doing (Luke 23:24)."

Within our society, there must be laws and order to thrive. However, we must be mindful of the institutions within our community, culture, and the world and boldly act to keep God's love and commands within the systems. So how should one interpret this verse to allow the boldness of action that our Lord empowers? We are commanded in Luke 6:27-28 to "Love your enemies, do good to those who hate you, bless those who curse you, and pray for those who abuse you." Instead of ignoring the problem, seek ways to insert God's love into the lives of those involved and in the situation. We should utilize wisdom, action, creativity, and nonviolent challenges to the unacceptable situation, boldly challenging injustice, contesting exploitation, oppression, poverty, inequality, and destruction.

"Have you heard that it was said, 'An eye for an eye and a tooth for a tooth.' But I say to you, do not resist an evil doer. But if anyone strikes you on the right cheek, turn the other also." Matthew 5:38-39

Living on Earth - Why Is It So Difficult?

> "So God created humankind in his image...
> God blessed them, and God said to them,
> 'Be fruitful and multiply, and fill the earth and subdue it;
> and have dominion over the fish of the sea
> and over the birds of the air
> and over every living thing that moves on the earth.'
> God said, 'See, I have given you every plant yielding seed
> that is upon the face of all the earth,
> and every tree with a seed in its fruit;
> you shall have them for food.
> Every beast of the earth, and every bird of the air,
> and to everything that creeps on the earth,
> everything that has the breath of life,
> I have given every green plant for food.'
> God saw everything he made, and indeed it was very good."
>
> Genesis 1:27-31

WHEN GOD CREATED the heavens and the earth, he blessed them and provided all the creatures of the earth and its habitat for man, and man was to have dominion (ownership, authority) over it. That is a beautiful gift and a responsibility. You will notice the last sentence in the scripture above states, "God saw everything he made, and indeed it was very good" (Genesis 1:31). It is important to realize that God did not create sin, nor does he approve or desire evil in the world. James 1:13 tells you, "No one when tempted should say, 'I am being tempted by God.'" God cannot be tempted by evil and he himself tempts no one. However, one is tempted by one's own desire, being lured and enticed by it. God's original design did not include the suffering that exists in the world today; suffering is a result of our sin.

Although the earth is full of beauty and wonder, since the original sin of Adam and Eve, described in the book of Genesis Chapter 3, it may sometimes be a harsh, cruel place, and you may have often asked yourself, "If God really loves us, why does he let this happen?" This question is not easy, but can be partially answered in God's desire to allow us the choice.

The Lord offers people freedom of choice. Even when choices prove hurtful or damaging to yourself or others, God allows you to choose. God does not force his will on people. Even if you preferred he took control to save the pain. God does not want slaves to his will. God gives opportunities to learn about him and allows each person the choice to share life and relationship with him. Many of us want a God who will just take control and remove the heartache and pain. That is not the nature of our God.

God is just, and justice requires the penalty. Punishment from God is intended to help the sinner realize the sinful choice, repent and turn to God. "Bodily afflictions, loss of property, misfortunes, etc., may constitute real punishment to the ungodly, but...to Christians, they are administered not in the spirit of wrath and vengeance, but in the spirit of love for the purposes of correction and trial."[39] Paul tells you in Hebrew 12:5-6, "My child, do not regard lightly the discipline of the Lord, or lose heart when you are punished by him; for the Lord disciplines those whom he loves, and chastises every child whom he accepts."

LIVING ON EARTH - WHY IS IT SO DIFFICULT?

The Bible tells you that the punishment for sin against God is death. The book of Romans 6:23 explains, "For the wages of sin is death." Death may be a spiritual death that occurs when an individual no longer seeks God. Death may be a bodily, temporal death, when the body dies, and the soul separates. Finally, there is eternal death which occurs when an individual fails and is no longer in the presence of God but receives everlasting punishment in hell. The scripture John 3:16, shares the powerful story of Christ's gift of salvation for you. "For God so loves the world that he gave his only Son so that everyone who believes in him may not perish but may have eternal life."

God wants to have a relationship with you. He did not choose to create people as robots. He created each individual with a mind to reason and make choices. Throughout the Bible, God provides you with the roadmap to guide your choices. You will face temptations and your choices matter. He does not promise everything will be perfect. He promises to be with you, you will not stand alone, and he will give you his strength and inner peace. God will consistently deliver you, and he will accomplish your delivery in one of three ways. God will deliver you: 1) from your trials, 2) through your trials, or 3) into the realms of heaven. When you choose to walk with God, he will see you through the trials of this life and reward you in heaven.

"Long ago you laid the foundation of the earth, and the heavens are the work of your hands. They will perish, but you endure."
Psalm 102:25-26

Trials for God – Bearing a Cross

"Righteous art Thou, O Lord,
that I would plead my case with Thee;
Indeed I would discuss matters of justice with Thee:
Why has the way of the wicked prospered?
Why are all those who deal in treachery at ease?"

Jeremiah 12:1 (NASB)

IT IS NOT difficult to find people suffering hardship, strife, or lack of fairness in this life, The Bible is full of writings and stories of people who faced similar challenges. King David and Jeremiah, both men of God, describe the trials of life in their own books within the Old Testament. In his book of Psalms, King David, many times, wrote both praise and complaint to God because of repeated trials in his life. Jeremiah is often referred to as the "weeping prophet" because of his trials as he served God prophetically to Israel. These men spoke to God in honesty and truth. They shared their heartfelt feelings with their Lord.

Studying these godly men in the Bible allows you to better understand the handling of difficulties and trials. In addition, studying these men's stories may shed light on the purpose for suffering. For example, in the book James 1:2-4, you learn, "Whenever you face trials of any kind, consider it nothing but joy, because you know that the testing of your faith produces endurance; and let endurance have its full effect, so that you may be mature and complete, lacking in nothing." James continues in 1:5, "If any of you is lacking in wisdom, ask God, who gives to all generously and ungrudgingly, it will be given you."

God does not create difficulties, nor does he desire them. However, when life's challenges and suffering confront you, God will make good come from them. While suffering, it is difficult to see beyond the pain to the goodness and growth God will bring to this situation. As James recommends, when you are suffering and feel broken, confused, or lost, God will give you wisdom if you ask. The challenges of life can draw you closer to God and open your heart to such qualities as compassion, patience, kindness, faithfulness, gentleness, and self-control.

Jesus tells his followers in Mark 8:34, "If any want to become my followers, let them deny themselves and take up their cross and follow me." Koehler defines bearing a cross as, "… whatever Christians endure because they are Christians, whatever they suffer because they follow the Savior and in word and deed confess His name before men."[40] Each follower of Christ will bear a cross. Matthew 10:22 tells you, "You will be hated by all because of my name. But the one who endures to the end will be saved."

Unlike the result of sin, which creates guilt and punishment, the bearing of a cross is a sign of God's love, not his anger. "If you are reviled for the name of Christ, you are blessed, because the spirit of glory, which is the Spirit of God, is resting on you" (1 Peter 4:14). When your opportunity comes to bear the cross for your Lord, it is not an accident. Throughout the challenge, God will be by your side.

Life isn't fair, a sad fact of life. Good, kind people suffer, and bad, cruel people prosper. Being a follower of Christ does not promise a life free of struggles, pain, suffering or persecution. You have the choice of how to accept life's trials. During your trials and difficulty, the choices you make may allow others to discover the gifts and powers of Christ. He alone can provide comfort, hope, strength, and peace. When suffering is present, God's grace may also be found. When the time comes, and you feel overwhelmed or discouraged by circumstances, choose contentment, knowing that God is in control and you can trust him. "No testing has overtaken you that is not common to everyone. God is faithful, and he will not let you be tested beyond your strength, but with the testing he will also provide the way so that you may be able to endure it." (1 Corinthians 10:13)

Pray that you will seek God's guidance, strength, and peace as you face trials throughout your life. That God will help you learn to be content whatever the circumstances and that you will find comfort in knowing God is with you. Pray that God will use your suffering for his good purposes.

"We know that all things work together for good for those who love God." Romans 8:28

"The Lord is near to the brokenhearted and saves the crushed in spirit." Psalm 34:18

Onward Christian Soldiers

Onward Christian soldiers, marching as to war,
With the cross of Jesus, going on before!
Christ, the royal Master, leads against the foe;
Forward into battle, see His banner go!

(Refrain)
Onward, Christian Soldiers,
Marching as to war,
With the cross of Jesus
Going on before!

Like a mighty army moves the church of God;
Brothers, we are treading where the saints have trod;
We are not divided; all one body we
One in hope and doctrine, one in charity.

S. Baring-Gould

Service Requirements

"Those who find their life will lose it,
and those who lose their life for my sake will find it."

Matthew 10:39

"For those who want to save their life will lose it,
and those who lose their life for my sake,
and for the sake of the gospel, will save it."

Mark 8:35

"For those who want to save their life will lose it,
and those who lose their life for my sake will save it."

Luke 9:24

JESUS IS QUOTED in the gospels Matthew, Mark, and Luke with this repeated message. Scriptures often repeat concepts that are powerful statements about how you must live your faith. In these statements, Jesus tells you the type of service you must be willing to give to follow him.

Consider the following passage, "whoever wants to save his life will lose it." This passage means choosing the immediate and worldly goods of this earthly life over the opportunity to serve God will cause you to lose the gift of eternal life in heaven. Barclay tells you,

SERVICE REQUIREMENTS

"Christians must realize that life is given, not to keep for themselves, but to spend for others; not to nurture its flame but to burn it out for Christ and for others."[41] If a person comes to be comfortable with life on earth and the earthy ways, which are often greed, selfishness, dishonesty, lack of integrity, etc., this person will lose the opportunity of everlasting life. Earthly practices tend to be evil and hurtful, creating sickness, sadness, and hopelessness. You must never become comfortable with these conditions, but you must always seek to show God's love and care through your words and actions. To live a godly life, you must hate the ways of evil and seek the ways of the Lord.

The scripture, "whoever loses his life for my sake will find it," gives insight and wisdom in that you must spend your life selflessly to fulfill God's purpose and discover genuine contentment. "The persons who seek first ease and comfort and security and fulfillment of personal ambition may well get all these things-but they will not be happy people; for we were sent into this world to serve God and our fellow-men."[42]

It would be easy to assume that these verses mean that you have to give up all your dreams to be willing to do God's will. That thought is not correct. In fact, it may be that God is the one who planted the seed for your dreams. He needs you to be the best dentist, teacher, coach, crime fighter, etc., possible and he wants to work with you in that service. If God has a need for you as a missionary in Africa, a seed will be planted in your heart and the idea will blossom. Where he needs you, he will support you and guide your journey. However, you must invite him to drive. With God on your team, your dreams may grow and take on new meaning and joy. Remember, with God's influence on your goals and ambitions, your life on this earth will be one of excellent service to humanity and to God. Allow your goals to be to the glory to God. It is indeed a win, win alternative!

Hardened Hearts

> "They are darkened in their understanding,
> alienated from the life of God
> because of their ignorance and hardness of heart."
>
> Ephesians 4:18

ONE'S RELATIONSHIP WITH Christ is personal; it is about God and you. You must choose to let Him into your heart and life. God will make a personal invitation to your heart, not to a group, but to you. People become children of God because they made a choice to seek God; they are not chosen because of anything special in their lives. Their political status, their family background, or the goodness of their actions--none of that matters. To be a child of God is a personal decision of the heart and mind! God desires all of humankind to love him and worship him; however, he will only open that door to one's heart if the individual asks.

As noted in the scripture above, in the book of Ephesians, the apostle Paul tells us that there are people who have "hardening of their hearts." What does Paul mean about a hardened heart? According to William Barclay, "it loses feeling. It becomes insensitive. The minds of the mass of the people have become insensitive; they can no longer hear and feel the appeal of God."[43] These individuals have had opportunities to see and hear the call of God, but they have chosen to turn away. Who is that individual? Characteristics of individuals who

HARDENED HEARTS

have grown to have hardened hearts might be seen in self-satisfaction or pride. However, it may also be seen in eyes blinded to the struggles of others; hardened feelings insensitive to others; or in the loss of understanding sinful acts, no longer differentiating right and wrong.

A hardened heart is a tragedy! Reach out to help others to see the love of God so the gentleness of heart and spirit may grow and your heart will not grow hard. Pray for God to give you eyes to see, ears to hear, a voice of kindness, and a touch of gentleness.

"God gave them a sluggish spirit, eyes that would not see and ears that would not hear." Romans 11:7

Prayer

> "The prayer of the righteous is powerful and effective."
>
> James 5:16

JESUS WENT TO God in prayer often. In prayer, Jesus asked for God's will and direction, he asked for courage and strength, he prayed for others, and offered thanksgiving. As Jesus directs you to pray, he guides you so that you too can experience the gifts provided by a close relationship to our Father in Heaven. God's directions are made clear in Ephesians 6:18 when Paul writes, "Pray in the Spirit at all times."

A primary reason for prayer is that it helps establish and maintain a relationship with our Lord. Prayer is a discipline. It is necessary to make time to talk to God and quiet your mind, so you are not hurried or distracted. You are having a conversation with God and he promises always to listen. When you take time to pray or talk with God, you are in a continual relationship with him. As Jesus gave his disciples the Lord's Prayer (Matthew 6:9-13), he provided insight to prayer. However, there is no set formula for prayer. You must pray with your heart, mind, and soul. For what do we pray? Consider the following concepts:

- Worship and honor God, his power, his goodness, his love.
- Offer thanksgiving for his gift of your Lord and Savior, Jesus Christ.

- Confess your sins, ask for, and accept his forgiveness.
- Thank Him for the Holy Spirit and ask that you have a will to allow the Spirit's guidance toward greater spiritual understanding and wisdom.
- Thank God for your many blessings.
- Speak to God when you or others face trials of illness, insecurity, family, or other crises. Intercede for others facing complex challenges (talk to God on their behalf).
- Always acknowledge that you desire his will for your life.

"Have faith in God. Truly I tell you, if you say to this mountain, 'Be taken up and thrown into the sea,' and if you do not doubt in your heart, but believe that what you say will come to pass, it will be done for you. So I tell you, whatever you ask for in prayer, believe that you have received it, and it will be yours" (Mark 11: 22-24). Matthew 17:20 also tells you that faith can move mountains. Just as the apostles tell you of God's great power given to the faithful, God's power can indeed make miraculous changes in your life and in our sinful world. As you pray for miraculous happenings, you must have faith that God is powerful and can accomplish your request. Be willing to take your concern to God and be obedient - willing to follow his guidance, and wait patiently and expectantly for him. In addition, your prayer must be a request of love, some bond of caring.

If you are struggling with praying or what to say, remember the Holy Spirit will intercede for you. There are, however, actions you may take that will help if you are struggling with prayer: listen to sermons, read faith-based materials, schedule quiet time in your day, or write to God in a journal. Remember, the Holy Spirit is with you always, even in prayer.

As Jesus asked for direction throughout his life, you too can find the Father's guidance if you ask. You must be willing to ask, and you must know that the Lord hears your prayer and will respond to your needs according to his will, and as he sees what's best for you. God's answer to your prayers may be immediate, and it may be "wait" or possibly "no." You may rest with assurance, however, that God will answer your prayer.

Finally, if you want God's help, ask! Be bold and persistent in prayer. Matthew writes in his book 7:7, "Ask and it will be given you; search, and you will find; knock, and the door will be opened for you." Be honest in your message and always seek God's will. Pray with adoration to God. Pray for your provisions. Pray for forgiveness of sin. Pray for others. Pray that God's will be done. Pray.

"Devote yourselves to prayer, keeping alert in it with thanksgiving. At the same time pray for us as well that God will open to us a door for the word, that we may declare the mystery of Christ." Colossians 4:2

"So I tell you, whatever you ask for in prayer, believe that you have received it and it will be yours." Mark 11:24

"I call upon you, for you will answer me, O God; incline your ear to me, hear my words. Wondrously show your steadfast love."
Psalm 17:6-7

Right with God

> "The righteousness of God is through faith in Jesus Christ
> for all who believe. For there is no distinction,
> since all have sinned and fall short of the glory of God;
> For they are now justified by his grace as a gift,
> through the redemption that is in Christ Jesus."
>
> Romans 3:22-24

IT IS NOT uncommon for people to want to be in God's favor or have a close relationship with God. How does the feeling of "being right with God" happen? Some people try to develop this relationship by good works. However, God asks us to have faith in his Word. There is a great deal of difference between these two ideas.

God desires you to have faith in his Word, and doing so, brings joy and inner peace. On the other hand, the attempt to earn God's favor creates stress and sadness. What is the difference between these two avenues to become right with God? Let's take a look at each.

Humans often try to earn God's love, attempting to follow God's Word perfectly. To try that road to a relationship with God is painful because you continue to fall short regardless of your best efforts. No human being can live a perfect life. No one can earn God's love. All are sinful beings. Great sadness can result from this attempt because one can never be perfect and will always fall to disappointment.

FOLLOWING CHRIST

To develop a right relationship with God, the apostle Paul, in the book of Romans, reminds you that God only requires that you have faith in God and his Word. Trust his Word entirely and trust his love for you, even when you are undeserving. Sometimes your behaviors make him happy, and other times, your choices make him sad. Either way, God continues to love you. Steven Furtick, New York Times bestselling author, and founder and lead pastor of Elevation Church in North Carolina, shares these encouraging words, "You'll always be chosen. Nothing can stop God's work in your life."[44]

God's love for you is unearned and undeserved; however, God loves you! Unearned love is God's gift of grace, freely given to you and me. People who love God do good works because of their love for God, their Father in Heaven. Therefore, they feel compelled to do God's will, not because they are forced or feel it is needed to earn God's favor. "My joy is not determined by what happens to me but by what Christ is doing in me and through me."[45]

God wants a relationship with you! He is not asking you to perform miracles or be perfect. He knows you are sinful and undeserving. But, God loves you anyway and wants you to trust his Word and believe in his love for you.

"For the Lord is good, His steadfast love endures forever, and his faithfulness to all generations." Psalm 100:5

It Is Well With My Soul

When peace like a river attendeth my way,
When sorrows like sea billows roll,
Whatever my lot, Thou hast taught me to say,
"It is well, it is well with my soul."

(Refrain)
It is well with my soul.
It is well, it is well with my soul.

Though Satan should buffet, though trails should come,
Let this blest assurance control,
That Christ has regarded my helpless estate,
And hath shed His own blood for my soul.

My sin, oh, the bliss of this glorious thought,
My sin not in part but the whole,
Is nailed to the cross and I bear it no more,
Praise the Lord, praise the Lord, oh my soul!

And, Lord, haste the day when the faith shall be sight,
The clouds be rolled back as a scroll,
The trump shall resound and the Lord shall descend,
Even so it is well with my soul.

Horatio G. Spafford

Learn by Doing - Start Today

"On the day I called, you answered me,
you increased my strength of soul."

Psalm 138:3

"IF WE WAIT until we have understood everything, we will never start at all. But if we begin by doing God's will as we know it, God's truth will become clearer and clearer to us. We learn by doing."[46] As with most things, if you wait to begin until you know all the facts, or until you are the most skilled, you will never start and never have the joy of the experience. If you desire to experience the joy of Christ in your life, you must start. Begin today! Be watchful! Look for God's hand in your life each day: kind words, thoughtful actions, beautiful views, fortunate happenings, wise friends, etc.

We all learn by doing! The growing process will continue throughout your lifetime in scriptural knowledge (the Bible) and life experiences in which the Lord touches your world. As you live the Christian life, you will grow to understand more each day. There are no perfect Christians. We are all continuing to learn and grow in our walk with the Lord.

When you ask and seek God's will in your life, the Holy Spirit will be with you. The Holy Spirit promises a cleansing (the gift of peace) from past mistakes and offers the strength and power of renewal. (Wow!

That alone is wonderful!) The Holy Spirit will help guide you to the spiritual peace in life which we each long to experience.

You must begin! You learn by doing! Get started! Always remember, God loves you! God Bless You!

"Christians are always listening for a voice of God above the noise of the many voices of the world to tell them where to go and what to do." John Brown of Haddington

This Little Light of Mine

This little light of mine, I'm gonna let it shine!
This little light of mine, I'm gonna let it shine!
This little light of mine, I'm gonna let it shine!
Let it shine, let it shine, all the time.

Unknown

Count Your Blessings

Count your blessings name them one by one;
Count your blessings see what God hath done;
Count your blessings name them one by one;
Count your many blessings, see what God hath done.

Johnson Oatman

The Christian Frame of Mind

> "Do your best to present yourself to God
> as one approved by him,
> a worker who has no need to be ashamed
> rightly explaining the word of truth."
>
> 2 Timothy 2:15

LIFE IS A complex mixture of moments of peace and joy intermingled with conflict, pain, and suffering. For the Christian, there is great comfort in realizing that their Lord and Savior, Jesus, has lived on this earth and can understand our experiences because he, too, has experienced happenings and emotions of humans. Jesus, as a man, was the kindest and most compassionate person ever to live. He was tried in courts and, although he was innocent, he was found guilty and sentenced to death on the cross. Jesus experienced ridicule and great suffering, which is thought by many as the greatest tragedy of all time. But our Lord did not end this story with sadness and loss but brought joy and victory. Jesus was raised from the dead and ascended into heaven with the promise that we might join him there. Jesus' life, death, and resurrection show that he will see us through earthly trials and bring us to victory at the end of our journey.

Jesus' presence will change how one views trials of life. As humans, both Christians and non-Christians, we desire to control our destiny, seek justice, and be loved. A Christian's mindset on these points makes a clear distinction on who is in charge and impacts the Christian's life.

Control

We often desire to control our world. An infinite number of disappointments occur due to our lack of control of variables on this earth. It may be aspects of nature, weather, health, accidents, or people/systems such as parents, employers, law, etc. Yes, this life is brutal, unjust, and one in which evil sometimes appears to have control. However, if one believes in Christ, the trials are lightened by understanding that our Lord is ultimately in control. If a situation does not unfold as expected or desired, the Lord has control of the situation, and his followers' circumstances. If a door closes, and we ask the Lord to be our guide, he will open a window and allow success and peace of mind in service to him.

Injustice

Injustice in this world is a reality that is often difficult to accept. As decisions unfold, they may have severe consequences to one's life; the individual who lives the consequences may not believe it was the best decision. The person who has the authority to make the decision, to instill justice, may be well-intentioned. Still, the view of justice in the situation will be varied by those involved, and the decision may not appear as justice to all parties.

Another type of injustice in this world is when the sinner seems to prosper, and the righteous man knows pain and suffering. The Lord will bring justice to all on Judgment Day. At that time, we will all stand accountable to God for our thoughts and actions on this earth. Until then, we are to forgive others as our Lord has forgiven us and to pray for their well-being. This concept allows us to look at the injustice with eyes open for each person involved without feeling the need to make it just. Jesus will make it right in his time.

Love

An additional factor that is significant in this life is the need for love. As children, we first are touched by the love of parents or a significant adult. The circle may expand to include siblings, a spouse in the home, friends in society, and colleagues at work. These individuals may have a genuine love and commitment to you, but as humans, being less than perfect, they will, at some time, make a decision that will prove hurtful or disappointing. A Christian will know that Christ lives and is our friend always. We are not alone. He is here with us, he loves us, and he will not disappoint!

Following Christ gives one freedom from the need to be in control. Persons who are followers of Christ will feel the security of Jesus Christ at their side, and that fact will make the trials of this life more tolerable and comfortable. Knowing that Christ is in control and he is our friend lessens our need to control the variables in life. A Christian will continue to seek justice but can rest because Christ will bring justice on Judgment Day. Jesus sees the picture with clarity. The Lord can bring goodness to difficult situations if one trusts in Him.

Finally, Jesus is with his followers always. They wake up with Jesus: eat with him, sing, dance, cry, work, play, sleep, etc., with him. A Christian takes time to appreciate his constant presence and talks with him in prayer, praise, and thanksgiving. Christians may talk to God in the car, in the shower, during exercises, taking that test, etc. Even when we are broken, Jesus is with us and loves us. No need to be lonely. Jesus is our friend. He is our constant companion.

Jesus requires that we believe in him as the Son of God, repent of our sins, and ask for forgiveness that we may be with him in heaven. We are to seek God's will in our lives and boldly act upon that will. We are responsible for using the gifts and talents given us. We are called to care for humanity and, in diligence, work for the health, happiness, and welfare of others.

This Is My Father's World

This is my Father's world:
And to my listening ears
All nature sings, and 'round me rings
The music of the spheres.
This is my Father's world:
I rest me in the thought
Of rocks and trees, of skies and seas –
His hand the wonders wrought.

This is my Father's world:
O let me never forget
That though the wrong seems oft' so strong,
God is the Ruler yet.
This is my Father's world:
Why should my heart be sad?
The Lord is King: let the heavens ring!
God reigns; let earth be glad.

Maltbie D. Babcock

Related Scriptures

"Be imitators of God, as beloved children, and live in love, as Christ loved us and gave himself up for us." Ephesians 5:1-2

"Come to me, all you that are weary and carrying heavy burdens, and I will give you rest." Matthew 11:28

"Keep your voice from weeping, and your eyes from tears; there is a reward for your work, says the Lord." Jeremiah 31:16

"For surely I know the plans I have for you, say the Lord, plans for your welfare and not for harm, to give you a future with hope." Jeremiah 29:11

"Come to me all of you who are weary and carry heavy burdens, and I will give you rest. Take my yoke upon you. Let me teach you, because I am humble and gentle, and you will find rest for your soul. For my yoke fits perfectly and the burden I give you is light." Matthew 11:28-30

"Make your ear attentive to wisdom; incline your heart to understanding." Proverbs 2:2

"I can do all things through Christ who strengthens me." Philippians 4:13

RELATED SCRIPTURES

"I am continually with Thee, Thou hast taken hold of my right hand, with thy counsel Thou wilt guide me, and afterward receive me to glory." Psalm 73:23-24

"Let your heart hold fast to my words; keep my commandments, and live. Get wisdom; get insight: do not forget, nor turn away from the words of my mouth. Do not forsake her and she will keep you; love her, and she will guard you." Proverbs 4:4-6

"May the God of hope fill you with all joy and peace in believing, that you may abound in hope by the power of the Holy Spirit."
Romans 15:13

"I will always thank my God as I remember you in my prayers, because I hear about your faith in the Lord Jesus and your love for all the saints…Your love has given me great joy and encouragement."
Philemon 4:7

"O Lord, be not far off, O Thou, my help, hasten to my assistance. Deliver my soul." Psalm 22:19

Developing Godly Character

◆▶────────◀◆

A person's actions speak of the values and beliefs they hold. For example, a follower of Christ will strive to make choices that bring honor to the Lord. If the person loves the Lord, the choices made should reflect that love and respect. This section highlights areas where a person's character is often challenged. The readings will offer examples of using God's guidance when making daily decisions regarding the character that will prove pleasing to God, to you, and to others.

The Bible identifies character traits that, if practiced, show honor to God. Therefore, the development and use of godly character traits will allow you to serve God and bring greater peace and fulfillment to your life. Character traits include but are not limited to the following: integrity, sense of humor, responsibility, time usage, obedience, dealing with anger, and forgiveness.

Praise God from Whom All Blessings Flow

Praise God, from whom all blessings flow;
Praise Him, all creatures here below;
Praise Him above, you heavenly hosts;
Praise Father, Son, and Holy Ghost.
Amen

Thomas Ken

"I do not ask for mighty words
To leave the crowd impressed.
Just grant my life may ring so true
My neighbor shall be blessed."

Unknown

The Gift of God's Armor – Understand and Use It

> Finally, be strong in the Lord, and in the strength of His might.
> Put on the full armor of God, that you may be able
> to stand firm against the schemes of the devil.
> For our struggle is not against flesh and blood,
> but against the rulers, against the powers,
> against the world forces of this darkness,
> against the spiritual forces of wickedness
> in the heavenly places.
> Therefore, take up the full armor of God."
>
> Ephesians 6: 10-12 (NASB)

GOD WANTS US to be prepared and to be strong as we face the challenges of this world. Consequently, he provides protection and power for us through the gift of his armor. In the book of Ephesians 6:13-18 (MSG), Paul gives additional insight into the meaning of this gift of armor.

> "Be prepared. You're up against far more than you can handle on your own. Take all the help you can get, every weapon God has issued, so that when it's all over but the shouting you'll still be on your feet. Truth, righteousness, peace, faith, and salvation are more than words. Learn how to apply them.

> You'll need them throughout your life. God's Word is an indispensable weapon. In the same way, prayer is essential in the ongoing warfare. Pray hard and long. Pray for your brothers and sisters. Keep your eyes open. Keep each other's spirit's up so that no one falls behind or drops out."

We are facing a spiritual battle each day. To be prepared, we must act. First, understand the nature of each of these gifts of armor and rely on their power and protection. The specific advantages provided by the armor of God are briefly explained below.

Truth - To a Christian, the truth is that God exists in the Father, the Son, and the Holy Ghost. In addition, the Bible is the Word of God. This belief brings wisdom, courage and strength.

Righteousness – To be righteous, one acts according to what is morally right. It is a genuine attempt to be free from guilt or sin.

Peace – "Don't worry about anything, but in all your prayers ask God for what you need, always asking him with a thankful heart. And God's peace, which is far beyond human understanding, will keep your hearts and minds safe in union with Christ Jesus."
Philippians 4:6-7 (GNB)

Faith - "Now faith is the assurance of things hoped for, the conviction of things not seen." Hebrews 11:1

Salvation - We are sinners and behave in ways that are against God's will. God sent his Son, Jesus, who took on our sins when he died on the cross and thus, restored our relationship with God. Because of God's grace, we can experience a newness that allows us to strive to live according to God's will. To accept God's gift of salvation, we invite the Holy Spirit to abide in us and guide our everyday life.

THE GIFT OF GOD'S ARMOR – UNDERSTAND AND USE IT

The best way to be prepared to use the armor of God is to learn through Bible study and prayer. The armor is designed for protection and defense against evil. It is to be used as a unit, not individual parts. Grow to understand the tools you have been given, and use them. Keep your focus on the Lord, his gifts, and his glory. His love and armor will shield you all day long.

The Whole Armor of God

Soldiers of Christ, arise,
And put your armor on,
Strong in the strength which God supplies,
Through His eternal Son;
Strong in the Lord of Hosts,
And in His mighty power,
Who in the strength of Jesus trusts
Is more than conqueror.

Leave no unguarded place.
No weakness of the soul,
Take every virtue, every grace,
And fortify the whole.
To keep your armor bright
attend with constant care.
Still walking in your Captain's sight
And watching unto prayer.

Charles Wesley

Defining Yourself – Self-worth

> "You must make every effort
> to support your faith with goodness,
> and goodness with knowledge,
> and knowledge with self-control,
> and self-control with endurance,
> and endurance with godliness,
> and godliness with mutual affection,
> and mutual affection with love."
>
> 2 Peter 1:5-7

IT IS EASY to get lost searching for who you are or your value as a person and individual. In reality, it's not about self-worth. Your job is to esteem not yourself but God. The only valid opinion of yourself is determined by all that you are in his creation. God defines your nature and your character when he claims you. From that point forward, you strive for the picture he has of you as his redeemed child. The apostle Paul tells you in 2 Corinthians 12:10, "I am content with weaknesses, insults, hardships, persecutions, and calamities for the sake of Christ; for whenever I am weak, then I am strong."

Life events are constantly challenging your self-worth. Consider two situations common in life: 1) You have done something you wish you had handled differently, or 2) You are disappointed with life's circumstances and unmet expectations. Either of these concerns can cause unhappiness, disappointment, disillusionment, causing your self-worth to spiral downward, making it difficult to think positively. These concerns, and the anxiety they produce, make it difficult to function normally. Your best option is to take these concerns to God.

If you have made a mistake or a poor choice, admit your mistake and ask God to forgive you. Accept his forgiveness and take heart. God forgives you, and you must forgive yourself. Learn from this experience. In addition, when you have expectations for your life that do not fall into place, you must remember, God does not value you or me for our accomplishments. He sees your heart, your dreams, hurts, strengths, shortcomings, etc., and he wants to help. He values you. If you bring your trials and brokenness to him, he will open doors and help build your character to overcome the obstacles. You can look forward to the new opportunities God has prepared for you. He will grow your heart for service, love, compassion, caring, kindness, responsibility, integrity, etc. God will help you be the best you it is possible to be.

Each of us is unique and complex. There are a number of variables with which the world defines or differentiates individuals: career choice, friends, family, hobbies, circumstances, appearance, intelligence, etc. To describe oneself by achievements or genetic gifts is a tool used to increase self-worth by worldly standards. However, neither your achievements nor your genetic contributions are as crucial to your identity as the character you demonstrate in your daily living. Kindness, generosity, respect, integrity, honesty, etc., are the best judges of a person. Define yourself by your character. This practice will allow others to recognize you as a child of God!

Place your needs and desires in God's hands and desire his way. Then you can have hope knowing he can use these difficult situations to draw you closer to him and his purpose for your life. God knows you best. According to his needs for your service, God will build your self-worth on your unique strengths, weaknesses, hopes, dreams, skills and gifts. God wants the best for you, so include him in the journey of discovery. Look to him for guidance regarding who you should become, and how you will define yourself.

All Things Bright and Beautiful

All things bright and beautiful,
All creatures great and small,
All things wise and wonderful;
The Lord God made them all.

He gave us eyes to see them,
And lips that we might tell
How great is God Almighty
Who has made all things well.

Cecil Francis Alexander

Your Own Unique Character

"What no one ever saw or heard,
what no one ever thought could happen,
is the very thing God prepared for those who love him."
1 Corinthians 2:9 (GNB)

GOD CREATED YOU with a unique purpose, and he will help you to exercise the skills and character to serve that purpose. So, be open to the possibilities and know that God will use your character in miraculous ways if you are willing. The collective experiences, trials and adversity, and the joys and delights you face in this life, are at work to create the unique, wonderful person of character you are becoming.

Character traits are a piece of your personality and a window to your values. As you consider your character, always be mindful that God has a plan for you. His plan for your development may be something you did not imagine. The traits you currently have may change throughout your life; God is working with you. Changing these traits may be swift or slow; however, it often takes effort and persistence to change. Below is a partial list of positive character traits.

FOLLOWING CHRIST

Adventurous	Generous	Persevering
Ambitious	Gentle	Principled
Capable	Grateful	Respectful
Compassionate	Honest	Right-minded
Confident	Humble	Sense-of-humor
Considerate	Imaginative	Shy
Cooperative	Joyful	Sincere
Dependable	Just	Teachable
Determined	Kind	Thoughtful
Devoted	Loyal	Trustworthy
Enthusiastic	Patient	Understanding
Faithful	Peaceful	Unselfish

God's chosen path for you will allow the development of traits unique to you. Value your uniqueness. Kerry and Chris Shook explain that you were designed to leave a lasting impact, "Never underestimate the power of one. It's the ability each of us has every day, to be used by God to bless the rest of the world."[47]

"For those whom he fore-knew he also predestined to be conformed to the image of his Son." Romans 8:29

Seek Wisdom

"Do not abandon wisdom, and she will protect you;
love her, and she will keep you safe.
Getting wisdom is the most important thing you can do.
Whatever else you get, get insight.
Love wisdom, and she will make you great.
Embrace her, and she will bring you honor."

Proverbs 4: 5-7 (GNB)

MUCH HAS BEEN written about the variety of ways to gain wisdom. The quest for greater understanding is not new. You can positively impact your future by choices in word and deed that build toward greater wisdom. The past is behind you, and is unchangeable. However, you can make a difference regarding your future if you are willing to change your actions. Train yourself to be alert, using your senses, eyes, ears, mind, etc., to discover areas of need, examine situations and make wise decisions.

Below are three areas of choice in which you should pay careful attention as you seek wisdom in your life: carefully choosing friends, seeking and listening to the counsel of wise people, and a willingness to be a servant to others. Implementing these personal, daily choices can significantly influence your journey toward greater wisdom and smart choices.

The choice of friendships: Associate with people you admire whose lives, lifestyles, conversation and choices are uplifting and positive. King Solomon's counsel in Proverbs 10:20 states, "The tongue of the righteous is choice silver; the mind of the wicked is of little worth." Therefore, choose friends with care, do not consent to relationships that drag you down and hurt your walk with God.

The choice of counsel, seeking godly individuals of wisdom: Making decisions without the input of respected others limits knowledge to your own experiences. By consulting with a wise person, the knowledge and experience tremendously increase your chance of success. Therefore, seek the counsel of those you respect. If you seek wisdom, God will give you a godly, wise person to listen to, learn from, and with whom to spend quality time.

The choice to serve others: Service to others brings untold wisdom. As you serve others, they will freely share with you. Instead of waiting for someone to set the table, you can prepare the table for your friends or family. A person who develops a servant's heart becomes wealthy beyond measure. The Lord has given you unique gifts; He wants you to use these gifts to his service. He needs his followers in all walks of life, the ball field, the courthouse, the classroom, etc. To whatever arena you are drawn, the service you provide other people is service to your Lord. The blessings for a servant's heart will give honor to others as you gain wisdom.

The quest for wisdom requires careful choice, listening, and service. True understanding is not dependent upon book knowledge, street smarts, advanced degrees, or careers. The world-renowned New Testament interpreter William Barclay offers still a different look at a means to attain wisdom. He shares a list of personal qualities developed through time that build understanding. As you will determine from these two insights to gaining wisdom, they are different. However, they both align with the Word of God. Personal qualities developed through time are the basis of true wisdom. William Barclay describes these qualities.[48]

- Peaceable – creating right relationships, not aggressive or self-assertive. The truth should always be spoken but with gentleness. Avoid strife…. If peace is not forthcoming, shake the dust off your feet and prayerfully go on.
- Gentle – mindful of the feelings of others; listen and honor others; be patient, considerate, restrained, and respectful; work toward forgiveness and seek fairness.
- Open to Reason – approachable, not stubborn, can be persuaded, not self-righteous, seeking additional truths, being agreeable.
- Full of Mercy – for those who suffer unjustly as well as those who create their troubles. Be compassionate, helpful; value and work for justice.
- Full of Good Fruits – make choices that benefit others (the hungry, weak, sick, young, old, etc.). Do not let the ways of the world dictate life; make responsible choices.
- Without Uncertainty – know and act on your values, do not be two-faced or wishy-washy. God's will is the force that drives, and you should always be ready to serve and obey God.
- Sincere – no masks, no games. Be genuine, straightforward, and honest.

In the search for wisdom, it is a wise person who includes outside influences carefully. Many wonderful books, great movies, soothing or inspirational music, powerful speeches and other materials can be assets to attaining greater wisdom. These sources of wisdom may be joyful, tender, uplifting, and positive. The choices for these materials, however, must be made carefully. Pray for discernment to help fend off messages that run counter to the Christian worldview.

FOLLOWING CHRIST

It is also essential to not overlook the wisdom gained as you learn from mistakes--yours or others. Pay attention. Mistakes give learning opportunities. To learn, you must take time to rethink the situation and determine why you made the mistake. Accept the fact that we are all human and sometimes make a poor or careless choice, then seek ways to avoid that behavior in the future. God uses mishaps for growth and purpose. Take advantage of these uncomfortable situations to learn and grow in wisdom.

The search for wisdom is universal. Seeking an understanding of the Christian faith will allow you an awareness of the sources and personal qualities that build for greater comprehension. Biblical guidance and that of godly people will ensure the growth of wisdom.

God Loves You! You are special to God and are like no other person! God made you as you are on purpose! God wants good things for you! He has plans for you, and has provided you a Bible to teach you the way. He has given his Son for your salvation. He has given you the Holy Spirit to provide you with understanding and guidance. He acknowledges that you are less than perfect, and he forgives you if you ask. God will show you the way to grow in wisdom. So ask and look for his answers each day; you will find them. Thank the Lord for his love, his goodness, his faithfulness!

"The fear of the Lord is the beginning of knowledge, but fools despise wisdom and discipline. Hear, my son, your father's instruction, and do not forsake your mother's teaching." Proverbs 1:7-8

Know and Honor Boundaries

"Love must be completely sincere.
Hate what is evil, hold on to what is good.
Love one another warmly as Christian brothers,
and be eager to show respect for one another.
Work hard and do not be lazy.
Serve the Lord with a heart full of devotion.
Let your hope keep you joyful, be patient in your troubles,
and pray at all times."

Romans 12: 9-12 (GNB)

BOUNDARIES ARE VALUES or rules by which you choose to live your life. So much of life is out of your control. However, if you control the things that are within your realm, your sense of stability and power in life is much greater. No person enjoys life when they feel others' rules and wishes are pulling them. The power to determine your destiny is given to others to decide (detentions, suspensions, failing grades, lost jobs, lost opportunities, etc.), when choices are made that break rules (tardiness, back-talk, laziness). Even though the decision regarding your consequences may be displeasing, you must accept the decision. Every person feels the need to control their life. Unfortunately, at some time, choices are made which are irresponsible, ill-prepared, unkind, etc. We all have a past and an opportunity to choose to change. Every day is a new day offering new opportunities; take charge of your life and make wise choices.

Boundaries help keep your actions and behaviors in line with the values you hold; they allow you to have greater control as you experience different situations. Boundaries are not barriers, but they are personal standards designed to offer strength and security to your decisions and life. Everyone needs boundaries or limits. Throughout life you will see them: rules govern the game in competitive sports, rules keep the roadways safer, and rules help create joyful music.

You have a choice in boundaries. You can choose limits that follow the Lord and his plan for your life, or you may choose limits from this world, following your plan and your own will. It may be challenging to determine your boundaries in this world of seemingly limitless possibilities and varying values displayed through television, movies, books, etc. Paul tells you in   1 Corinthians 10:23, "'All things are lawful,' but not all things are beneficial. 'All things are lawful,' but not all things build up."

What do you want to stand for? What are your limits, your convictions? The Prophet Isaiah in his book tells us, "The grass withers, the flower fades; but the word of our God will stand forever" (Isaiah 40:8). Things of this world are fleeting and will not last, but God's Word is everlasting. Therefore, the limits that have the everlasting power to bring peace, joy, contentment, and purpose, are those that are established to follow God's commands and his will for your life.

People with high levels of self-esteem usually have boundaries, and they do not allow people to take advantage of them. To become an emotionally healthy person, you need to develop firm personal boundaries. Are you pleased with the limits you have currently established? You should ask yourself that question throughout life and adjust the areas in which you are uncomfortable. Bible study is an excellent source in determining boundaries. As you learn about Jesus, you will see how his boundaries established a life of action, showing love for his Lord and people. You may also find it helpful to seek a

KNOW AND HONOR BOUNDARIES

godly person with whom you can share. Find a person whose character you admire and talk to them.

Just as you need to establish your personal boundaries, you need to respect and honor other people's boundaries. Again, Paul tells us, "Do not seek your own advantage, but that of the other" 1 Corinthians 10:24). When another person does not do what you want or does not respond as you wish, it is human nature to try to change that person's decision to be more pleasing for you. As much as you might prefer their response was different, you must accept it as their decision. Your acceptance will show respect for the other person's boundaries. You must learn not to manipulate or control others but take responsibility for your actions and emotions.

Having personal boundaries in place can make life easier because you do not have to make last minute decisions. You have already thought about what is important and have chosen to be prepared to act on that decision. You must be unafraid to stand up for the boundaries you have established. Boundaries aligned with God's Word, and the willingness to act on these boundaries, will bring you more excellent health emotionally and spiritually.

"Trust in the Lord, and do good; so you will live in the land and enjoy security. Take delight in the Lord, and he will give you the desires of your heart. Commit your way to the Lord, and trust in him and he will act." Psalm 37:3-5

"Son, hold on to your wisdom and insight. Never let them get away from you. They will provide you with life – a pleasant and happy life. You can go safely on your way and never even stumble. You will not be afraid when you go to bed, and you will sleep soundly through the night." Proverbs 3:21-24 (GNB)

Be Careful

Be careful of your thoughts
For your thoughts become your words.
Be careful of your words
For your words become your actions.
Be careful of your actions
For your actions become your habits.
Be careful of your habits
For your habits become your character.
Be careful of your character
For your character becomes your destiny.

Unknown

Courage – Integrity

"Be strong and bold; have no fear or dread of them,
because it is the Lord your God who goes with you;
He will not fail you or forsake you."

Deuteronomy 31:6

HAVING DETERMINED YOUR boundaries, it is often necessary to have the courage to uphold those boundaries. Courage is the strength to stand up against situations that create fear, danger, or discomfort. You will have situations in life that will require courage to act in a godly manner, or uphold your boundaries. These situations may create fear and discomfort for you. Those discomforts may be from physical pain, or loss of friends, family, finances, or careers. The possibilities of problematic situations are limitless. Your choices are powerful in communicating the values you hold dear, your boundaries. If you are a follower of Christ, you must choose accordingly.

When you have acted in a manner that upholds your boundaries, you are said to have integrity. Integrity is when a person strives to align personal conduct with personal values, to do the right thing, even in difficult or challenging circumstances. Integrity follows closely when personal boundaries are established and honored with action. A person of integrity is true to themselves. Your responses to life's challenges are met with confidence and firm resolve when boundaries are in place. Your decisions and actions bring honor to your values and your life. You will be a person with integrity.

FOLLOWING CHRIST

When you display courage, it does not mean you are unafraid. You know the right thing to do, and you choose to act accordingly. You may be scared, but you do the right thing. This determination is the courage Jesus Christ demonstrated on the cross. As a human, Jesus was not eager to face death on the cross. He was 33 years old, and he knew the pain and agony of death on a cross. Crucifixion was a familiar manner of civil punishment in Jesus' day. Jesus' willingness to die on the cross is a tremendous example of courage and selflessness. "God's will meant the cross and Jesus had the nerve himself to accept it."[49] Life everlasting is available to you and me because Christ courageously dared to face the pain of the cross for us.

God made you in his image for his purposes; and he needs your service, just as you are. You were created to uphold godly standards and he will provide strength of character, and courage so you may honor those standards. As you face challenges, be thankful that you were designed to honor justice and righteousness; to stand against injustice and wrongdoing. It is not always easy to stand for your beliefs, but it is essential to be true to yourself and your God even in the face of opposition or ridicule. God has given you knowledge of right and wrong, and he will be with you as you stand for what is good and right. Remember, you should always choose to act because it is the right thing to do, honoring your boundaries. You did not act to become popular, famous, or rewarded; you acted to change a situation for the better. You acted with strength of character, courage and integrity.

"Put your trust in the Lord your God, and you will stand your ground. Believe what his prophets tell you, and you will succeed."
2 Chronicles 20:20 (GNB)

"Be alert, stand firm in the faith, be brave, be strong. Do all your work in love." 1 Corinthians 16:13 (GNB)

I'm in the Lord's Army

I may never march in the infantry,
Ride in the cavalry, shoot the artillery;
I may never zoom o'er the enemy,
But I'm in the Lord's army.
I'm in the Lord's army.
I'm in the Lord's army.
I may never march in the infantry,
Ride in the cavalry, shoot the artillery;
I may never zoom o'er the enemy,
But I'm in the lord's army.

Unknown

Responsibility

> "For the Spirit God has given us does not make us timid;
> instead, his Spirit fills us with power, love, and self-control."
>
> 2 Timothy 1:7 (GNB)

TO BE RESPONSIBLE means to be obligated to do something, to be morally accountable for your behavior. Simply stated, to be responsible means recognizing a task that needs to be done and performing the task. Terms such as reliable, trustworthy, dependable, committed, and accountable are often interchangeable with responsibility. Responsibility is significantly impacted by your faith, and it has relevance to your walk with God. To be responsible, you must be willing to stand for what you believe. First, let's look at the development and characteristics of individuals who display responsible behaviors.

Responsible behavior, doing the right thing, results from motivation and guidance from within the individual, not external sources. That sounds so easy, but in reality, it is not! Obedience to rules, strictly based upon rewards and punishments may not withstand the challenges of everyday living. Accepting responsibility involves sacrifice; it may mean sacrificing your time, money, dreams, etc. It is easier when parents help develop this trait from childhood, but that is often not the case. Therefore, at whatever stage a person is in life, the development of responsibility takes desire, time and practice. People who practice responsible behaviors display the following characteristics:

- They have a sense of personal ethics: honesty, compassion, accountability, justice, and courage, etc.
- They are problem solvers. However, they accept responsibility only when they can honor the task. They get it done. They do not procrastinate. They have the ability to say, "No" to a task.
- They do not make excuses. Instead, they own their mistakes and learn from them.
- They act appropriately and demonstrate respect for others.

Responsibility is about choices. A person may be responsible in some areas of life and not in others. If you struggle with responsibility in one or all areas of your life: home, school, work, relationships, etc., you will face difficulties and suffer. However, responsibility is a choice and you can make great gains if you desire to improve. As an adult, the initial steps must come from within you. You must be willing to face the situation calling for responsible behavior and act responsibly. Begin with small steps but begin the growth to become accountable. The personal rewards in the sense of helping others and the acceptance of the responsibility are great.

"The perverse get what their ways deserve, and the good, what their deeds deserve." Proverbs 14:14

Responsibility to God

> "So let us not grow weary in doing what is right
> for we will reap at harvest time, if we do not give up.
> So then, whenever we have an opportunity,
> let us work for the good of all,
> and especially for those of the family of faith."
> Galatians 6:9-10

CHRISTIANS HAVE A responsibility to God. Paul shares this message in 1 Corinthians 15:55, 57-58, "Where O death is your victory? Where, O death is your sting? Thanks be to God, who gives us the victory through our Lord Jesus Christ. Therefore, my beloved, be steadfast, immovable, always excelling in the work of the Lord, because you know that in the Lord your labor is not in vain." Paul knew that humankind is fearful of death. With the knowledge of salvation through Jesus Christ's death on the cross, as a Christian, fears may be abolished. The gift of salvation brings the Christian a challenge to step up and show honor and be of service to God through actions. As a follower of Christ, you have a responsibility to the Lord.

Colossians 3:2-4 tells you, "Set your minds on things that are above, not on things that are on the earth, for you have died, and your life is hidden with Christ in God." This passage makes clear that your focus should be on God. As a follower of Christ, your motivations and actions should be chosen to honor God. Paul continues in his letter to the Colossians 3:23-24, "Whatever your task, put yourselves into it, as done for the Lord and not for our master, since you know that from the Lord you will receive the inheritance as your reward; you serve the Lord Christ."

Whatever you are undertaking, it is your responsibility to make sure the work serves the Lord to reach souls for him. In Matthew 28:19, Matthew tells you of the commission that Jesus gave to his followers. "Go therefore and make disciples of all nations baptizing them in the name of the Father and of the Son and of the Holy Spirit, and teaching them to obey everything that I have commanded you." Share His Story, His Word, and together, change a life forever, this command was given to all God's followers. That is your responsibility.

There are many passages in scripture directing God's people how to serve him. Matthew 25:34-36 shares Jesus' guidance as to what is expected of his followers, "Come, you who are blessed by my Father, inherit the kingdom prepared for you from the foundation of the world; for I was hungry and you gave me food, I was thirsty and you gave me something to drink, I was a stranger and you welcomed me, I was naked and you gave me clothing, I was sick and you took care of me, I was in prison and you visited me." James also gives guidance as to the responsibility of the Christian in his book, James 1:27. "Religion that is pure and undefiled before God, the Father, is this: to care for orphans and widows in their distress, and to keep oneself unstained by the world."

Hold yourself accountable for your choices and behaviors. Remind yourself of the characteristics of responsible people: delay gratification, accept some frustration with a task, seek assistance, be patient, and less self-serving. Appreciate and use your gifts, money, time, and energy in service to God. That is your responsibility.

FOLLOWING CHRIST

"In everything do to others as you would have them do to you." Matthew 7:12

"For just as the body without the spirit is dead, so faith without works is also dead." James 2: 26

O Jesus, I Have Promised

O Jesus, I have promised to serve Thee to the end;
Be Thou forever near me, my Master and my Friend;
I shall not fear the battle if Thou art by my side,
Nor wander from the pathway if Thou wilt be my Guide.

O let me feel Thee near me! The world is ever near;
I see the sights that dazzle, the tempting sounds I hear;
My foes are ever near me, around me and within;
But Jesus, draw Thou nearer and shield my soul from sin.

O let me see Thy footprints, and in them plant mine own;
My hope to follow duly is in Thy strength alone.
O guide me, call me, draw me, uphold me to the end;
And then in Heaven receive me, my Savior and my Friend.

John Ernest Bode

Time Used Wisely

> "Teach us to live well!
> Teach us to live wisely and well!"
> Psalm 90:12 (MSG)

TWENTY-FOUR HOURS EACH day is the time given to everyone. In today's society, it is common for individuals to over-extend their schedules. The theme of many lives is hurried, rush and run--never enough time. How you choose to use the time depends on the values you hold, your priorities. It is crucial to learn how to manage your time effectively, so the things valued most are the focus of your time. To arrange time each day for godly activities is essential to living life as God intended. Time should not be wasted; it is a valuable resource and can only be spent once. A common reason for over-extended (busy) schedules is that we fill our calendars with unnecessary tasks that clutter our lives, taking time away from prayer or Bible study. Below is a listing of reasons why people choose to stay busy:

1. to avoid feelings, people, or activities. It is similar to running away from what is uncomfortable.
2. to feel a sense of accomplishment with the completion of tasks.
3. because they want to appear valuable.

FOLLOWING CHRIST

4. because they equate being busy as a means to a successful life. They may be materialistic and never have enough.
5. to avoid more critical, sometimes complex tasks. They procrastinate.
6. because they are often unaware of the need to relax and provide for themselves self-care.
7. because they may be unable to say "no." God desires that each person set priorities determined by God's will, not human will.

The goal is not to get busier but to use your time to best fulfill your purpose in life. Each person must answer that question for themselves; however, some choices are more fulfilling and offer greater rewards. The choices of how to fill your time come down to two options: God's way or humanity's way. In <u>God's way</u>, one seeks to glorify God in all actions, and choices are made in preparation for life after this world in heaven. God desires for us to have personal relationships with him, family, and friends. In <u>Humanity's way</u>, a person seeks power, prestige, pleasure and possessions for the here and now. The world's way is following a dream that is elusive and ever-changing. God's way brings the blessings of immeasurable peace and joy to life. Make an effort to determine your use of time regarding what is pleasing to God, not the wants and needs of humans.

Examine how you use your time each day. If you do not have time for prayer or Bible study, you are doing something God didn't put on your task list. Be cautious of scheduling your life to be so good that you have little time to be godly. It requires a strong sense of self-discipline to make these tough choices regarding your use of time. However, tomorrow is a new day. When the day begins, include God and face the challenges with new hope.

When you plan to use your time for God's purposes, you will plan your time around biblical principles; honoring God, family, service, caring, compassion, etc. Your schedule will still incorporate time for work, play, and other necessary activities, but the focus will be God-centered and uplifting, including prayer, and possibly Bible reading, scripture memorization, random acts of kindness, or exercise. Listen to your heart, and God will speak to you about your life, your future, and the best way to serve him. Choose your dreams wisely. Plan your time wisely.

"Everything that happens in this world happens at the time God chooses." Ecclesiastes 3:1 (GNB)

"Forget what lies behind and reach forward to what lies ahead." Philippians 3:13

A New Day

This is the beginning of a new day.
God has given me this day to use as I will.
I can waste it or grow in its light and be of service to others.
But what I do with this day is important because
I have exchanged a day of my life for it.
When tomorrow comes, today will be gone forever.
I hope I will not regret the price I paid for it.

Unknown

Heartaches – Pain and Confusion

"Cast all your anxiety on him because he cares for you."
1 Peter 5:7

DOES YOUR HEART ache? Is your heart full of pain and confusion? You are not alone in these feelings. Many have had a similar frustration. The scriptures tell of many people who experience difficulties and dark times. In 1 Samuel 18 we learn about King Saul's relationship with David that developed into Saul's intense jealousy and rivalry. The intensity was so great that David had to flee as Saul was attempting to kill him. Following this dark time, David is eventually crowned king. Our Lord Jesus also faced dark and difficult times on earth. The Pharisees opposed him and plotted his death. The story of Jesus suffering is told in Isaiah 53. However, following Christ's death on the cross, he was victorious and left the grave to enter into heaven.

God understands, and he is there for you! Sometimes in our pain, we assume the worst of God. If we can only trust that he will be with us and see us through the pain, we may experience a sense of greater peace. When you start to feel these distressing emotions, you may want to pray this simple, powerful prayer: Dear Lord, rescue me, and give me peace! Amen. And remember, the Holy Spirit is praying for us even when we do not pray for ourselves.

Good and evil exist in the world. Typically, each of us makes our

HEARTACHES – PAIN AND CONFUSION

determination of good and evil based on our situations. If, however, we would look to God's goodness and his ideas of evil or darkness, the pain and confusion felt may take on new meaning. Your life is a journey with God, and he will see you through the pain and confusion to victory. During these difficult, painful times, it may be helpful to remember three things about our Lord and his relationship with you. 1) God is with you, 2) God can bring light to darkness, and 3) God is working on a purpose in your heart.

1. God is with you. To feel lost is a helpless feeling. But God is with you, and he is not lost. There is hope. He will show you the way and see you through the trials to victory. You don't have to depend on yourself. You have a dear constant companion! Go to him in prayer!

2. God can bring light to darkness. You are a survivor! Life has hurt you in many ways. Life can be a dark place, but God can bring light and goodness from the hurt. God gives a sense of safety and security. He cares for you! Trust in his timing. He will see you through the storm to joy!

3. Together, you and God are working on developing your life. When you are walking through times of fire, remember God will use this opportunity to refine you. As much as you are able, rest in what trust you have in God. Although at times it may be difficult, it is incredible!

W. Paul Young, in his book, *The Shack*, tells God's message to each of us. "This mess is you! Together, you and I (God), we have been working with a purpose in your heart. And it is wild and beautiful and perfectly in process. To you it seems like a mess, but I see a perfect pattern emerging and growing and alive."[50] In times of darkness, look for the light. God is at work and the light will shine for you again.

"If you suffer because you are a Christian, don't be ashamed of it, but thank God that you bear Christ's name." 1 Peter 4:16 (GNB)

"My dear friends, do not be surprised at the painful test you are suffering, as though something unusual were happening to you. Rather be glad that you are sharing Christ's sufferings, so that you may be full of joy when his glory is revealed." 1 Peter 4:12-13 (GNB)

What a Friend We Have in Jesus

What a friend we have in Jesus,
All our sins and griefs to bear!
What a privilege to carry
Everything to God in prayer!

Oh, what peace we often forfeit,
Oh, what needless pain we bear,
All because we do not carry
Everything to God in prayer!

Can we find a friend so faithful?
Who will all our sorrows share?
Jesus knows our every weakness,
Take it to the Lord in prayer.

Joseph M. Scriven

Spiritual Obedience

> "This love I speak of means that
> we must live in obedience to God's commands.
> The command, as you have all heard from the beginning,
> is that you must all live in love."
>
> 2 John 1:6 (GNB)

PAUL WRITES IN Romans 7:15, "I do not understand my own action. For I do not do what I want, but I do the very thing I hate." It is common that we know what we should do; we just simply choose not to do it. Consequently, we spend time dealing with the uncomfortable, sometimes painful consequences of our unwise choice. It may be satisfying, exciting, or adventurous to disobey, however, the consequences of disobedience can be painful and create a great loss. Obedience in life helps us avoid pain.

God's guidance is given directly through his Word in the Bible and through godly people with whom you may come in contact: a parent, friend, teacher, coach, etc. Train yourself to listen and seek God's guidance and pray for strength and courage to stand firm in times of temptation. You must become wise and courageous to counteract disobedience. God freely gives wisdom to all who ask.

Sometimes, we fail to respond appropriately to corrections or reproofs. If you find yourself in this situation, consider the factors below and determine why you responded with indifference to the correction. Understanding your reasoning may help you overcome the rebellion and grow toward a spirit desirous of a greater willingness to learn and grow. Consider the following reasons why people sometimes fail to respond to corrections.

1. Stubborn. It means literally refusing correction or advice. An attitude of pride.
2. Lack of caring or awareness. The individuals truly don't care about the situation, they are insensitive. This may be evidence of low self-esteem.
3. Defensive. These persons are not willing to be wrong. They often display a prideful manner and have not learned to be humble.

God's Word provides guidance for you to follow. His Word gives insight into choices that make life on earth more meaningful and purposeful. His guidance is not to limit or lessen the "good times" life can offer but to enrich and add depth to the relationships and interactions. Always be alert to life's reproaches from others in your life. The wisdom they offer may be powerful and enrich your life. Take advantage of the opportunity to learn the ways of a wise person. Pray for God to give you strength to withstand temptations, and for the Holy Spirit to give you the will and desire to stand firm in obedience to the guidance and will of the Lord.

"Thanks be to God that you, having once been slaves of sin, have become obedient from the heart to the form of teaching to which you were entrusted, and that you having been set free from sin, have become slaves of righteousness." Romans 6:17

Wisdom and Wealth - A Spiritual Guide -1-

"For where your treasure is, there your heart will be also."

Matthew 6:21

THE TOPIC OF money can be complicated and confusing as one thinks of budgets, basic needs, wants, rising costs, debt, etc. However, having a plan for earning and spending money can help. John Wesley, an English clergyman, theologian, and evangelist, in his sermon titled "The Use of Money," suggests three points about money: gain all you can; save all you can, and; give all you can. This simple plan can offer insight and clarity to a healthy attitude and the wise use of money.

> <u>Gain all you can</u>. We ought to make money, be industrious and work hard. There is nothing wrong with making money; it is one's duty to gain what one can. However, money should be gained in appropriate and honorable means, not secured in ways that are evil and wrong. Wesley cited examples:
>
> 1) Do not gain money at the expense of life or health. (Harmful chemical environments, extreme working hours, etc.)

2) Do not gain money through an occupation that harms the mind, is contrary to the law of God, or country. (Career that involves lying, cheating, etc.)

3) Do not make money by hurting your neighbor. We are not allowed to do evil that good may come. (Gambling, usury, pawn-broker, etc.).

4) Do not make money by practicing improper medicine. Do not sell anything that impairs health. And finally,

5) Do not make money at the expense of your neighbor's soul or your own. (Establishments that lower the state of humanity--taverns, playhouses, etc.)

<u>Save all you can</u>. The meaning of this phrase is to be frugal. Be careful with spending, and spend wisely. Avoid extravagant, expensive, and showy things. When buying food, clothing, shelter, equipment, and other items, seek simplicity and quality rather than grandeur. Seek to save all you can in living expenses. This idea of saving does not mean putting your money into savings accounts and never using it. However, it does mean to consider carefully how you use your money.

<u>Give all you can</u>. Wesley suggests you gain all you can and save all you can so you might have money to give. Wesley listed four considerations to help discern how to give: 1) give to yourself all you need for the basics, 2) give your family and employees their fair share, 3) next give to other Christians and the church, and 4) give to other people in need, the poor and less fortunate.

The scriptures report two miracles regarding small gifts and tremendous results. Each of the Gospels record the feeding of 5000 people with only five loaves of bread and two fish. Additionally, Matthew and Mark describe another happening as they tell of feeding 4000 people with only seven loaves of bread and a few small fish. The significance of these stories is to recognize that God can do great things with small gifts. Regardless the size of your gift, God can make it grow and bless others in amazing ways. Give all you can.

Money can be a great encouragement, but it can bring tremendous stress if mishandled. If this becomes a problem area in your life, you should seek reliable resources and proceed in a responsible and accountable manner. Churches, banks, libraries may all have resources to guide you. Resources are available in books, tapes, seminars, etc. One of the best ways in which to manage finances is a simple personal budget. If you need help, ask someone you respect for guidance. Be prayerful as you set priorities using money, and be conscientious in your spending habits.

Wisdom and Wealth – A Spiritual Guide -2-

> "Take care!
> Be on your guard against all kinds of greed;
> one's life does not consist in the
> abundance of one's possessions."
>
> Luke 12:15

WEALTH CAN BE a blessing if you have an appropriate attitude toward money; however, improper use brings strife to many homes. Careful management of funds and debt repayment allow people to enjoy the simple beauty of life rather than worry and struggle to pay bills. Unfortunately, people often place great value on securing money. There are, however, many qualities of life that money cannot buy. King Solomon offers great insight into financial accountability in the book of Proverbs. Below are numerous passages from this text.

- "Take my instruction instead of silver, and knowledge rather than choice gold; for wisdom is better than jewels, and all that you may desire cannot compare with her." Proverbs 8:10-11
- "Better is a little with righteousness than a large income with injustice." Proverbs 16:8
- "How much better to get wisdom than gold! To get

understanding is to be chosen rather than silver." Proverbs 16:16
- "Better is a dry morsel with quiet than a house full of feasting with strife." Proverbs 17:1
- "Some friends play at friendship but a true friend sticks closer than one's nearest kin." Proverbs 18:24
- "Better is a poor man who walks in his integrity than he who is perverse in speech and is a fool." Proverbs 19:1
- "What is desirable in a man is his loyalty, and it is better to be a poor man than a liar." Proverbs 19:22
- "A good name is to be chosen rather than great riches, and favor is better than silver or gold." Proverbs 22:1
- "Do not wear yourself out to get rich; be wise enough to desist. When your eyes light upon it, it is gone." Proverbs 23:4-5

THE BOOK OF Proverbs identifies a godly character of integrity, honesty, and kindness as worthy goals for which to strive. A reputation of respect and a good name is more excellent than money. Peace and love, warm affection, admiration, or devotion to another person is the desire of a wise person. Money cannot buy these fine character qualities. To use wealth wisely, you must seek knowledge and practice restraint. However, a truly wise man is not revealed by the amount of money he possesses but rather by how he handles his money. Seek wisdom, and be mindful of attitudes toward money, how it is acquired, and the way it is used. Wisdom begins with the life-long search for relationships and insight into family and the Word of God. Throughout the Proverbs, God tells us that those who honor God with their money are blessed in return.

I'd Rather Have Jesus

I'd rather have Jesus than silver or gold;
I'd rather be His than have riches untold;
I'd rather have Jesus than houses or lands.
I'd rather be led by His nail-pierced hand.

(Refrain)
Than to be the king of a vast domain,
Or be held in sin's dread sway.
I'd rather have Jesus than anything
This world affords today.

I'd rather have Jesus than men's applause;
I'd rather be faithful to His dear cause;
I'd rather have Jesus than worldwide fame.
I'd rather be true to His holy name.

He's fairer than lilies of rarest bloom;
He's sweeter than honey from out of the comb;
He's all that my hungering spirit needs.
I'd rather have Jesus and let Him lead.

Rhea F. Miller

Sense of Humor

"Be joyful and glad in heart
for all the good things the Lord has done."

1 Kings 8:66

WHEN YOU THINK of the Bible and faith, it is serious and sobering information. It seldom brings to mind humor and laughter. God chose to create human beings in his image and we as humans tend to find pleasure in laughter. That understanding alone is reason to believe God also appreciates humor. In Ecclesiastes 3:1 and 4 the scriptures tell you, "For everything there is a season, and a time for every matter under heaven: a time to weep, and a time to laugh; a time to mourn, and a time to dance."

Although the Bible, as the most valued and precious book of faith should be taken seriously, you may see touches of humor within its pages. Consider the animals God created each unique and varied: the skunk with its pungent odor for protection, the porcupine with quills, the giraffe with a long neck, the elephant with a long trunk, the highly poisonous pufferfish, the walking stick, and the multi-legged millipede. There are many creatures with qualities that are purposeful but are so unique they may be considered humorous. God created them all as the Bible tells you in Genesis 1:25, "God made the wild animals of the earth of every kind, and the cattle of every kind, and everything that creeps upon the ground of every kind. And God saw that it was good."

Experiences that occurred with a burst of unabated laughter are likely to be fondly remembered. It often comes unexpectedly, but if well-timed and uplifting it is a most joyful experience; a blessing from God. There are, unfortunately, some types of humor that are inappropriate and create negative feelings. It is common in our society for an individual to display a public smile while inwardly holding back tears from hurtful words of others. Paul, in Ephesians 4:29, addresses this situation, "Let no evil talk come out of your mouths, but only what is useful for building up, as there is need, so that your words may give grace to those who hear." Paul continues in his letter to the Ephesians, "Entirely out of place is obscene, silly, and vulgar talk; but instead, let there be thanksgiving" (Ephesians 5:4). Below is a listing of various aspects of humor to consider as you share the gift of laugher with others.

1. Appropriate humor can strengthen relationships, or it can be destructive and demeaning. Although humor should build confidence and joy in people, it should not be used to belittle or mock others.

2. Humor is an excellent technique to help people relax and feel comfortable. However, be cautious with the use of sarcasm, gags and practical jokes.

3. Be sure of the appropriate timeliness of the humor. Tragedies, deaths, life crises, weather crises may not be the time for fun. Be gracious in your words and cautious of remarks that may be regarded as offensive to sensitive occurrences and emotions.

4. When humor points to qualities and events in our personal lives, it may be enjoyed. However, avoid racist, sexist, dirty, or discriminating humor.

What a wonderful blessing is a good sense of humor; a funny statement, a well-chosen phrase, a witty comment, an amusing tasteful joke. Life can be difficult, and it is easy to become too severe, uptight, and critical. During these times, there is a tendency to shut down, thereby creating a limited ability to understand. Humor can bring light to these tense situations. It may change the atmosphere in the workplace, a home, or a heart.

Laughter is healing! Some people have the gift of bringing blessed laughter, not foolish, distasteful, hurtful words, but kind unexpected funny responses. We can all enjoy that God-centered, joyful person with an open heart who can create humor to make us laugh. You may not have the gift of bringing laughter, but you should cultivate a spirit to seek the joy given by humor. Give yourself a healthy sense of humor and enjoy life! Start now! Ask God to lighten your heart.

"A joyful heart makes a cheerful face." Proverbs 15:13 (NASB)

"Pleasant words are like a honeycomb, sweetness to the soul and health to the body." Proverbs 16:24.

Broken Dreams

As children bring their broken toys
With tears for us to mend,
I brought my broken dreams to God
Because He was my Friend.

But then instead of leaving Him
In peace to work alone,
I hung around and tried to help
With ways that were my own.
At last I snatched them back and cried,
"How could You be so slow?"
"My child," He said,
"What could I do?
You never did let go."

Unknown

Anger – Give It to God

> "My beloved: let everyone be quick to listen,
> slow to speak, slow to anger;
> for your anger does not produce God's righteousness."
> James 1:19-20

ANGER IS A natural human emotion that everyone experiences at some time. Anger is not a sin in itself. The scriptures tell us in Mark 3:5 that Jesus got angry at the moneychangers in the Temple; "He looked around at them with anger; he was grieved at their hardness of heart." Jesus was mad because these men were misleading and taking advantage of people who loved God, and they were doing it in God's house. His anger was not selfish but was addressing their wicked lack of respect for God. Jesus' anger was not sinful. Anger is not a preferred emotion. However, there may be times in your life when it is justified. A disregard for God's standards may justify anger. Evil, be it personal or social, is in our world and should not stand unchallenged.

Anger is typically motivated as a result of something you wanted and didn't receive. This anger is selfishly motivated and is sinful. Anger can be a normal human reaction to feeling frustrated, hurt, rejected, or threatened. Uncomfortable memories from the past can also lead to angry feelings. If you feel angry about the past, hanging on to the feelings of hurt and pain can cause you more problems, more significant pain. When someone you care about hurts you, you have choices. You can hold onto anger, which often causes you to not speak to the other person or throw a fit, raise your voice, or explode with emotion. Still another typical manner in dealing with anger is to have thoughts of revenge. These choices do not create healing or honor God. There is a choice that does both, creates healing, and brings honor to God. The healthiest choice to resolve anger is to turn the situation over to God. You can pray for God's help, give the anger to him and leave it in his hands, forgive and move forward. Peace and resolution may take time, but you can rest assured that God will give you peace in the situation.

Anger is a powerful emotion, and when expressed as shouting, lashing out, or becoming violent, it can destroy your family, career, peace of mind, and overall well-being. However, it is important to learn how to assert yourself, your boundaries, or your needs. Confrontation is a reality most people do not enjoy and often avoid. As noted above, there are many ways to express your frustration, displeasure, or anger that are destructive. Therefore, it is necessary to learn and practice the tools of expression that work better toward getting the results you desire. Here are a few ideas to help develop skills to express anger in a healthy manner.

1. Remember, God is in control.
2. Maintain your composure. If the situation has created intense emotion for you, breathe, pray, step back, distract yourself, excuse yourself for a walk, or for time alone. Allow yourself time to process the emotions and the reality of the situation before discussing possible solutions. If necessary, agree to discuss this topic at a later time and then make sure you do.
3. Uncover the real reason the situation is creating frustration for you. The reason may be rejection, sorrow, or pain. Once you have discovered why, it may be easier to communicate your concerns. Don't take comments personally.

4. The frustration may be from a source not connected to the problem area. For example, you may be tired, hungry, or just fed up. These daily human factors make sensitive discussions more difficult. If possible, resolve these issues before tackling an unrelated yet a significant concern.

5. Try to understand the other person's viewpoint. Talk in a casual yet concerned manner, avoiding confrontational tones. Show genuine interest in their viewpoint.

6. Demonstrate care and compassion. Honor the person's right to be frustrated. Respect their feelings. Make every effort to move forward with a healing tone of civility and empathy.

7. Communicate skillfully. Show respect for each other by listening, and talking with clarity, composure, and civility. Ask questions to learn what feelings have surfaced. Respond with sincerity and compassion.

The best outcome for discussing frustrations or anger is that both parties are willing to discuss the issue, compromise, forgive and move forward. Unfortunately, this is not always the case. You must accept that you are not in control of the response of the other individual. If the other individual is unwilling to resolve the situation at that time, you should give the concern to God. Release your hold on the anger and frustration, and let God be your healer. Seeking God's help, turning your anger over to him, and pursuing forgiveness is a challenging process but one which will allow you to feel inner peace, joy, and hope for the future.

People develop habits for dealing with anger, and these can be difficult to break. If you tend to practice the behaviors associated with unresolved anger, ask God for forgiveness and help to change. As you seek a change in your patterns of expressing anger, you should be encouraged that God is with you; he is trustworthy and just. As you seek his will and wisdom, you will gain insight to trust in him to handle the issue. Turning your anger over to God will indeed bring you greater peace, joy, and contentment. As my dear Christian friend, Marilyn Moore, often says, "Sometimes God calms the storm, sometimes God calms the person in the storm."

"Do not say, 'I will repay evil'; wait for the Lord, and he will help you." Proverbs 20:22

"If you become angry, do not let your anger lead you into sin, and do not stay angry all day. Don't give the Devil a chance."
Ephesians 4:26-27 (GNB)

I Need Thee Every Hour

I need Thee every hour,
Most gracious Lord;
No tender voice like Thine
Can peace afford.

(Refrain)
I need Thee, Oh, I need Thee;
Every hour I need Thee;
Oh bless me now, my Savior,
I come to Thee.

I need Thee every hour,
Stay Thou nearby;
Temptations lose their power
When Thou art nigh.

I need Thee every hour,
Teach me Thy will;
And Thy rich promises,
In me fulfill.

Annie Sherwood Hawks

Forgiveness: Let Go of Grudges/Bitterness

"Be kind and tender-hearted to one another,
and forgive one another,
as God has forgiven you through Christ."
Ephesians 4:32 (GNB)

WHEN SOMEONE YOU care about hurts you, the pain can be tremendous. The behavior that caused the hurt can break your trust, dream, friendship, or heart. The persons most likely to hurt you are those closest to you--friends, siblings, parents. It may be difficult to overcome when you are hurt by someone you love and trust, because of a lie, rejection, abuse, or an insult. You may feel trapped and see no way out of the hurt and pain.

These experiences cause negative feelings such as anger, confusion or sadness. The emotions begin small but can grow bigger and very powerful. If not resolved, they can take root and replay in your mind. For example, when you are struggling to forgive, it is expected that you have personal thoughts and reruns of conversations in your mind concerning the individual and how they offended you. These thoughts and conversations accomplish nothing, but will likely create more intense pain for you.

FORGIVENESS: LET GO OF GRUDGES/BITTERNESS

Forgiveness is a process of change. It can be difficult, and it can take time. Forgiveness can be very challenging, especially if the individual does not admit wrong. Remember, the benefits of forgiveness are for you. If you desire to forgive, forgiveness will come in time. However, forgiveness is not a one-time thing. It begins with a decision but memories, words, or actions may trigger old feelings and you may need to recommit to forgiveness repeatedly.

If you do not practice forgiveness, you may be the one who pays most dearly. By seeking forgiveness, you seek peace, hope, gratitude, and joy. Forgiving is not forgetting what happened to you. The act that hurt you may always remain a part of your life. Your forgiveness does not deny the other person's responsibility for breaking you. You can forgive the person without excusing the act.

When you are unforgiving, you may bring anger, bitterness, or sadness into every relationship and experience. You fail to enjoy the present when the hurt is so great that your life is wrapped up in the pain. The bottom line is you may feel miserable in your current life. If this is how you think, it is time to practice forgiveness! According to an old Arabic Proverb, "Write the wrongs that are done to you in sand, but engrave the good things that happen to you on a piece of marble. Let go of all emotions such as resentment and retaliation, which diminish you, and hold onto the emotions, such as gratitude and joy, which increase you."

Forgiveness brings peace that helps you go on with life. The offense is no longer at the center of your thoughts or feelings. Instead of resentment and misery, you have made way for compassion, kindness, and peace. Forgiveness will allow you to let go of grudges and bitterness, so that you may find new freedom and joyfulness. Remember: God works miracles! God makes good come out of difficulty. When there is suffering, you will find grace.

FOLLOWING CHRIST

"Forgive each other; just as the Lord has forgiven you, so you also must forgive." Colossians 3:13

Amazing Grace

Amazing grace how sweet the sound
That saved a wretch like me!
I once was lost, but now am found,
Was blind, but now I see.

'Twas grace that taught my heart to fear,
And grace my fears relieved;
How precious did that grace appear
The hour I first believed!

Through many dangers, toils and snares
I have already come:
'tis grace has brought me safe thus far,
And grace will lead me home.

The Lord has promised good to me,
His word my hope secures;
He will my shield and portion be
As long as life endures.

John Newton

Asking For Forgiveness

> "For Thou, Lord, art good, and ready to forgive,
> and abundant in loving kindness to all who call upon Thee."
>
> Psalm 86:5 (NASB)

THE ABILITY TO forgive people who have treated you or others unjustly is only one aspect of forgiveness. It is also essential that you be willing to accept responsibility if your behavior has hurt others. Our Lord does not expect perfection and forgives you when you ask. However, he does expect you to seek forgiveness and make an effort to correct your mistakes. A factor of genuine sorrow is when you attempt to make better decisions in the future. An apology involves more than the admission of an error. It includes the understanding that you are responsible for behaviors that have hurt the relationship. A genuine apology must also send the message that you care about the relationship and want to do what is necessary to repair and reconnect.

Decisions, especially major decisions, should be made thoughtfully and prayerfully. Each of us has made mistakes and has wronged others and God. Poor choices can create pain for all individuals involved. Take the risk of honesty. If you mess up, ask for forgiveness. If you mess up again, ask for forgiveness again. Remember, asking forgiveness and being forgiven does not stop the damage done or the hurt caused toward others, but it can help heal the pain. If the other individual is unable to forgive, understand they may need time. Pray for their hurts to ease and that they may feel God's peace. God does work miracles.

> "Unless people speak the truth about what they have done and change their mind and behavior, a relationship of trust is not possible... But should he finally confess and repent, you will discover a miracle in your own heart that allows you to reach out and begin to build a bridge of reconciliation."[51]

If there are places in your life where forgiveness is needed, consider the example below. With heartfelt repentance, you will find comfort in seeking forgiveness. Remember: God will work through this difficult situation with you. You may just need the courage to ask.

> It is not my intention to stir old waters, but I know that I have made choices that have caused you pain. It was never my intention to hurt you, but that fact does not take away your pain. Please accept my apology and I ask your forgiveness. If you are aware of actions I might take today that would help remove the hurt, I invite you to trust me enough to tell me so I can help.

"Everyone who believes in him receives forgiveness of sins through his name." Acts 10:43

I Surrender All

All to Jesus I surrender,
All to him I freely give;
I will ever love and trust him,
In his presence daily live.

(Refrain:)
I surrender all,
I surrender all,
All to thee, my blessed Savior,
I surrender all.

Judson W. Van De Venter

Power of the Tongue – Choose Your Words Wisely

*"A soft answer turns away wrath,
but a harsh word stirs up anger.
The tongue of the wise dispenses knowledge,
but the mouths of fools pour out folly."*

Proverbs 15:1-2

WORDS ARE POWERFUL! The Book of Genesis tells us that God spoke words to create the world. Words are used in stories and songs to build courage, instill comfort and inspire camaraderie. Families with children, students in schools, colleges and universities, and soldiers in service to our country, use stories and songs to strengthen ties.

Once spoken, you cannot take comments back. It is important to understand this power and discover how words can be used most effectively to strengthen relationships and relay the correct message. As you choose what to say, take time to consider your message and the intent. The words you choose can bring joy or hurt, build up or destroy. Use your tongue to bring joy. Praise God. Sing to the Lord. Pray to the Lord. Witness for the Lord. Build Community.

The book of Proverbs gives examples of ways in which the tongue can be used in positive and helpful ways. Examples of encouragement, teaching, witnessing, sharing humor, offering corrections, or providing wisdom to someone in need, are all written about in Proverbs. Consider the messages in each of the verses below:

- "Without consultation, plans are frustrated, but with counselors they succeed." Proverbs: 15:22
- "He who listens to life-giving reproof will dwell among the wise. He who neglects discipline despises himself, but he who listens to reproof acquires understanding." Proverbs 15:31-32
- "Kind words are like honey - sweet to the taste and good for your health." Proverbs 16:24 (GNB)
- "The mouth of the righteous is a fountain of life." Proverbs 10:11
- "A joyful heart makes a cheerful face, but when the heart is sad, the spirit is broken." Proverbs 15:13

Choose a joyful controlled tongue. Ask the Holy Spirit to help you learn to control your language and to speak in ways pleasing to God. What you say can have the power to change lives; use that power for good; use that power for God.

"One who spares words is knowledgeable; one who is cool in spirit has understanding. Even fools who keep silent are considered wise; when they close their lips, they are deemed intelligent." Proverbs 17:27-28

"Rash words are like sword thrusts, but the tongue of the wise brings healing. Truthful lips endure forever, but a lying tongue lasts only a moment." Proverbs 12:18-19

"Avoid worldly and empty chatter, for it will lead to further ungodliness." 2 Timothy 2:16 (NASB)

Self-Talk – The Voice in Your Head

> "The Lord is my light and my salvation – whom shall I fear?
> The Lord is the stronghold of my life -
> of whom shall I be afraid?"
>
> Psalm 27:1

GOD DESIRES YOU to be at your best. That is how he created you, and that is how he wants you to function. He made you with a need for food and rest, and he allows opportunities for the provision of those needs. Each day, you face challenges that may hinder the precision of your focus and function. You must learn to plan for and utilize the opportunities God has given to keep functioning. A busy day may require you sacrifice to make time for lunch, but you should eat. It is appropriate and necessary that you take time to take care of yourself. Just as God provides for the needs of your physical body, he will give you tools to quiet the voice in your head.

A challenge for many people is learning to appropriately respond to the voice in their head, often called self-talk. This voice may be cheerful and positive, which creates uplifting thoughts that build confidence, efficiency, and motivation. However, much of the time, the message is negative and critical, causing damage and pain. Just as it is crucial to understand the power of the tongue, you must understand

SELF-TALK – THE VOICE IN YOUR HEAD

the power and influence of the voice in your head. Self-talk can cause damage to your best self. If uncontrolled, this negative voice may limit your potential as it creates self-doubt and can destroy your self-worth.

Positive and negative self-talk has a powerful impact on your life; it affects your body, mind, life, and relationships. The power of this negative voice cannot be understated. The voice in your head impacts all aspects of living if it is not controlled. It is essential to learn to quiet this voice and get it out of your head. You are not powerless. Quiet this negative voice and build confidence and self-esteem.

Dealing with self-talk can be difficult. But Steven Furtick, founder of the Elevation Church in Charlotte, North Carolina, and best-selling author, has a refreshing idea, "I wish I had a little devil on my left shoulder. I could flick him off and tell him to go to hell. Then I would fist-bump the angel sitting on my right shoulder and get on with doing all the things God has called me to do."[52] Furtick suggests that you express this sentiment when your thoughts keep you from responding to God's call in the manner he prefers. Therefore, it is necessary to practice the skill of quieting the voice.

Negative voices are often distorted, focused on blame, and unrealistic. Therefore, you need to learn to silence these voices. "The key is training your mind to know the difference between the Enemy's threats and God's whispers – and conditioning your heart to respond accordingly." Furtick offers the following to help discern the voices.

> The Enemy's threats are embedded in lies.
> God's whispers are rooted in truth.
> The Enemy's threats are designed to paralyze.
> God's whispers are empowered to mobilize.
> The Enemy's threats condemn vaguely.
> God's whispers instruct specifically.

> The Enemy's threats conspire to diminish hope.
>
> God's whispers empower change.
>
> The Enemy's threats are aimed to take you out.
>
> God's whispers speak a better word to keep you in and move you forward.
>
> The secret to overpowering the spirit of fear is recovering the signal, then attuning your spirit to the One who is always speaking. His voice resounds, not at 210 decibels like a blast of TNT (dynamite), but in a silence that can be heard if you have ears to hear.[53]

Furtick gives the devil, the Enemy, responsibility for the negative voices in your head. "The devil wasn't telling me outright lies – he was just giving me half the truth."[54] He suggests you need to finish the narrative. Yes, you made a mistake and sinned. Repent and accept God's forgiveness. Then when the devil begins to replay the tape, let him know you've taken care of the matter with God. He, the devil, should go.

The power of negativity can be overwhelming. A goal in dealing with it is to change it. First, become aware of the intensity of the voice and language. Then, soften the tone, select more gentle words. This process takes commitment; it is challenging, but firmly take charge. Change the "It's the worst day" to "I've had better days," change "I can't" to "this may be hard." The more gentle tone and language will lessen the power of the negative voice. You can quiet this harmful negative voice. Below are pointers to help control your self-talk.

1. Realize, the voice is not telling the whole story and is likely not true. Realize this voice may not be authentic but a small part of a larger story with a happy ending ahead. Believe that you do have the power to change the story.

SELF-TALK – THE VOICE IN YOUR HEAD

2. You deserve compassion! So, when this negative voice begins dragging you down, remember, don't bash yourself. You deserve the same compassion as a friend.

3. You control your mind, so take control and stop the voice. Breathe and remain calm. Sing a song, think of a beautiful place in nature, and stop the thought.

4. Be more kind and gentle to yourself. Remind yourself of your positive qualities, strengths, accomplishments, etc. Do not let the negative comments stand unchallenged.

5. Bring joy and humor to the mind. Music speaks to some people, sing the message. This practice can diminish the power of negativity.

6. Mentally place this image in a place of less significance: the back seat, the other side of the room, etc. Make the voice less personal, less powerful.

7. Change the narrative and elevate a more positive outlook. Regardless of the error, you are worthy, remind yourself.

8. If you continually struggle with this negative voice, consider talking to a trusted friend or professional.

God needs you at your best. The Holy Spirit will help you challenge the message of the enemy. The enemy is speaking to you in the form of self-talk. Confront the messenger. With the Holy Spirit's guidance, you can discover a different reality of truth and grace. You can quiet these voices and break their power. Pray for God to help you conquer the negative voices and give him your best.

Peace, Trust, and Mercy

May today there be peace within your mind, body and spirit.
May you trust that you are exactly where you are meant to be.
May you not forget the infinite possibilities
that are born of faith in yourself and others.
May you use the gifts that you have received,
and pass on the love that has been given to you.
May you be content with yourself just the way you are.
May this knowledge settle into your bones,
and allow your soul the freedom to sing,
dance, praise, and love.
For peace, trust, and mercy are there for you every day.

Anonymous

What Attracts Others to You?

> "Do you not know that your body
> Is a temple of the Holy Spirit who is in you,
> whom you have from God,
> and that you are not your own?
> For you have been bought with a price:
> therefore glorify God with your body."
>
> 1 Corinthians 6:19-20 (NASB)

LET'S LOOK AT what attracts others to you. Personal attributes are powerful. What makes one sexy? What attracts the attention of the opposite sex? The answers to these questions will vary depending on the respondent, but a few factors are consistent. Aside from the warm smile that communicates a friendly demeanor, these are personal qualities that attract others:

- A spirit that is full of joy – contentment and an excitement for living.
- A spirit that is full of peace – harmony and respect in relationships, tranquility, and order.
- A passion for life – go for it, give it your best shot! Take action!
- Self-confidence – a belief in one's abilities and potential.
- A well-groomed body – a clean and fit body.

Feeling good about who you are is priceless but looking good is also important. Now that we have considered the personal attributes that others find attractive let's examine how to maintain a healthy, fit body. The foundations for good physical health are:

1. Physical Activity – Discover ways to exercise your body each day, it takes only minutes, not hours. It does not have to be grueling, but it does need to be consistent.

2. Proper Nutrition – Learn healthy food choices and select those foods for your daily diet.

3. Stress Management – Learn and practice healthy techniques that help you defuse the stresses of everyday life. (For many people, this can be a daily physical workout, or time spent sitting quietly with God's Word.)

4. Adequate Sleep – The human body works most efficiently when it has rested. Without rest, one's body is tired; food choices are often comfort foods that are less healthy choices. Proper rest and physical activity make it possible to maintain a healthy perspective on stressful events.

Make time each day to focus on maintaining your physical and mental health. Although you have twenty-four hours a day to live life, carve out a small portion to focus on your health. Your healthy life choices will be an example for others and a gift for those who love and care about you. You will also reap great benefits as you will have a robust, vibrant mind and body that look and feel great. Give God your best in mind, body, and spirit.

"I can do everything through him who gives me strength."
Philippians 4:13

WHAT ATTRACTS OTHERS TO YOU?

The Serenity Prayer

"God, grant me the serenity
to accept the things I cannot change,
Courage to change the things I can,
And wisdom to know the difference."

Reinhold Niebuhr

You've always been beautiful.
Now you're just deciding to be healthier,
More fit, faster and stronger.
Remember that.

Unknown

Healthy Habits

"Do you not know that you are God's temple
and that God's Spirit dwells in you?
If anyone destroys God's temple, God will destroy that person.
God's temple is holy and you are that temple."

1 Corinthians 3:16

TIME PASSES QUICKLY and practices in one's life can quickly become habits, either good or bad. It is essential in life for daily routines to make each of us stronger, healthier, and wiser. Hope alone does not change one's situation. It does take effort; even a small amount of effort can produce tremendous results. Take time to review your habits and adjust them as appropriate for healthy positive behaviors. Abigail Van Buren, also known as Jeanne Phillips, the columnist of Dear Abby, shares a list of "New Year's Resolutions" adapted by her mother from the original credo of Al-Anon. Consider the following synopsis of her ideas: Just For Today...[55]

Just For Today, I will live through this day only.

- I will not brood about yesterday or obsess about tomorrow.
- I will not set far-reaching goals or try to overcome all of my problems at once.
- I know I can do something for 24 hours that would overwhelm me if I had to keep it up for a lifetime.

Just For Today, I will be happy.

- I will not dwell on thoughts that depress me.
- If my mind fills with clouds, I will chase them away and fill it with sunshine.

Just For Today, I will accept what is.

- I will face reality.
- I will correct those things that I can correct and accept those I cannot.

Just For Today, I will improve my mind.

- I will read something that requires effort, thought and concentration.
- I will not be a mental loafer.

Just For Today, I will make a conscious effort to be agreeable.

- I will be kind and courteous to those who cross my path.
- I will not speak ill of others.

Just For Today, I will refrain from improving anybody but myself.

- I will improve my appearance.
- I will speak softly.
- I will not interrupt when someone else is talking.

Just For Today, I'll do something positive to improve my health.

- If I'm a smoker, I will quit.
- If I'm overweight, I will eat healthily – if only just for today.
- I will get off the couch and take a brisk walk even if it's only around the block.

Just For Today, I will gather the courage to do what is right and take responsibility for my own actions.

The list above is really about setting goals and priorities. Setting a goal helps focus time and effort on what you believe to be important. When you identify a goal and follow with intentional effort, God willing, you will succeed in achieving the dream. Set goals and take small steps each day to achieve your dream. Take one day at a time. Pray.

"Let your gentleness be evident to all. The Lord is near. Do not be anxious about anything, but in everything, by prayer and petition, with thanksgiving, present your requests to God." Philippians 4:6

Extend Hospitality – Greetings and Farewells

> "Do not neglect to show hospitality to strangers,
> for by doing that some have entertained angels
> without knowing it."
>
> Hebrews 13:2

GOD DIRECTS US to extend hospitality to others. God does not mean the hospitality that is thought of in our world today when it requires one to clean the house, cook fancy foods, decorate, or even plan entertainment. Hospitality, as described in the Bible, may be defined as extending services to others. God does not direct us to do any of the tasks above. Instead, the scriptures guide us to bring worship opportunities into our home and our world, including strangers, families, church-goers, colleagues from work, etc. The fellowship offered in hospitality can be life-changing, healing and may open the door for God's work in many lives. Welcome others into the knowledge of the gospel of our Lord Jesus Christ. Practice hospitality.

Jesus gives us guidance on how to say good-bye as he prepared his disciples for his own leaving. He begins by announcing his departure and preparing them for his leaving. In John 13:33, we learn that during the Last Supper, the evening before Jesus was crucified, Jesus tells the disciples, "I am with you only a little longer. Where I am going, you cannot come." Jesus then tells his disciples the purpose for his leaving, and assures them that he will return and they will be together again. In John 14:3, "I go and prepare a place for you, I will come again and will take you to myself, so that where I am, there you may be also." John continues to share Jesus' message in his book, John 14:16-17, as he explains that he has made arrangements for the Holy Spirit to come and help and teach them what they needed to know and understand. "I will ask the Father and he will give you another Advocate, to be with you forever. This is the Spirit of truth. You know him, because he abides with you and he will be in you." "The Advocate, the Holy Spirit, whom the Father will send in my name, will teach you everything and remind you of all that I have said to you" (John 14:26).

The Bible describes Jesus' last moments before leaving his disciples to return to his Father. The scriptures record Jesus' ascension into heaven in the book of Luke 24:50-51, "lifting up his hands, he blessed them. While he was blessing them, he withdrew from them and was carried up into heaven." Jesus knew that it was essential to meet with his disciples before he left them on earth and ascended to heaven. So, he didn't leave them without saying goodbye.

We can learn from Jesus' powerful example of extending farewells. He demonstrated four areas in which we might offer comfort and support to our families and friends at such times. Consider the following:

1. He announced his departure, allowing time for the disciples to process his leaving.
2. He shares the reason for his leaving and offers the assurance of returning and being together again.
3. He informs them that he has planned for another to help and care for them in his absence.
4. He is with them in the final moments and offers a blessing. Then he leaves them.

Jesus shared with his disciples the information children often ask when someone they care about is leaving. Where are you going? When will you be back, etc.? Although they did not fully understand what Jesus was saying to them, Jesus shared information they were interested in knowing about his leaving and returning. Make a routine of saying good-bye. It builds security, value, and a sense of purpose for those you are leaving. Take time to say "good-bye," and, if appropriate, give a warm embrace. These behaviors reassure people of your love and care for them.

"Welcome one another, therefore, just as Christ has welcomed you, for the glory of God." Romans 15:7

"God's steward must be...hospitable, a lover of goodness, prudent, upright, devout, and self-controlled." Titus 1:8

Traditional Gaelic Blessing

May the road rise up to meet you.
may the wind be always at your back.
May the sun shine warm upon your face;
the rains fall soft upon our fields
and until we meet again,
may God hold you in the palm of His hand.

God Be With You

God be with you till we meet again;
Loving counsels guide, uphold you,
May the Shepherd's care enfold you;
God be with you till we meet again.

God be with you till we meet again;
Unseen wings, protecting, hide you,
Daily manna still provide you;
God be with you till we meet again.

God be with you till we meet again;
When life's perils thick confound you,
Put unfailing arms around you;
God be with you till we meet again.

God be with you till we meet again;
Keep love's banner floating o'er you,
Smite death's threat'ning wave before you;
God be with you till we meet again.

Jeremiah E. Rankin

Allow People to Be Human – Love or Respect Them Regardless

> "Don't hit back; discover beauty in everyone.
> If you've got it in you, get along with everybody.
> Don't insist on getting even; that's not for you to do.
> "I'll do the judging," says God. "I'll take care of it."
> Romans 12:17-19 (MSG)

IN HIS BOOK, *Twelve Things I Want My Kids to Remember Forever*, Jerry Jenkins, has included a chapter entitled, Some People Have the Right to Be Wrong. He takes this serious topic and adds a touch of humor and reality as he writes, "I believe these truths and I urgently want you to listen, hear, understand, and apply them, but I confess I learned too many of these the hard way."[56]

We are all human. Being human means we are imperfect, no one does everything correctly. With that in mind, it is important to understand that a person's position, (mom, dad, teacher, coach, etc.) should earn them respect and some privilege. Training, experience, and/or age have allowed this person to earn the role. This experience should provide them some latitude for mistakes. In short, because of their position and the magnitude of their responsibility, we should allow some leeway for errors. Their decision or error may be unfair, foolish, or just shortsighted, and it may be a poor decision, but don't be too critical. There should be no misunderstanding, these individuals do not have free rein to break the law. But in many instances, when the decisions are not monumental, allow them the right to be wrong; respect and love them regardless. "The person in authority has the responsibility, is accountable, is compensated, and will have to answer for his decisions...Offer polite counsel, then keep your mouth shut and do your job."[57]

"Above all, clothe yourselves with love, which binds everything together in perfect harmony. And let the peace of Christ rule in your hearts." Colossians 3:14-15

"Put away from you all bitterness and wrath and anger and wrangling and slander, together with all malice, and be kind to one another, tenderhearted, forgiving one another, as God in Christ has forgiven you." Ephesians 4:31-32

Christian Responsibilities to the Community

> "Let your light shine before men,
> that they may see your good deeds
> and praise your Father in heaven."
>
> Matthew 5:16

WE ARE A part of a greater society on earth, towns, cities, states, countries, and the world. In any community, we are given benefits and have responsibilities. If we enjoy the privileges of society, then we should accept the duties. Therefore, the teaching of the church is for Christians to be obedient to the laws and prayerful for the leaders.

As was previously written, God has given each individual a task on this earth. Some people are given gifts to govern societies. It is the responsibility of all Christians to be mindful and help the decision-making processes within the organization or the government. Pray for the wisdom and health of individuals making decisions for these communities.

A healthy community is a reflection of wholesome families. An emotionally healthy family practices the qualities of love, commitment, faithfulness, patience, etc. Consequently, children develop skills in communication and relationships that enable them to relate well to others, and resolve differences and conflicts. Healthy families are a vital component for building healthy communities.

Pray to have the strength and wisdom to do the responsible thing as you live and work in the community with your fellow human. Your gifts, your family, and your prayers can each powerfully impact the health of your community.

"Let every person be subject to the governing authorities; for there is no authority except from God, and those authorities that exist have been instituted by God." Romans 13:1

"For the same reason you also pay taxes, for the authorities are God's servants, busy with this very thing. Pay to all what is due them – taxes to whom taxes are due, revenue to whom revenue is due, respect to whom respect is due, honor to whom honor is due." Romans 13:6-7

Because of you...
I looked around at all the children suffering in the world.
I saw the abuse, the neglect, the pain.
I looked up to heaven and said "WHY?
Why don't you do something to help these children?"
The reply came back:

"I did do something. I created you!!!"

Unknown

Hope – Reliance upon God

> "May the God of hope fill you with all joy
> and peace in believing,
> that you may abound in hope
> by the power of the Holy Spirit."
>
> Romans 15:13

THE WORD OF God, his love and power, are the basis of Christian hope. When Jesus came to earth, he changed our relationship with God. Before Jesus' coming, God was viewed as untouchable, with many rules to follow. During that time, the people's relationship with God was often one of tension and stress. Jesus changed that into a new, close, and intimate relationship with God. In this new relationship, we find hope and grace; "…not condemnation, not judgment, not vengeance; but undeserved, incredible kindness of God."[58]

God gives us hope! Christ brings a spirit that can overcome trials. Life in Christ does not provide a spirit that waits idly and lets things happen. He provides a spirit that prayerfully meets the challenges and will prevail with God's grace and strength. Although, trials can be difficult, they are opportunities to grow in reliance on God, creating a stronger, purer, and closer relationship with him.

Reliance on your own devices creates a world that is restless and stormy. When this world brings tough times, sorrow, persecution, and loneliness, it can bring despair and close our hearts to the possibility of hope. Yet, when we rely on the Word of God, we find peace and comfort in our trials, God's grace.

It is powerful to realize that nothing can separate us from the love of God. He is with us in life and death. The powers of evil, the unknown and things of the past, present or the future, are unable to separate a Christian from the love and care of God. Therefore, find hope in knowing that God loves you, he cares, and he is with you always.

"Even those who are young grow weak; young men will fall exhausted. But those who trust in the Lord for help will find their strength renewed. They will rise on wings like eagles; they will run and not get weary; they will walk and not grow weak." Isaiah 40:30-31(GNB)

Now The Day is Over

Now the day is over,
night is drawing nigh;
shadows of the evening
steal across the sky.

Jesus give the weary
calm and sweet repose;
with your tenderest blessing
may my eyelids close.

Comfort every sufferer
watching late in pain;
those who plan some evil,
from their sin restrain.

Thro' the long night-watches
may your angels spread
their bright wings above me,
watching round my bed.

When the morning wakens,
then may I arise
pure and fresh and sinless
in your holy eyes.

S. Baring-Gould

Related Scriptures

"There is no one who always does what is right, not even one." Romans 3:10

"Do not work for the food that perishes, but for the food that endures for eternal life, which the Son of Man will give you." John 6:27

"By wisdom is a house built, and by understanding it is established." Proverbs 24:3

"Trust in the Lord with all your heart, and do not lean on your own understanding. In all your ways acknowledge Him, and He will make your paths straight." Proverbs 3:5-6 (NASB)

"Now as they observed the confidence of Peter and John, and understood that they were uneducated and untrained men, they were marveling, and began to recognize them as having been with Jesus." Acts 4:13 (NASB)

"Do not be fooled. 'Bad companions ruin good character.' Come back to your right senses and stop your sinful ways."
1 Corinthians 15:33 (GNB)

"Whoever is faithful in small matters will be faithful in large ones; whoever is dishonest in small matters well be dishonest in large ones." Luke 16:10 (GNB)

RELATED SCRIPTURES

"No one can serve two masters; for a slave will either hate the one and love the other, or be devoted to the one and despise the other. You cannot serve God and wealth." Matthew 6:24

"Don't burn out; keep yourselves fueled and aflame. Be alert servants of the Master, cheerfully expectant. Don't quit in hard times; pray all the harder. Help needy Christians; be inventive in hospitality." Romans 12:11-13 (MSG)

"Be hospitable to one another without complaint. As each one has received a special gift, employ it in serving one another, as good stewards of the manifold grace of God." 1 Peter 4:9 (NASB)

"We are pressed on every side by troubles, but we are not crushed and broken. We are perplexed, but we don't give up and quit. We are hunted down, but God never abandons us. We get knocked down, but we get up again and keep going." 2 Corinthians 4:8-9

"Do not judge and you will not be judged. Do not condemn and you will not be condemned. Forgive and you will be forgiven. Give and it will be given to you." Luke 6:37-38

"And what does the Lord require of you? To do justice, and to love kindness, and to walk humbly with your God." Micah 6:8

"The heart of the righteous ponders how it answers, but the mouth of the wicked pour out evil things." Proverbs 15:28

"Rash words are like sword thrusts, but the tongue of the wise brings healing. Truthful lips endure forever, but a lying tongue lasts only a moment." Proverbs 12:18-19

"One who spares words is knowledgeable; one who is cool in spirit has understanding. Even fools who keep silent are considered wise; when they close their lips, they are deemed intelligent."
Proverbs 17:27-28

"Misfortune pursues sinners, but prosperity rewards the righteous. The good leave an inheritance to their children's children but the sinner's wealth is laid up for righteous." Proverbs 13:21-22

"Teach us to number our days aright, that we may gain a heart of wisdom." Psalm 90:12.

"Wait for the Lord; be strong and take heart and wait for the Lord." Psalm 27:14

"Now that you have purified your souls by your obedience to the truth so that you have genuine mutual love, love one another deeply from the heart. You have been born anew." 1 Peter 1:22

"Bless those who persecute you; bless and do not curse. Rejoice with those who rejoice; mourn with those who mourn. Live in harmony with one another. Do not be proud, but be willing to associate with people of lower position. Do not be conceited. Do not repay evil for evil." Romans 12:14-17

Developing Healthy Relationships

◆▶────────◀◆

Each relationship is unique and a gift from God. Whoever you are, you need to develop and maintain a valued connection with another person, a healthy alliance. A healthy relationship brings joy, closeness, unity to life, and honor to God. Developing healthy partnerships is challenging. The values and choices you make each day can have a great impact on the outcome of your relationships.

Healthy relationships require effort to develop. The focus of this section will be on godly aspects of some of the critical components of behavior that impact associations. The writings address friendships and move through dating, marriage, and family. Examined are such concepts as sex, communication, heritage, tradition, broken families, and prayer.

Building healthy, loving relationships is one of the most important things you will do in life. God designed relationships to help each of us in our walk through life and bring us closer to him. Many of us do not have godly examples of living in healthy households that bring honor to Him. I pray that God will give you additional knowledge, skill, and a desire to allow him, working through you, to create stronger and more loving relationships. The words of the apostle Paul offer insight to healthy relationships and a more joyful life. Paul tells us, "Finally brethren, whatever is true, whatever is honorable, whatever is right, whatever is pure, whatever is lovely, whatever is of good repute, if there is any excellence and if anything worthy of praise, let your mind dwell on these things." Philippians 4:8 (NASB)

"Dear Lord,
Bless this home with Your love and peace.
Fill these rooms with Your joy and laughter.
Let these rooms be places of learning
of Your truth and grace.
Let Your glory shine
through these windows to the neighbors.
May the kind words, consideration,
and harmony draw others to You.
May Your rich blessings touch this family
and all who enter,
In the precious name of Jesus, amen."

Unknown

Love, Marriage, and Family

> "It (love) bears all things, believes all things,
> hopes all things, endures all things.
> Love never ends."
>
> 1Corinthians 13:7-8

FEW THINGS IMPACT one's life as love, marriage, and family. These are each huge topics, and this writing will barely touch the surface, but they are each worthy of further reading.

Love:
Christian love invites the Lord onto your team. Each member should feel cherished and treasured, being top priority after God. Members should strive to build a deep connection, emotionally and spiritually allowing each to develop a soft, tender heart. To maintain love, we must choose to love, be committed to the relationship, be forgiving, be self-sacrificing, etc. Each person's analysis of these factors within a relationship may be different, so it is essential to talk about these terms with the one you love and develop a mutual understanding when one says, "I love you."

Marriage:
There should be a closeness or greater depth of feeling for one another in the marriage relationship, than for others. Marriage partners benefit by being companions and caring for one another in a wide

variety of ways. At the same time, there must be a level of trust and respect that allows the freedom for each individual to grow. The level of involvement with one another or amount of independence depends on the couple. Marriage is also about creating a healthy home. This means creating four walls within which one finds, love, joy, security, peace and honor to God.

Family:
One of the greatest gifts God has given humans is to feel a close connection with family members. Having knowledge and sharing details of each other's lives: joys, heartaches, dreams, secret loves, magical moments, and God's story in your lives. May you be fortunate to be a member of a family who cherish each other, share comfort in sorrow and unrest, care for each other's needs, and who you may trust to talk about everything, nothing, or just sit in silence.

Unfortunately, not everyone has a healthy family. This topic is discussed further in the sections entitled "Family Matters" and "Broken Families." If you are from a family you feel is broken, it is important to remember that the Lord Jesus Christ is a God of healing and love. He too wants to heal your broken family. There is always hope with God.

In closing, recognize that everyone's life is complicated and different. Occurrences in life may shatter the peace, stability, or happiness within. Some of these happenings leave deep wounds, scars, and ugliness. Scars do not excuse poor behavior, but wounds will allow us to understand and show compassion. We must be willing to forgive people as they heal from the wounds and brokenness of spirit and body. We must also be patient with one another and share a genuine caring and closeness, supporting one another's hopes, dreams, and purpose for life.

LOVE, MARRIAGE, AND FAMILY

Pray that you will have a personal character of strength for the difficult times, a tender heart for love and compassion, a heart to forgive wrongdoings, and a desire to help build and support a family that honors God in its very existence.

Just a Closer Walk with Thee

I am weak but Thou art strong;
Jesus, keep me from all wrong;
I'll be satisfied as long
As I walk, let me walk close to Thee.

(Refrain)
Just a closer walk with Thee
Grant it, Jesus, is my plea.
Daily walking close to Thee,
Let it be, dear Lord, let it be.

Unknown

Friendship – A Precious Gift

"A friend loves at all times."
Proverbs 17:17

A FRIEND IS a tremendous blessing in life. A close friend can provide the loyalty, love, companionship, and growth that are vital for a healthy life. The goal should be to honor God as you strive, throughout your life, to become a better friend and better person.

Eddie Lyons is the pastor at High Street Church in Springfield, Missouri. Eddie and his wife, Cindy, served as missionaries in the Philippines for 20 years, and while there, he completed his MBA from the Ateneo University of Manila. Eddie retells the beautiful and personal friendship between David and Jonathan as described in 1 Samuel 18:1, 3-4, and again in chapter 20. The scripture tells of Jonathan, a prince who had experienced great wealth befriending David, a shepherd, the 8th son of Jesse, who was often overlooked and rejected. Both of these men shared a love for God. Jonathan willingly surrendered his right to be King because he recognized God's hand on David. Jonathan and David proved to be devoted friends as they were long-suffering and accepting of each other throughout life's challenges.[59]

How do we develop a devoted friendship similar to that of Jonathan and David? The following list explains the qualities of solid friendships and is not designed to be used as a yardstick to measure yourself

FRIENDSHIP – A PRECIOUS GIFT

or others harshly. Instead, seek friends and associate with individuals who display godly character. The following list identifies qualities and traits that build healthy, enduring relationships.

Traits of a True Friend:

1. A true friend is loyal. They stand with you through difficult times, keep secrets, and don't gossip.
2. A true friend is generally very dependable. Friends make great efforts to keep their word.
3. A true friend is trustworthy and speaks honestly from the heart.
4. A true friend is empathetic, kindhearted, respectful, and sensitive to your needs. A true friend offers encouragement and compassion as the situation requires. They are not judgmental.
5. A true friend stimulates thinking and helps to keep our minds sharp. They should be wise decision-makers and good thinkers. They listen. In difficult situations, they are willing to share sound advice and offer godly counsel and support.
6. A true friend is supportive and encourages in matters of faith.
7. A true friend is self-confident and helps your confidence elevate.
8. A true friend is fun to be with, can laugh, and sees the humor in life.

The qualities above are necessary to build a true and lasting friendship. However, encouragement to depend on God is the greatest gift a friend can give. Companionship is strengthened by a spiritual kinship. Time creates special closeness as the relationship will be enriched through shared memories. Honor these friendships; keep in touch!

Be careful of your choice of friends! Some people seem to enjoy pulling others down rather than uplifting and supporting. Individuals who would not be true friends or help you gain wisdom may have one or many of the following character traits: uncontrollable temper, evil practices, crude speech, or is prone to malicious or violent activities.

People need friends. Each of us desires a close relationship with someone. Being a good friend is essential to having a good friend. Commit yourself to be the kind of person that makes a quality friend. Seek and enjoy a blessed relationship with God and a genuine, spiritual friendship with another human being. Remember, your best friend is Jesus.

"Whoever walks with the wise becomes wise, but the companion of fools suffers harm." Proverbs 13:20

"Be happy with those who are happy, and weep with those who weep. Have the same concern for everyone. Do not be proud, but accept humble duties. Do not think of yourselves as wise."
Romans 12:15-16 (GNB)

May the Lord Bless and Keep You

"Grace to you and peace
from God our Father and the Lord Jesus Christ."

Philippians 1:2

THE APOSTLE PAUL wrote a letter to the church he started in Philippi, and it's recorded in the Bible in the book of Philippians. He opens with touching and beautiful sentiments from one friend to another. Paul's letter serves as a reminder that we should always rejoice in our friendships with other followers of Christ. In the opening statements, Paul expresses various uplifting sentiments that can serve as a lesson for acknowledging appreciation of qualities in friends, and ways to encourage and support their walk with Christ. Paul prays for them, gives thanks for them, encourages them, and acknowledges they are a gift to him from Christ Jesus. He concludes his opening remarks with encouragement to keep God in their hearts and follow God's commands. Following are Paul's opening comments in his letter to the Philippians 1:2-6, 8-11 (GNB).

> May God our Father and the Lord Jesus Christ give you grace and peace.
>
> I thank my God for you every time I think of you; and every time I pray for you all, I pray with joy because of the way in which you have helped me in the work of the gospel from the

> very first day until now. And so I am sure that God, who began this good work in you, will carry it on until it is finished on the Day of Christ Jesus. You are always in my heart! And so it is only right for me to feel as I do about you....God is my witness that I tell the truth when I say that my deep feeling for you all comes from the heart of Christ Jesus himself.
>
> I pray that your love will keep growing more and more, together with true knowledge and perfect judgment, so that you will be able to choose what is best. Then you will be free from all impurity and blame on the Day of Christ. Your lives will be filled with the truly good qualities which only Jesus Christ can produce, for the glory and praise of God.

Pray that God will give you a relationship with another person, a Christian friend, to which you may feel as close to as Paul's friends in Philippi. A friend of faith is a priceless and rare gift. Be that friend for someone.

Date with a Purpose

"Be subject one to another out of reverence for Christ."
Ephesians 5:21

THE BIBLE GIVES a great deal of insight into Christian marriage and a Christian household. As you begin considering your future partner, it is of great importance to seek wisdom. Setting dating guidelines will help you find a partner with values you admire and keep you out of situations with unhealthy people. In addition, dating sets the groundwork for your future friends, family and life. Carefully consider the four uniquely different aspects of dating outlined below. These concepts may impact the success and happiness of your dating life, as well as the commitment and fellowship of your marriage.

<u>Dating is an important ritual</u> in life and society. However, as you begin considering the process, it is powerful to first understand a few concepts that will tremendously influence your dating experiences. The considerations below address your innermost thoughts about you and your life expectations. This information may change your ideas about who to date.

- Before a relationship can blossom, you need to have your personal life in order. First, you must have an understanding of your own personal values, goals, and personality. Otherwise, it will be difficult, if not impossible, to nourish a healthy marital relationship.

- God values you, and you must grow and learn to value your gifts as well. You must respect yourself before others find value in you. God made you as he wanted and needed you. You are valuable! You will find a partner fitting the description of the person you believe you deserve.
- You will live life in many chapters: childhood, young adult, middle-aged adult, older adult, etc. Your marriage partner will not define you. Your relationship with God is the primary relationship in your life. He will be with you throughout your story, be faithful to him.

<u>Before you enter the dating scene, prepare yourself</u>:

- Have a list of your values and consider the cost if you were to compromise them.
- Understand, it is ok to want to get married, but it is also ok not to get married.
- Have a community of Christians around you, and LISTEN to them.
- Are you willing to date non-Christians? Dating is not the place to be a missionary. If your date needs evangelism, they may not yet be a candidate for your serious dating partner.

<u>If you are a person of faith, Paul tells us in 2 Corinthians 6:14, "do not be mismatched with unbelievers."</u> Paul continues to compare life lived in righteousness or lawlessness, light and dark. As a follower of Jesus, consider the principles for Christian dating outlined below:

- Look for the commitment to faith. Does the individual attend church or have a Bible? Is their reputation one that reflects the life of a person of faith? Does this person cultivate healthy desires and demonstrate patience to honor the stated values.
- Trust your senses. If you think you should slow this relationship, consider why?

- Be cautious of social media. It is easy to hide behind the screen with a flurry of descriptive words. Instead, look for words that are followed with action and evidence of commitment.
- Look first for a friendship that slowly grows into a more significant relationship. Discover a shared sense of faith, values, interests, and activities. Also, consider commonality in education, family background, income, expectations in life, etc. Move slowly in the relationship, so it may grow into a commitment and long-lasting love affair for life.
- Remain Pure: The Song of Solomon 1:16 describes the setting in which the young lovers abide. "Our couch is green; the beams of our house are cedar, our rafters are pine." The scene described is out of doors, a location much easier to escape the temptations of inevitable desires. To uphold this standard requires discipline, restraint, and abstinence from activities that don't promote holiness.
- Date to discover a partner to marry. Genesis 1:28 reads, "So God created humankind in his image, in the image of God he created them; male and female he created them. God blessed them, and God said to them, 'Be fruitful and multiply.'" Chapter 1:31 continues, "God saw everything that he had made, and indeed, it was very good." God planned on men and women uniting in marriage. He intended this union to strengthen each individual's growth as a person and follower of Christ.

<u>There are yet a few final, powerful topics to discuss</u> as you are dating. It is essential to discover and stand in agreement regarding these goals before you marry. This strong foundation will save frustration, conflict, and unhappiness. These areas are:

- Money – Find common ground regarding how you plan to earn, save and spend the money.
- Religion –As a couple, you must have an understanding about

how you will honor faith as a family. You must decide what values and traditions of faith you will practice. Each person must feel at ease with this agreement.
- Children: Talk about if you want children and how many. Discuss if you are unable to have children. Also, decide how as a family, you will address the issue of faith.
- Activities: Couples must spend time together in pleasurable activities they both enjoy. It is equally important that each member of the partnership be allowed time alone. Discuss what activities you enjoy together and when you want time on your own.

The dating process should be exciting and fun! As you have previously read, the Book of Proverbs is full of wisdom regarding the characteristics of godly people who make a good mate. The qualities of a good friend blend well with those of a godly mate. The above principles are worthy for you to consider as you begin dating. Knowing yourself and upholding your values will allow the dating process to be exciting and fun with fewer wrong places and wrong people. Look for a partner that will build, with you, a fun and rewarding marriage. Always remember, no one is perfect!

Choosing a mate is one of life's most significant decisions! Pray that God will guide you to discover a loving and compatible mate with whom to share your life!

"Let your gentleness be evident to all. The Lord is near. Do not be anxious about anything, but in everything by prayer and petition, with thanksgiving, present your requests to God." Philippians 4:6

Stages in Relationships

> "Let love be genuine; hate what is evil;
> hold fast to what is good;
> love one another with mutual affection;
> outdo one another in showing honor."
>
> Romans 12:9-10

RELATIONSHIPS TAKE WORK and effort, but they are worth it! Falling in love seems so easy but staying in love requires commitment and relational skills. There are identifiable differences in which relationships vary: parents, siblings, friends, colleagues, and couples. Some of these relationships may last a lifetime, while others come and go throughout life. However, regardless of the duration, each of them requires both parties to work through situations and circumstances in a healthy, positive manner, so the relationship will grow to become stronger and more committed.

Below, are four stages of development in which a relationship may journey to create a strong connection. These stages focus on the relationship of courtship.

The first stage is that of enchantment. You know you feel differently about this person. They are the center of your thoughts throughout the day; you're eagerly looking forward to seeing or talking with them again. If you notice their faults, you forgive them easily. You are eager to know this person better. During this phase, it is difficult to sleep, the person is on your mind almost every waking hour.

The second stage is spending time together - getting to know each other. In this stage, it is common to share thoughts and ideas as you take risks. Sometimes, the relationship grows stronger as you discover more about each other and trust builds. In different situations, time together and the risks taken allow those involved to find out if the relationship is a good fit. It is not uncommon for a relationship to end during this stage.

The third stage deals with difficult situations or a crisis. These situations are uncomfortable but allow the opportunity for working together and building trust. Dealing with difficulty is a critical stage in a relationship. If you can manage a stressful situation and work as a team, it provides an excellent opportunity for growth as a couple. Relationships are always growing and changing. Your reactions to these tough happenings impact this change and dictate a strengthening or weakening of the relationship. It is also possible that handling this situation may alienate the individuals and drive them apart. Another factor that can create conflict is from individuals outside the relationship. Be cautious of allowing others to get into the middle of your relationship. If you are considering a long-term commitment, you must honor your partner and make significant attempts to stand together. Relationships are powerful when the pair knows they can work through tough times together.

The final stage is the challenge of trust and security. The challenge must be defeated; trust and security must prevail. The memories through the years have grown and created joy, affection, caring, and trust. The major conflicts have been resolved, and the relationship feels secure. You share a deep attachment to the other individual and genuinely enjoy and pleasure in each other's company.

STAGES IN RELATIONSHIPS

Relationships create both joys and challenges in life. Understanding the development of stages in relationships helps you discover the level of commitment and attachment. Not all relationships will bring trust, reward, and comfort. Carefully consider the dynamics of the relationship as you journey from one stage to the next. Pray for God to guide you and the dynamics of the relationship.

"Let no evil talk come out of your mouths, but only what is useful for building up, as there is need, so that your words may give grace to those who hear." Ephesians 4:29

"You will make your plans, but God directs your actions. The king speaks with divine authority his decisions are always right." Proverbs 16:9 (GNB)

How Serious Is Your Relationship

"Love is patient; love is kind;
love is not envious or boastful or arrogant or rude.
It does not insist on its own way; it is not irritable or resentful;
it does not rejoice in wrongdoing, but rejoices in the truth.
It bears all things, believes all things,
hopes all things, endures all things."

1 Corinthians 13:4-7

INFORMATION ABOUT DATING rules and stages in a relationship may be helpful. Still, they may also be a bit tedious and overwhelming in finding a lifetime partner. As you manage your dating life, there are considerations outside the relationship that have value and deserve consideration.

- Always remember the focus of life: "You shall love the Lord your God with all your heart and with all your soul and with all your mind and with all your strength." Mark 12:30.
- Listen to those who love you and care about your life and your future. They know you well, your unique needs, and they will be honest and help you make good decisions. You need truth, wisdom, and possibly correction as you continue on this journey.
- Remain true to yourself and accountable for your values.

- Include Christian friends and family in your dating life. They are part of your world and should be part of your future. Do not become isolated.

Before long it is apparent that you need godly people in your life to support your efforts in finding a godly life-long partner. You need people who are willing to speak honestly, lovingly and courageously, even when you are not eager to hear their comments. People who choose to serve God, who know you, love you, and want the best for you are gifts from God to help you; allow them a voice as you seek a lifetime partner.

As your relationship grows stronger, you should evaluate your personal reactions as you share time with this potential partner. Listen to your voice and trust the message. Remember, you are looking for a person to be your lifelong companion. Below are a few familiar voices that may guide your thinking regarding the suitability of this person as your potential partner.

- You are at ease and find the values of this person to be pleasing to you. You feel comfortable introducing the person to family and friends. If this is not the case, be bold enough to be honest with yourself and the other person. If you have reservations, it may be time to reevaluate the relationship.
- You can be yourself and find this person seems to enjoy and appreciate your gifts of personality and character. On the flip side, you are comfortable with the other person's true self and accept and appreciate the talents, personality and character they bring to the relationship. If this comfort level is not present for both parties, it is likely time to look further.
- As you anticipate your next time together, you are eager and envision a rewarding time together. However, if you have a sense of dread, prefer being with other people or doing other activities, you need to be truthful with yourself

and acknowledge this may be developing into a mediocre relationship.

The considerations outlined above are both varied and vital. The mate who is chosen with prayer for wisdom, purpose, and care can be a beautiful and wonderful gift! A truly healthy relationship is built with God and develops a deep and abiding love resulting from a lifetime of shared joys, trials, survivals, and growth.

"Above all, maintain constant love for one another, for love covers a multitude of sins." 1 Peter 4:8

"Then the Lord God said, 'It is not good that the man should be alone; I will make him a helper as his partner." Genesis 2:18

Choose a Godly Mate

> "If I speak in the tongues of mortals and of angels,
> but do not have love, I am a noisy gong or a clanging cymbal.
> And if I have prophetic powers,
> and understand all mysteries and all knowledge,
> and if I have all faith so as to move mountains,
> but do not have love, I am nothing."
>
> 1Corinthians 13:1-2

IT IS COMMON that people seek a companion with whom to spend their lives; a marriage partner. The choice of a life-partner is a huge decision that should not be taken lightly. The first considerations should be whether the individual has character qualities you admire and can be a person whom you would consider a true friend. If these qualities are present in the relationship, it is wise to look further still and consider the qualities of an ideal mate. The qualities listed below are to provide insight as you date, looking to make this critical decision. We are all imperfect human beings and cannot fulfill all of these qualities at the highest level. However, a person with a heart for God will seek to honor these qualities and demonstrate maturity in these areas.

Consider these qualities as character traits of a choice partner:

1. The individual loves and fears God. The Lord's will is priority, and decisions are made based on biblical principles.

2. The individual seeks wisdom and speaks in wisdom and kindness.
3. The individual can be depended upon, they look for and give help, and they will pick you up in difficult times.
4. The individual is gracious, friendly, courteous, kind, agreeable, approachable, and neighborly.
5. The individual is a person in whom you have complete trust.

When you choose to date with a purpose and move toward choosing a godly mate, it is also vital to evaluate your personal feelings about the relationship. For example, do you feel: loved, appreciated, desired, trusted, and encouraged? These are feelings that may need to be discussed and resolved before you marry.

A godly marriage partner will allow her mate to be a separate unique person. The partnership should complement one another's lives and share many significant components. It is, however, also important that each person maintain a sense of personal identity and be allowed to pursue this identity. No member of the relationship should exercise over-powering control but each should encourage the individual's unique gifts.

Although the process should be pleasant, the choice of a partner must be made carefully and deliberately, for a poor choice is both painful and permanent. Society sends mixed messages regarding marriage partners and their relationships. Commercials, television programs, and movies present a liberal and often sad view of this potentially excellent relationship and show relationships practicing poor, ungodly behaviors. Society puts a tremendous emphasis on physical beauty and charm. These are fine qualities, but they should not be the basis by which a mate is chosen. "Charm is deceitful and beauty is vain, but a woman who fears the Lord, she shall be praised" (Proverbs 31:30). Proverbs continues to tell you that if you associate with a fool, your life will, unfortunately, be challenging.

A final note: The Book of Proverbs has much to say about marriage; it is an excellent guide for personal behaviors and character qualities of people with whom you should or should not associate. However, in 1 Corinthians 7:8, Paul shares information regarding the choice of single life. "To the unmarried and the widows I say that it is well for them to remain unmarried as I am. But if they are not practicing self-control, they should marry."

If you are not yet married, choosing a mate based on positive character qualities will bring a lifetime of joy. If you are married, the characteristics identified can guide self-awareness and provide goals for which to strive. Whether you choose to be married or single, good character brings honor to your life and glory to God.

Unacceptable Behaviors in a Partner

"For where your treasure is, there your heart will be also."
Matthew 6:21

TROUBLESOME BEHAVIORS CAN be a sign that this relationship is not built to last. Although these "red flags" are not a guarantee of a troubled relationship, they are undoubtedly worthy of your caution and awareness. Don't make the common mistake of believing you can change a person or their traits. That is between the individual and God.

If you are dating an individual with tendencies toward one or more of these traits, you may want to step back and give the relationship a break. Knowing the qualities of both a healthy and an unhealthy relationship will help equip you with the necessary skill to maintain a healthy relationship. The following is a list of behaviors that give insight to unacceptable behaviors in a relationship:

- Control – These individuals are always the decision-maker. They may be manipulative and jealous and tell you what to do and with whom to spend time. They also are often closed to new experiences, and excessively rigid. It is expected for these individuals to try to isolate you from friends and

UNACCEPTABLE BEHAVIORS IN A PARTNER

family. Controlling behaviors will rob you of your life and your identity.
- Dishonesty – Lying keeps information from you. These people may steal from you or others.
- Disrespect – Rather than build the partner up with honor, they may make fun of opinions or interests.
- Dependence – These individuals do not develop a life interest other than the partner. The sense of "I cannot live without you" is a red flag.
- Intimidation – This controlling behavior occurs when one partner is made to feel fearful. The threat is often in the form of intense anger, violence, or a danger of breaking up.
- Physical Violence – This unfortunate trait becomes apparent when one partner uses physical force to get their way. The behavior may be grabbing, shoving, slapping, etc.
- Unresolved Anger Issues - Excessive anger is a source of stress. These people are argumentative, aggressive, possessive, and often verbally abusive. Give your attention to people who have a healthy manner in dealing with their anger.
- Sexual Violence – This is when sexual activity occurs without consent.
- Addictions: Addictions can seriously damage relationships. They serve as a trap for people. Addictions come in a variety of forms including substances, activities, objects, etc. Addictions damage not only the individual but also relationships.
- Self-involved – These people are takers, not givers. They think only of themselves rather than others. Often unkind, unsupportive, condescending, rude, and demonstrating a lack of respect for their partner. Because of selfishness, this situation can drain the life out of a relationship.
- Emotionally Detached - Some people are unwilling or unable to open themselves emotionally. They may appear defensive and avoid discussions of sensitive topics. When asked about feelings, they are quiet or change the subject.

- Lack of Spiritual Connection - People are spiritual creatures. God should be the priority in life, followed by family. God should be the center and the purpose of life.
- Misguided Parental Relations – This may be a two-fold area of concern. First, it is important to respect and honor parents but you need to be the top priority in looking toward a marital relationship. Your desires are to be celebrated! Secondly, be watchful for the person who is looking for someone to take care of them, as a nurturing parent. These people may be selfish and lazy.
- Unhealthy Fears - Everyone experiences fear. Healthy fears help save lives. Unhealthy fears are triggered by imagined or exaggerated dangers, and cause people to make irrational, unwise decisions. People consumed by fear are blocked from developing healthy relationships.

Don't compromise! It is essential to pay attention to troublesome behavioral and emotional problems that could create severe difficulties in a long-term relationship. There must be resolution to these troublesome behaviors before you marry. Living together or getting married will not change anything. Healing, and change, is between this individual and God. The person with these behavior problems is the one who must seek to change him or herself. Change is possible if the individual seeks help and actively commits to the goal. Your relationship is headed for trouble unless your partner looks for help, sees a therapist, or participates in couple's or group counseling to resolve the problem behavior. This is not the time to compromise.

Hopefully, you have come to realize an individual with the concerns identified above is, at this time, not ready to become a healthy lifetime partner. Although you are not the one directly responsible for helping change a person's behavior, God commands us to love the individual regardless of the behavior. The words of the apostle John remind us of Jesus' command in John 13:34-35 (MSG), "Love one another. In the same way I loved you, you love one another. This is how everyone will recognize you are my disciples – when they see the love you have for each other." Love in action may be that you lift a prayer on their behalf. Pray for the person and ask God to come into their heart and heal their life of brokenness and pain.

Be patient and purposeful as you seek a marriage partner. Seek the qualities of a godly, wise, gracious, faithful, down-to-earth, genuine, transparent, and honest person. These qualities will bring joy and honor to your life and glory to your God.

Prepare Yourself for Marriage

"Love is patient and kind;
it is not jealous or conceited or proud;
love is not ill-mannered or selfish or irritable;
love does not keep a record of wrongs,
love is not happy with evil, but is happy with truth.
Love never gives up;
and its faith, hope, and patience never fail."

I Corinthians 13: 4-8 (GNB)

IF YOU SHOULD choose to marry, the second most significant decision you will make in your lifetime involves the person you decide to make your life partner. (The most significant decision is your faith.) As you prepare for marriage, there are practices you can begin that will lay a firm foundation for a healthy marriage. Erin Smalley and Lilo and Gerald Leeds have each given insight for couples to consider as marriage approaches.

Erin Smalley, a strategic marriage spokesperson for Focus on the Family's marriage ministry, reminds you that the marriage covenant is made and is designed to be lived out for the rest of your life. She offers the following tips with brief excerpts (The author's comments are italicized):[60]

- Have a clear understanding of God's purpose in marriage. Malachi 2:15 clarifies for us, "God, not you, made marriage. His Spirit inhabits even the smallest detail of marriage" (MSG). God desires that you become more like Him (holy) through your marriage. Marriage is a wonderful gift from the Lord, but there are days when loving your spouse just may draw you closer to God and work holiness in you as a result. That is why it is important to fully understand the purpose of the vows you are taking as you enter the covenant of marriage.
- Spend plenty of time getting to know each other prior to getting engaged. There may not be a set amount of time, but it's essential that you share many experiences together in order to know if this is really the person with whom you desire to spend the rest of your life. Watch to see how he or she handles your heart during times of disappointment, conflict or when you are stressed.
- Get plugged into quality premarital education or counseling. Talk to pastors or church leaders concerning who they would recommend for counseling or mentoring. Most churches offer a group format for training engaged couples or have designated premarital mentors for engaged couples. *There are also community resources and books that provide premarital education. The benefits are great. Take advantage of the opportunity.*
- Set aside time to just be together and enjoy. Plan a weekly date night that keeps your relationship a top priority. Take time to laugh and have fun together.
- Commit to a lifetime together. The commitment brings a sense of safety and security as a result of knowing that you are both in this for the long haul. *In addition, with this commitment, there is a willingness to seek help and support toward building a trusting, strong, and rewarding marriage.*
- Build a community of support. One of the key components of creating a healthy marriage is having the support of those

> close to you. Make sure that your friends and family are in agreement with the upcoming marriage. If there are concerns, sit down and seek to understand them. Ultimately you get to decide who you will spend the rest of your life with, but it's helpful to have a strong community of believers standing by you.
>
> Excerpted and adapted from the article "Are You Planning for a Marriage or Just a Wedding?" by Erin Smalley. Copyright 2017 Focus on the Family. All rights reserved. Used with permission.

In addition to the above listing, a decisive action you should practice prior to, and throughout your marriage, is to pray for each other and your marriage. Marriage creates joy and complications that may be eased with prayer. Finding time to read together is still another decisive action to strengthen your marriage. Read your Bibles, and read materials giving you wisdom regarding other topics relative to your partnership: money, sex, romance, etc. Each of these practices will strengthen your commitment to your God, your spouse and your marriage.

The late Lilo and Gerald Leeds, earned degrees in math and science respectively, received their Master's degrees together in liberal arts, and between them held seven honorary doctorate degrees. They offer additional insight:

> "Being healthy and having fun keep you and your relationship full of energy, joy, and passion. Without shared activities and pleasures, a circle of loving friends and relatives, and satisfying individual pursuits, a relationship can seem like it's all work and no play. When two partners maintain a playful, optimistic spirit, they are well on their way to achieving a happy and satisfying lifetime partnership."[61]

A wonderful marriage requires effort to remain strong. The previous list of behaviors is designed to help nurture a deeper connection with your partner and the Lord. In this uncertain world, it is difficult to be sure about anything. However, one thing is sure, your marriage will be blessed if you and your partner include God, and decide to serve Him.

"Surely there is a reward for the righteous; surely there is a God who judges on earth." Psalm 58:11

Have Thine Own Way, Lord

Have thine own way, Lord! Have thine own way!
Thou art the potter, I am the clay!
Mold me and make me after thy will,
While I am waiting yielded and still.

Have thine own way, Lord! Have thine own way!
Wounded and weary, help me, I pray!
Power, all power, surely is thine,
Touch me and heal me, Savior divine.

Have thine own way, Lord! Have thine own way!
Hold o'er my being absolute sway!
Fill with thy Spirit 'till all shall see,
Christ only, always, living in me.

Adelaide Pollard

Effective Communication - Levels

> "But speaking the truth in love,
> we must grow up in every way
> into him who is the head, into Christ."
>
> Ephesians, 4:15

COMMUNICATION IS A key to healthy relationships. It is helpful to understand the progression of communication from casual to heartfelt exchanges so that you may cultivate expertise in this area. Understanding this progression is valuable as it will help create an awareness that may cause you to choose words and topics more carefully as you communicate with others. The steps or levels of communication are not skills to attain, or behaviors to practice--they are for your understanding. The levels of communication are listed below:

1. Cliché is a common, simple phrase or greeting, that is a socially accepted behavior. Although no response is required, these short exchanges can make another person feel valued in that you cared to share a greeting. Examples include comments such as *Good morning, Have a nice day,* or *How are you?*
2. Expanded greetings are communications that go beyond a simple greeting as the exchange shares a bit more information.

Examples of an expanded greeting may be in conversation with a receptionist, cashier or colleague when you incorporate facts, yet nothing personal is offered. You may discuss the weather, your workplace, or the approaching holiday.

The above areas are essential steps in communication as they build on one's sense of ease, comfort, and trust. At this point, very little has been shared regarding personal qualities. There has been little or no risk, no emotional investment. You may have gained a greater sense of comfort. The comfort created from these conversations build a foundation for deeper personal exchanges. The conversations identified below detail more personal sharing and greater risk; they may serve to strengthen and enrich the relationship between the two people.

1. Sharing ideas, stories, and judgments about a topic in which both people have shown interest. As a result, conversations grow deeper and both parties are willing to listen and share. These conversations may revolve around topics including hobbies, vacations, work, etc. This is an initial step in adding depth to exchanges.

2. Sharing personal feelings and emotions requires both parties to be open, empathetic, and compassionate as they each demonstrate a more significant investment in the relationship. Consequently, the speaker puts great trust in the listener. This level opens the door to the risk of rejection.

3. Peak Communication, as it is often called, occurs when complete openness and honesty are shared, leading to deep understanding and sincerity within a relationship. Each person may share joys, heartaches, or concerns. These reflections offer clarity and feedback. As a result, trust and confidentiality in the relationship have been proven strong.

Each level serves as its own testing ground, building trust and a comfortable atmosphere. If, at any time, on any level, the speaker is met with rolling eyes, impatient body movements, or words that are not gentle, accepting, and kind, the speaker will likely back away to a lesser level. Trust and safety have been broken or lost, and the relationship has been damaged. An effort must be made to repair the hurt, and both parties must be willing to move forward. The speaker must be willing to risk again, and the listener must be diligent in behaviors that build trust and support. Waste no time if damage occurs; work to repair the hurt! The rewards will be great!

Be an individual who encourages others to talk of ideas. Welcome the conversation and treat the topic with seriousness. Individuals have dreams--encourage and embrace the dreams. Create a home that nourishes and challenges creative thoughts and new ideas. The potential depth of power and joy inside your relationship is wonderful. It is exciting to discover the secrets and unexpected twists of this beautiful journey.

Effective Communication – Set the Stage

> "Rash words are like sword thrusts,
> but the tongue of the wise brings healing."
> Proverbs 12:18

SUPPOSE YOU WANT a relationship to last and grow deeper. In that case, it is essential that you are able to express yourself and allow your partner to express herself in an emotionally safe, accepting environment. A great deal has been written on ways to communicate effectively and the answers may seem simple, but when entwined with emotion and human nature, the task becomes more complicated. Below are fundamental principles of communication as outlined by Lilo and Gerald Leeds.[62] A brief synopsis of each principle follows. Those paraphrased by this author are identified in italics.

- Just listen! *As a listener, you show interest by, gestures, body language, eye contact, or simple words. Unless asked, there is no need to give advice or make a judgment. However, as a recipient, it is sometimes helpful or healing to thank the person for the honesty and say you will think about what was said.*
- Speak lovingly and with respect. *Avoid harsh words and loud voices. Both are damaging and cannot be undone. Instead, express appreciation and voice the positive whenever possible.*

EFFECTIVE COMMUNICATION – SET THE STAGE

- What is your communication style? Individuals have unique styles of communication. *Understand communication styles. People speak at different speeds, with different intensities, forces, or mildness. Some people are fast talkers, others slower. Accept and appreciate the differences. Regardless of your style, you must consider your words before you speak!*
- Ask for what you want – Especially if what you want changes over time. Happy partners realize they each have to figure out what they really want, be specific in explaining it, and ask for it clearly. *Partners do not magically know your desires.*
- Avoid criticism, blame, and silence. Try talking about how you feel. 'I feel hurt when you…' or 'I feel better when you…' It allows your partner to hear your concern without getting defensive.
- Body language counts. *Body language sends messages of openness, tension, defensiveness, impatience, etc. Be careful that the message sent is the message you intended.*
- Resolve disputes quickly. *Address issues when they present themselves or quickly thereafter. Unresolved issues may grow with the passage of time. However, when disputes are handled with honest, healthy, and constructive practices, differences can be opportunities for growth.*
- Get to the root of anger. View anger as a useful warning sign – a sign that somebody's needs or wants are not being met, that they are feeling hurt, or that something is not right. *Anger can create distance so it is important to let your partner know you listen and you care. A healthy marriage and a healthy family provide a safe place for individuals to express their anger.*
- Don't use anger to get attention. If your partner is angry, your first job is to remain calm. *If tensions are high, agree to continue the discussion later and let go of the anger. If you cannot resolve the problem in one sitting, that does not*

> *mean you must go to bed angry. Instead, remind each other how lucky you are to have each other and know that the disagreement will be resolved at a later time.*

Learning to communicate honestly, lovingly, and effectively with another human being takes practice. To control feelings, emotions, words, and listening is very difficult. We all fall short at times. Strive to develop skills in effective communication strategies, resolving conflict, and establishing growth and rapport. There are many areas in this life that will pay rewards as you practice communicating in a healthy manner. Make an effort to show admiration, love, and respect to your partner, your family, and others in your life. When strife and disagreements arise, seek meaningful ways to resolve the differences, remain calm, and speak gently.

Family Communication – Plan Ahead

> "Love from the center of who you are; don't fake it.
> Run for dear life from evil; hold on for dear life to good.
> Be good friends who love deeply;
> practice playing second fiddle."
> Romans 12:9-10 (MSG)

TO BEST ESTABLISH effective communication, there are a few things that you can do to aid in its success. It may be necessary to have a standard set of ground rules, a basic plan, and adjust the time and environment to limit distractions. As we explore these characteristics, it is important to realize that each one should be designed to meet the specific needs of the family or group. Every member of the group should be made aware of the rules and plan and have an opportunity to make suggestions for their revision or improvements. First, let's look at possible ground rules.

The ground rules should be succinct, offering clarity with no extra words. The ground rules should be personalized to fit your situation. Following is an example of ground rules.

- Open with a prayer
- Listen carefully

- Speak lovingly and with respect
- Each person has the opportunity to speak without interruption
- Offer support to each other
- The conversation is not to be discussed outside this group
- If young children are not needed in the matters discussed, they should be allowed to leave
- Close with a prayer

The plan or agenda is another component that may lead to more effective communication. Agendas are guidelines for how the time together will be used. The agenda below is a sample designed to be personalized as needed.

- Open with Prayer
- State purpose of gathering
- Each member has an opportunity to address the concerns
- Discussion should move forward to address joyfulness, other concerns or issues.
  » Regularly scheduled family meetings allow families to grow together. An effective family meeting allows for openness without judgment, and the privacy of the members is honored. Members can speak freely about any topic of interest: feelings, heartaches, complaints, dreams, goals, etc. The other members listen, offer support, and help find a resolution of the issue if necessary.
  » The coordination of schedules or other issues involving all members may be reviewed at this time.
  » Prayer requests are welcomed.
- Close with Prayer

The time of the meeting and the environment where the discussion takes place can be significant factors in the success of communication. The scheduled time should be when the members are relaxed and fresh, not at the end of a busy day. The area should be comfortable, provide appropriate seating and be well lighted. Those present should turn off telephones and other noise-making equipment. It is helpful to have a pencil and paper for everyone.

Preparation is an essential component of effective communication. The development of ground rules, a plan for the shared time, and setting the proper environment benefits each participant. This process will allow participants to feel a sense of belonging and safety as honor and respect are the norms for behaviors. Creating a family tradition of regularly planned and scheduled communication opportunities is a great way to create a bond of unity, support, closeness, and security among the members.

Build Opportunities to Communicate

> "Now go, and I will be with your mouth
> and teach you what you are to speak."
>
> Exodus 4:12

WORDS ARE THE tools of communication. Good communication is essential to a healthy relationship with both couples and families. Making a conscious effort to build opportunities to communicate can make a positive difference, showing love and appreciation. The guidelines below offer ways to create a positive attitude and environment that encourages positive family communication.

Intentionally, create everyday opportunities that allow for casual conversation. Show interest by listening attentively and asking questions. Unless requested, avoid the temptation to offer advice or lecture. Casual conversation shows an interest in the other person, other people, and current events. Conversation in these less complicated issues builds trust.

Some people find more comfort in conversing while involved in activities. Plan occasions to share that encourage dialogue. These activities may be as simple as eating meals together, family game nights, or driving to school. The activity may also be more involved like a camping trip or a church retreat. Whatever you do, create opportunities to talk.

Life provides many challenges, and these situations may create tough conversations. Therefore, it is essential to consider how to make the conversation comfortable, less tense, and productive. Take time to gather your thoughts and note, in advance, what you want to say, ask, and know. The subject is serious; acknowledge that as you display empathy and excellent listening skills.

The sensitive nature of the issue, emotions, or schedules might require patience as the conversation would be more productive if it were at a later time. However, be sure that the exchange does occur, and during the delay, communicate that you care.

Finally, understand that communication happens in many forms. Be alert to the non-verbal communication in a person's actions, body language, touch, and tone. These non-verbal messages are subtly given behind the words and tell details that are valuable for understanding. Another option for communication is the use of the many and varied platforms in technology. Be cautious regarding the security and privacy of these platforms. However, they can be helpful in reaching others to show you care and are interested in their lives.

Creating opportunities for talking requires effort. Look for opportunities to build communication, especially among those you love. As you strive to stay connected, be intentional, be creative, and maintain perspective. The traditions you create will fortify communication and strengthen the family's mutual understanding and love for one another.

Difficulties from Your Past – Trust God, Love Yourself, and Heal

> Do not fear, for I am with you,
> Do not be afraid, for I am your God;
> I will strengthen you; I will help you,
> I will uphold you with my victorious right hand.
>
> Isaiah 41:10

THE OLD TESTAMENT book of 1 Samuel chapter 17 shares the often-told story of David and Goliath. My friend and pastor, Eddie Lyons, retold this story to his congregation. The specifics and connections he brought forth are detailed as follows. David was an Israelite and a shepherd who cared for sheep. Goliath was a Philistine, a ferocious giant man. The entire Israelite community was afraid of Goliath, who, for forty days, taunted and challenged any Israelite to fight him. No one came forward to fight Goliath. Through a series of events, God sent young David to the encampment where the Israelite soldiers were preparing for battle against Goliath. Soon after, David was presented to King Saul to discuss the impending conflict, David recounted God's faithfulness and power which David had personally felt as he saved sheep from lions and bears (1 Samuel 17:37). King Saul was finally convinced of David's ability and faith in God and allowed the

DIFFICULTIES FROM YOUR PAST –
TRUST GOD, LOVE YOURSELF, AND HEAL

boy, David, to fight the giant, Goliath. As David went into battle, he proclaimed God's power as he called to Goliath and the others, "The Lord does not save by the sword and spear; for the battle is the Lord's and he will give you into our hand" (1 Samuel 17:47).[63]

The story of David and Goliath gives insight into the power of faith in our Lord. Despite the tremendous challenge, David found courage in his knowledge of God's history of kept promises, help in time of need, and demonstrated power. David understood the message paraphrased from the book of John 14:8, "If God is all you have, you have all you need."

The message below is uncomfortable to imagine and even more difficult if you live within its chains. However, the story of David reminds us to trust in God's promise to walk with us through challenges and bring us to victory. We can rely on God's power. Therefore, as you read the section below, if it speaks to your personal trials, know there is help in the Lord and you will overcome this challenge with his guidance and power. Let's get started.

Our first teachers are the individuals in our homes. Unfortunately, human beings are not born to be excellent communicators or problem solvers. We have all learned communication practices from imperfect people. People in our home, intentionally or not, send messages that weave into our emotional health, building up or breaking down one's self-concept. In some situations, emotions may not have been honored or lovingly validated; they may have been ignored or silenced. You may have been treated in a manner that suggested you were not important. A parent's criticism may have left you feeling rejected or possibly abandoned. As children, we accept the blame and often feel responsible. These difficult occurrences often cause individuals to bury hurtful feelings and emotions, only to have them resurface in intensity at surprising times. When emotions are ignored, they tend to grow more hurtful and powerful.

All people have past experiences that have caused painful and negative emotions. It is common for these harmful feelings to be unintentionally aroused in present-day life. Some situations awaken a furor, an intense emotion; even when your mind tells you it is a minor frustration or annoyance, you are furious. In other cases, the disappointments of life keep hanging on, causing more significant hurt and sadness. It might be an embarrassment or fear that continues to haunt your thoughts when the event is past and your sense of security should have returned. These negative feelings of abandonment, rejection, or other disappointments are genuine, painful, uncomfortable, and possibly harmful. Intense emotions are often generated from past experiences and relationships, as one has learned to suppress the hurt and bury the pain deep inside.

Buried pain will often present itself when circumstances are pleasant, and you are not expecting the emotion to arise. When a person feels safe and finds the love and compassion of another person, the feeling of security allows emotional tensions to relax, the barriers come down, and the past pains may begin to surface. This resurfacing of emotion can appear as unexplained reactions or moodiness during happy occasions. If you can talk to the individual with whom you feel safe, it can lead to healing as you open the door to being heard, accepted, and understood. You will more easily be freed from the deep sense of anger and resentment if you feel love, acceptance, understanding, and forgiveness, instead of judgment, criticism, or rejection.

When you reflect on these moments of intense emotion, take time to care for, and show kindness to yourself. Ask yourself questions to discover the reason for your pain. Why has this incident made you so angry? Why so frustrated? Why so sad? Why so afraid? As you listen, validate, and honor your hurts and brokenness. This practice will help you understand the reason for your intense emotions, and you will discover more loving feelings will enter your everyday existence. The frustrations, hurts, and sadness will still come, but you will be able to greet them with more loving and temperate emotions.

Society often complicates healing as it is a busy place providing many distractions and addictions to avoid the pain. However, to begin the healthy process of healing, consider writing the negative feelings and hurts onto paper. You might choose to write one or more letters to God, expressing your most intense, possibly irrational feelings. Although he already knows everything about you, lay it out to God. Through time, and possibly many letters, this process will help you heal from the brokenness and learn to handle and lovingly share these deep-seated emotions.

It is essential to understand the impact of unresolved negative feelings and emotions, as they have the power to steal your control and your joy. This emotional baggage is real and, left unresolved, the past pain will resurface in current situations and cause impatience, frustration, anger, sadness, etc. As David voiced his reliance and trust in God, you too can seek God's help to control and regain power over your emotions. You and God can change the grip and the intensity your feelings have on your life.

Unresolved emotions from your past can have a powerful hold on your reactions and behaviors regarding life's events. They can prevent loving communication with your spouse, family, co-workers, etc. Effective communication is not possible when emotions are high and you are upset. Pray for God to give guidance, support, courage, and love as you, together with God, tackle behaviors caused by past negative experiences. Seek to discover loving yourself and others in your life with the love each of you deserves. As David courageously challenged Goliath, you may courageously face your emotional baggage. Remember, as Goliath taunted David before the battle, David responded, "The whole world will know that there is an extraordinary

God in Israel. And everyone gathered here will learn that God doesn't save by means of sword or spear. The battle belongs to God –he's handing you to us on a platter!" (1 Samuel 17:47 MSG)

"It is the Lord your God who goes with you, to fight for you against your enemies, to give you victory." Deuteronomy 20:4

"Blessed be the Lord, for he has heard the sound of my pleadings. The Lord is my strength and my shield; in him my heart trusts; so I am helped, and my heart exults and with my song I give thanks to him." Psalm 28: 6-7

"Be strong and courageous; do not be frightened or dismayed, for the Lord your God is with you wherever you go." Joshua 1:9

DIFFICULTIES FROM YOUR PAST –
TRUST GOD, LOVE YOURSELF, AND HEAL

Abide With Me

Abide with me: fast falls the eventide;
The darkness deepens; Lord, with me abide.
When other helpers fail and comforts flee,
Help of the helpless, O abide with me.

I need thy presence every passing hour.
What but thy grace can foil the tempter's power?
Who like try self my guide and strength can be?
Through cloud and sunshine, O abide with me.

I fear no foe with thee at hand to bless,
Ills have no weight, and tears no bitterness.
Where is death's sting? Where, grave, thy victory?
I triumph still, if thou abide with me.

Hold thou thy cross before my closing eyes.
Shine through the gloom and point me to the skies.
Heaven's morning breaks and earth's vain shadows flee;
In life, in death, O Lord, abide with me.

Henry Francis Lyte

Husbands, Wives and Children – Powerful Choices

> "By wisdom a house is built,
> and by understanding it is established;
> and by knowledge the rooms are filled
> with all precious and pleasant riches."
>
> Proverbs 24:3-4 (NASB)

GOD CREATED THE first man and woman, and with them he established the institution of marriage. God's creations come with the promise of purpose and blessing. In the Garden of Eden, God planned for male and female to share their lives in love and understanding. He created a unique balance of attributes for each of them. He knew that, together, they would confront challenges, which upon overcoming, would strengthen their commitment, trust, and respect for one another. God planned circumstances to bring a wide range of emotions, laughter, and tears, so the senses of trust, compassion, and love could grow. God made each of us to serve, to teach, to hug, and to love.

The husband and wife team must practice thoughtful choices and responsible behaviors if the relationship is to grow and flourish. As we examine some of these choices and behaviors, remember spiritual beliefs and spirituality should be our foundation. We can choose to respect or discount each other, we decide to share or withhold from one another, we can discuss goals and work together or be solely independent, and finally, we can be forgiving or choose to hold grudges. The choice will determine whether the relationship and the family will enjoy fulfilling rewards or face misery. These components, shared lives, respect, loyalty, commitment, working together, common goals, love, and forgiveness are all qualities of a solid religious foundation.

A religious foundation is where a strong relationship begins. But, in addition to the religious foundation, there are other important choices one makes in marriage that can strengthen the relationship. Below is a look at some of these areas: religious foundations, commitment, spending time together, individual freedom, loving communication, forgiveness, and responsibility.

Regarding the development of a **religious foundation**, the Bible tells us, "That their hearts may be encouraged, being together in love, and attaining to all riches of the full assurance of understanding, to the knowledge of the mystery of God, both of the Father and of Christ" (Colossians 2:2). The message shared in this scripture tells of the blessing and mystery that unfolds for you as you seek to create a religious foundation for your family. Share your lives in prayer as you include God in joys, concerns, problems, and at mealtime. Make spiritual connections in your social life as you attend church and develop relationships with other believers.

God gives parents the responsibility to teach and share with their children the knowledge and understanding of our Lord. As parents make the conscious choice to include spiritual practices and beliefs in everyday life experiences, this happens. Repeated routines of prayers at meals and bedtime, regular church attendance, time set aside for Bible study, or simply the willingness to vocalize the many daily seen blessings from God allow children to grow in knowledge and love of the Lord.

Commitment is necessary to remain strong and grow as a family because times can become challenging in life and relationships. Things do not always turn out as you wished or hoped. However, strong families adjust and find ways to grow when it seems impossible. Commitment involves being willing to pay the price and sacrifice time, money, and energy. Support your family with your love, time, talents, and focus. It may require sacrifice and commitment beyond your imagination, but family should always be the priority.

A commitment that offers great blessings and untold rewards is **spending time together** as a family. Try to build into daily life schedules time to share as a family. It may be a morning devotional, mealtime, or an evening game, but this time builds bonds of caring, understanding, and growth. Our culture has the unfortunate tendency to promote the idea that giving things and possessions shows love and caring. Love is not for sale, nor is it an item to be purchased. Love blossoms as a result of time shared.

A delightful way to share time with your family is to create celebrations. Look for ways to celebrate with your family. Of course, individual joys and successes are always to be celebrated but also challenges and obstacles overcome are worthy of celebration. Life is to be celebrated! Celebrate!

Families need time together, celebrations, and traditions (repeated routines) to feel connected. Additionally, it is also important that each member have a place they can call their own which allows them solitude for thinking and personal reflection. The site does not have to be a room, but a small area in which can be stored prized possessions and dreams. Nothing elaborate is required, only the fact that it belongs to them. Privacy professes a person's dignity.

Another area of choice is allowing your partner **individual freedom**. A loving marriage relationship allows partners to be close companions, care for, trust, respect and accept one another. However, the partners must also allow the freedom for each partner to be an individual. The partnership will flourish if each is allowed and encouraged to discover personal fulfillment, growth, and creativity.

In the realm of family, the concepts of **loving communication, forgiveness and responsibility** have additional merits for consideration. The first teacher of these concepts is and should be parents. The many hours of shared time should offer sound examples of the principles of effective, loving communication, forgiveness, and responsibility. When children observe parents demonstrating these godly qualities, they will learn to value them and incorporate these practices into their own lives.

The discipline of work is one of life's most important lessons. Jobs require specific adaptations, concentrations, and effort. First, one must learn how to work. It takes practice to understand completing a task in small steps and then carrying the task to completion. Teaching children how to work and to enjoy working are valuable contributions parents instill in children. Look each day for ways to help your children become responsible and independent citizens of the family and the world. Taking out the trash, setting the table, helping with dinner, etc., are tasks that build self-discipline, responsible behaviors, and strengthen family bonds. A child will build confidence as he understands that his contribution to the family is valuable to the function of the household.

Choices are powerful and create lasting consequences. Make prayerful, intentional choices when creating a religious foundation within your family--spend time together, allow individual freedom, communicate lovingly, forgive, and be responsible. Attention to these choices helps build a family unit that is faithful, loyal, and honest. A family with a strong religious foundation will demonstrate integrity and deep respect for one another, and the family.

Never forget, you are not alone, and the Lord will make the journey with you if you ask him. His guidance is always available to you through his Bible and through trusted friends and family. Finally, remember who you are! You are a child of our wonderful God, and he loves you and your family!

God is the Fountain

God is the fountain whence
Ten thousand blessings flow;
To Him my life, my health, and friends,
And every good, I owe.

The comforts He affords
Are neither few nor small;
He is the source of fresh delights,
My portion and my all.

He fills my heart with joy,
My lips attune for praise;
And to His glory I'll devote
The remnant of my days.

Benjamin Beddome

Love In Action – God's Perfect Example

"We love, because he first loved us."

1 John 4:19

LOVE IS ONE of the great mysteries of humankind. Humans need one another, and they need God. This need appears to be innate. However, the ability to establish a loving, healthy relationship is learned. God designed us to seek and enjoy deep personal relationships with others. Through our relationship with him, he shows us how to love.

Knowing and feeling God's love will help you better understand the broad scope of what love means. God's love demonstrates that he indeed loves you and will be by your side every minute, providing for your needs, regardless of your shortcomings. God's love also demonstrates that he cares and will give you guidance to make better choices throughout life's journey. Below are a few of the major aspects of a loving relationship inspired by God. However, God's love can never be fully described by lists or breakdowns.

Love is action. Love is not a term that only identifies a feeling, but it is a verb that means action. Action is the most important aspect of love. In mature love, both individuals involved choose to behave lovingly for the sake of the other person and the relationship. Love in action will reach out to provide for the other in need by means of patience, kindness, hope, perseverance, and truth. However, love in action also sacrifices. There are times when one must give up their desires for the good of the relationship or the other person. Sacrifice is a difficult choice because it may have costs in time, inconvenience, finances, or altered dreams.

Love is unconditional. It is easy to love those who please us. Unfulfilled people will not always live up to the highest mark. Unconditional love will be strong and ever-present even when the shortcomings of the loved one are most pronounced. When the spouse is inattentive to your needs, or the child is unwilling to obey, love will remain.

Love is comforting. To love someone enough to set limits, guide behaviors, and discipline when they violate the rules shows you genuinely care. It can be a love of a parent to a child, a love of friends or spouses. In any case, the individual is willing to endure the unpleasantness of addressing wrongdoing for the other individual's benefit. This gift brings the security of true and lasting love. This action is a more extraordinary gift than money can ever buy.

God is the ideal example of a loving father as he shows love in action by making the greatest sacrifice for our benefit. God gave his Son! God's love is unconditional! He offers his love when we do not respond to it or deserve it. God's love is comforting! Through the example of Christ's life and throughout the Bible, God tells us the best way to live on this earth. However, we continually fall short of his expectations; God continues to send us godly individuals and earthly challenges to help set our footsteps straight. God loves us!

"God designed us to be in relationship both vertically with Him and horizontally with the people around us."[64] God created you to love him and to love others. His example of how to love others is evident as he demonstrates his love for you. When you feel God's love personally, it has the power to instill in you the desire to share his passion with others. To unconditionally reach out in patience, kindness, hope, forgiveness, and truth.

"Therefore prepare your minds for action; discipline yourselves; set all your hope on the grace that Jesus Christ will bring you."
1 Peter 1:13

Wonderful Words of Life

Sing them over again to me,
Wonderful words of life;
Let me more of their beauty see,
Wonderful words of life;
Words of life and beauty
Teach me faith and duty.

(Refrain)
Beautiful words, wonderful words,
Wonderful words of life;
Beautiful words, wonderful words,
Wonderful words of life.

Sweetly echo the gospel call,
Wonderful words of life;
Offer pardon and peace to all,
Wonderful words of life;
Jesus, only Savior,
Sanctify forever.

P. P. Bliss

Honor One Another

> "Be devoted to one another in brotherly love;
> give preference to one another in honor."
> Romans 12:10 (NASB)

THE TERM HONOR describes a behavior worthy of our focus. It is a powerful word that has an admirable quality of class and dignity. Honor means to place great value on another person, giving preference, respect, and high esteem to them.

A marriage must have honor between the two individuals, or they will struggle to maintain the love and nurture necessary to remain happy and healthy in the union. How does one show honor to another person? To begin, one must focus on positive qualities. We all have our shortcomings, but your thoughts and actions must communicate appreciation for the positive contributions and attributes of the individual--to show honor. The list below provides a few examples of activities that show honor to another person.

1. Study your partner. Make personal notes of things they enjoy, foods they prefer, and rewarding and fun activities. If you know these bits of information about your partner, you can personalize choices to give them value and honor. Allow them the knowledge that you respect and value them and this relationship.

2. Small acts are mighty. It is common to think that honor requires spectacular acts of consideration or generous gift-giving. However, it is important to do small things daily to show recognition for each other. Small actions such as cleaning the bathrooms, taking out the trash, cooking a meal, minor household repairs, and sharing time together show you care and honor this person. These small acts show consideration and caring. They do show evidence of honor.

3. When you make a mistake, ask for forgiveness. We are all human and make choices for which we are later sorry. Admit your mistake, and offer a heartfelt apology. No excuses. Be willing to be humble. Your apology shows honor for your partner and helps them to feel valued.

4. Focus on the traits you admire about your partner. Notice your partner's positive qualities and compliment them. List these qualities and visit the list often. Keep an open mind as you consider the possibilities. Possibilities include personality, appearance, manner of thinking, skill sets, character, values, and dedication to God. Do this activity together and share your lists. Honor your partner.

5. Take care of yourself – Your appearance reflects the value you place on yourself and those around you. Make sure you are prepared. Be a worthy partner for the person you choose to marry.

So to honor a person, you must place great value on the person, consider them a cherished treasure. Demonstrate honor as you stand together, prioritize the love for God, and celebrate the relationship. Value your partner as a unique and wonderful child of God.

Bring Out the Best in Your Partner

> "If I speak with the tongues of men and of angels,
> but do not have love,
> I have become a noisy gong or a clanging cymbal."
>
> Romans 13:1 (NASB)

TO LOVE AND be loved in return is what we look for in a partner. How a person interacts with another to make a strong, loving marriage is critical to the health of the relationship. It is wise to understand the components that help secure a loving marriage–to be conscious of them as you develop a relationship with a potential partner.

"When the Lord created man and woman, the man said, 'This at last is bone of my bones and flesh of my flesh; this one shall be called woman, for out of man this one was taken.' Therefore, a man leaves his father and his mother and clings to his wife, and they become one flesh" (Genesis 2:23-24). This sentiment is repeated in Matthew 19:4-6 and Ephesians 5:31. The above passage reminds us that we are a part of each other's bodies. They are part of us, and we care for them as we care for ourselves. We show them honor, love, and appreciation as we share our lives to honor our Lord.

When you are involved in a marriage, it is crucial to make conscious decisions regarding how to interact positively with love, service and honor for your partner. A significant decision is necessary to make each of these behaviors happen. Some decisions will come quickly in the relationship, and others will be forged over time. Below, is Lilo and Gerald Leeds' 20 identified behaviors that build strength in a relationship. Those paraphrased by this author are in italics.[65]

- Speak Lovingly – *Listen carefully to your partner and add comments of kindness, support, and love.*
- Show Your Respect – *Brag on your partner, ask for advice, notice your partner. Tell others of your partner's fine qualities.*
- Express Appreciation and Gratitude – *Notice and say thanks for the small gestures of kindness.*
- Be Kind and Understanding – *Show support for your partner in both good and challenging times. Be a team in resolving issues. Be sensitive to their feelings, thoughts, and experiences.*
- Put Your Partner First - Every time you need to make a significant decision, each of you should ask yourselves, 'How will my partner feel about this? Will this be good for my partner?'
- Be Affectionate, Touch Each Other – Be generous with hugs, kisses, and touches. *Touch is a powerful means of communicating care and affection and need not always lead to sex.*
- Show Love through Passion *(Sex)* – Both of you should make sex a top priority, with each of you aiming to delight and satisfy the other. If sex is not yet what you both would like it to be, work on it lovingly together until it is.
- Forge Loving Rituals – *Initiate rituals that belong to just the two of you. For example, morning routines, private nicknames, shared readings, notes, songs, etc. As a couple, build connections and everyday rituals to share.*
- Build Trust and Respect with Honesty – *There must be accountability with your partner regarding their word, honesty, truth, promises, etc.*

- Be Tactful - *Some topics and conversations may be more difficult than others. Always honor the relationship in a polite manner avoiding crude or cruel responses. Be sensitive to your partner's needs.*
- Be Faithful – *It is not enough to be faithful. You have to make sure not to give the appearance that you are anything but reliable. That means you never act like you're interested in anyone else romantically. And that you don't do anything in public or private that you wouldn't want your partner to see or know.*
- Be Positive – *Focus on shared values and qualities you admire in your partner. Allow your partner and yourself the freedom to grow and learn as you discover ways to address differences in your thinking and acting.*
- Be Flexible about Each Other's Habits and Temperament – *Always remember the essential matters in life. No person is perfect; be tolerant and patient as together you seek ways to overcome these minor irritants.*
- Take Time to Play Together – *Time shared in play reinforces memories and develops closeness in the relationship.*
- Respect Each Other's Privacy – *It can be challenging to share space with another. Things that were once private can now be seen easily by another. It is important to allow each other privacy. Therefore, it is beneficial to share information, so there is no fear of secrets but openness and a sense of honesty between the partners.*
- Give Each Other Time Alone – *It is important to do things together. It is equally important for each of you to be free to do things on your own.*
- Get to Know Each Other's Friends and Family – *Try to be open and accepting, not judgmental or critical. If this relationship is to flourish over the years, this network will be the source of love and support.*
- Explore Each Other's Dreams and Aspirations – *Dreams are*

> *powerful and personal. As you feel secure in the relationship, the willingness to share your dreams will grow. Respect and show honor to one another's plans, and work together to achieve them; this goal can create tremendous joy in a relationship.*

- Don't Do Things That Drive Your Partner Crazy – *Keep peace; don't push buttons. Encourage joy and happiness.*
- Do Everything with Love – Be consistent in showing love. Admit it when you are wrong. And forgive your partner when he or she turns out to be wrong.

"A great marriage is not a matter of luck. It is a product of careful thought, generous spirit, and hard work."[66] You will make choices many times throughout the days, months and years, to demonstrate love, respect, and caring for your partner. These behaviors lead to a happy, supportive relationship, and bring glory to God.

Love Life – Sex in Marriage

> "Let him kiss me with the kisses of his mouth!
> For your love is better than wine."
>
> Song of Solomon 1:2

THE BIBLE IS an excellent source of God's view of the purpose and joy provided by the physical relationship of sex; it is mentioned many times in the scriptures, both Old and New Testaments. To many people, the Bible is just God's way of telling us what we can and cannot do and has nothing to say to us of sex except to give additional rules. That concept is incorrect. The Christian view is that sex is intended for marriage between a man and a woman. The scripture below will show that God created males and females, created sex, and said it was good. Scripture will also be cited to share the pleasure and reward a husband and wife provide by a close sexual relationship.

The Old Testament book of Genesis 1:31 tells that God created males and females and said, "It is very good." Genesis 1:28 continues, "God blessed them, and God said to them, 'Be fruitful and multiply.'" The disciple Mark, in his gospel 10:6-8, adds insight as to the purpose of the sexual relationship between husband and wife as he writes, "From the beginning of creation, 'God made them male and female.' For this reason a man shall leave his father and mother and be joined to his wife, and the two shall become one flesh. So they are no longer two but one flesh." The sexual union is, therefore, a bond between the husband and wife, creating one flesh. Marriage establishes a partnership in which they are now a team and should act as such. They should try to gratify the other in both physical and spiritual needs. Hebrews 13:4 reads, "Let marriage be held in honor by all, and let the marriage bed be kept undefiled." Further insight is found in the book of Ecclesiastes 9:9, you learn, "Enjoy life with the wife whom you love, all the days of your life." The passages of scripture cited above give a clear picture that God designed and delights in the enjoyment and pleasure one receives through the sexual experience. However, it is intended to be enjoyed within the boundaries of a marriage.

The joy and value God intends to be placed on sexual relationships is detailed in the biblical texts of the Song of Solomon and Proverbs. The Song of Solomon is a beautiful love story. King Solomon speaks of the delight he receives from his wife. He draws a picture of how God intended physical relationships in marriage to add joy and a special closeness for the partners. Proverbs 5:18-19 shares godly advice of a father to his son regarding the sexual fulfillment he should enjoy with his wife. God intended the marriage sexual experience to be one of great joy, pleasure, and connection!

God finds each of us beautiful. In Genesis 2:25, it is written, "The man and his wife were both naked, and were not ashamed." It is sometimes difficult to feel comfortable with our bodies. The media is full of beautiful bodies with skin, curves, muscles, etc., all seemingly perfect. These pictures are not natural; they are images of a perspective of beauty created by the world. God is the creator of our body and soul, and he does not make anything shabby. Take care of your body as a gift from God. It is indeed beautiful!

There is nothing on earth that compares to the physical closeness between a husband and wife. The intimate experience of sexual intercourse is joyful and rewarding when it is in a permanent, loving relationship. Sex in a loving relationship is comfortable, satisfying, and beautiful.

A marriage relationship that includes a commitment to Christ will have security in physical and spiritual wholeness they can share. This intimacy takes time to develop. Those who are blessed to experience this profoundly fulfilling relationship understand and praise God for the blessing. Pray that God blesses you with this genuine loving commitment to both God and your marriage partner. It is among God's greatest gifts!

Moments

In the happy moments praise God.
In the difficult moments seek God.
In the quiet moments trust God.
In every moment thank God.

Unknown

Family Matters

"Whoever does not provide for relatives,
and especially for family members,
has denied the faith and is worse than an unbeliever."

1 Timothy 5:8

FAMILIES CAME INTO existence when Adam and Eve were created and united (Genesis 1:27, 2:22, 2:24). When a man and a woman make a covenant with God in marriage, they create a family until death. God blessed this union and said, "Be fruitful and multiply" (Genesis 1:28). This growing family serves important functions in life.

A strong, commonly recognized, functioning family is a gift of mothers, fathers, grandparents, aunts, uncles, cousins, etc., as God intended. Everyone has a family that shares bloodlines. That family gives individuals history and a heritage shared with other members. You may find you share physical attributes, talents, health, personality, etc., with this family. This shared history and heritage allow family members to feel belonging and roots in this complicated world. Families may share ancestors and bloodlines, but these are not the necessary ingredients for a well-functioning family.

Kinship is not the factor that determines the healthy, supportive concept of family. In some families, members do not share common threads with ancestors; your family may have backgrounds very different and no common heritage. However, if they serve as a bond of identity and support in your life, that makes them family. The companionship drives away loneliness and isolation. Disappointment, sorrow, and despair, may be lightened with shared hope and encouragement. You may not have the perfect family, but you can have a happy, supportive family. This group of people who support you through life may be called a clan, a tribe, or a family. Whether they are your bloodline or people in this world who love and care about you, they are your network, and you need them.

As with each of the relationships previously mentioned in this text, families need to spend time together to make memories and grow. Families should create opportunities to share laughter, tears, joys, concerns, faith, and traditions. Nothing can substitute for daily, personal interaction to strengthen family ties. Although the effort for a close family unit is intended to be led by parents, it is essential that all members have a willingness to participate.

Each family will build its unique purpose. The family that honors the Lord will place faith in God and His purposes at the center. With God in the center, the purpose may extend to sports, music, education, money, etc. Whatever the goal, it will determine what values you hold dear, how you prioritize your time, activities, money, where you live, and receive an education. The purpose of your family will impact many additional aspects of your life including, the quality of the relationships within your immediate family, extended family, and the community. Building a supportive, unified family with a defined purpose takes persistence and planning. It should create a foundation of:

- Spiritual beliefs that strengthen and replenish you and the other family members.
- Love that offers acceptance and nurture to each other in all aspects of life's joys and trials.

- Faithfulness and commitment that encourage your family and your convictions.
- Support and affirmation (build-up) of each family member.
- Shepherds or mentors to give advice or instruction to you and your family.

Strive to build a foundation for your family that develops a closeness and unity of spirit. Identify a purpose that includes your Lord, honors commitments, plans time together, seeks service opportunities, etc. Use your resources to strengthen family ties and relationships. A properly functioning family will offer support and depend on one another, preferring each other and looking to each other for help and guidance. If people in your life share these positive qualities, consider them family.

Pray that the love of your family should never fail. Ask that your family be one whose members believe in each other, support each other, understand and accept faults and gifts, are loyal and steadfast in time of need, and seek unity for the future together.

"A friend loves at all times and kinsfolk are born to share adversity." Proverbs 17:17

"There are also many rebellious people, idle talkers and deceivers… they must be silenced, since they are upsetting whole families by teaching for sordid gain what it is not right to teach." Titus 1:10-11

Tell Me the Story of Jesus

(Refrain)
Tell me the story of Jesus,
Write on my heart every word;
Tell me the story most precious,
Sweetest that ever was heard.

Tell how the angels, in chorus,
Sang as they welcomed His birth,
"Glory to God in the highest!
Peace and good tidings to earth."

Tell of the cross where they nailed Him,
Writhing in anguish and pain;
Tell of the grave where they laid Him,
Tell how He liveth again.

Love in that story so tender,
Clearer than ever I see:
Stay let me weep while you whisper,
Love paid the ransom for me.

Fanny Crosby

Broken Families

"I will never leave you or forsake you."

Hebrew 13:5

ALTHOUGH WE STRIVE for a perfect family, they are nonexistent. You may call them broken, fractured, wounded, or messed-up, but they are still family. The Bible gives many examples of these families. The first family beginning with Adam and Eve were thrown out of the Garden of Eden, and their son Cain killed his brother Abel (Genesis 3:23, 4:8). Jacob loved Rachel but married her sister Leah (Genesis 29:16-30). David committed adultery with Bathsheba and murdered her husband (2 Samuel 11:1-18). These are only a few of the many stories in the Bible of broken, wounded families. These examples show that God's families are not perfect; many are broken. But God does not leave them broken. God redeems families.

"But He was wounded for the wrong we did; He was crushed for the evil we did. The punishment, which made us well, was given to Him, and we are healed because of His wounds" (Isaiah: 53:3). This verse in scripture identifies that God will heal the many ways humanity may be broken. Be it a heart, a soul, or a family. God wants to heal your brokenness. Jesus' suffering and death on the cross was for your brokenness and sin. He gave his life so you and your family might heal. You are not alone. God is here to help!

BROKEN FAMILIES

It is essential to realize that brokenness is a part of us and that your broken family is not your fault. No one plans for it, and no one hopes for it; it is just that things change with time. The change may be due to health problems (physical, emotional, or mental), divorce, death, distance, financial or job transitions, or simply poor choices. You cannot control the choices of others, their responses, or the consequences. You should, however, take responsibility for your mistakes and ask forgiveness. Jesus is the source of healing. He has the power to bring healing and recovery to the wounds and scars. Each individual must come to Jesus and admit their hurt and ask God to help. God has the power to heal!

In every family, as in life, humans will certainly sin. Not one is above temptation. Interestingly, many people believe that their sin and personal shortcomings disqualify them from reaching others with the hope and power of faith. The fact that you can relate to others in similar situations may allow God to move through you to heal others. God can use your example of growth and deliverance to help encourage and guide others.

People are not perfect creatures. Change and conflict often cause people to become resentful, bitter, hateful, or hostile. They may actually leave, or spiritually and emotionally remove themselves from the hurts, and consequently, from the family. Although no one wanted it, the person, the relationships, the family has become broken and hurt.

Broken families need more than just time to heal. Healing takes intentional action, patience, tolerance, flexibility, a commitment to the goal, and a loving spirit. Members must be willing to forgive and be open to the rebuilding of trust. One must learn the varied ways to say, "I love you." The healing journey may be difficult, but it will be worth the time and effort.

A healthy family is constantly changing, growing, blending--never the same. The members are varied, as a family includes babies, growing children, parents, grandparents, aunts, uncles, and cousins. This family group is held in a bond as they share memories and qualities of love, trust, loyalty, kindness, and compassion. In a healthy family, these individuals can count on each other for giving and offering help, support, honor, and understanding. In a healthy family, you can count on family members to be there for you, looking out for you, enduring with you through it all. A healthy family shares the knowledge that God in heaven, is in charge, and is here to help!

When a family is broken or dysfunctional, God is there to open opportunities for other godly people to come and fill the void of family in your life. With that in mind, you will see a variety of family structures, shapes, sizes, and names. Each family is unique and no one's family is perfect. Some groups that offer support may be blended families, trusted friends, sporting team members, church members, colleagues, or neighbors. If your bloodline family is "broken," you should pray for their healing but also be prayerful for your healing. Tell God of your need to find a supportive family and ask for God's guidance in that endeavor.

A properly functioning family is beautiful. God designed the family, and with his blessing, it will be a beautiful functioning unit that will provide for the needs of those within and serve others beyond its walls.

"God did not give us a spirit of cowardice, but rather a spirit of power, of love and of self-discipline." 2 Timothy 1:7

"For this reason, I bow my knees before the Father, from whom every family in heaven and on earth takes its name."
Ephesians: 3:14

Tell Me the Old, Old Story

Tell me the old, old story
Of unseen things above,
Of Jesus and His glory,
Of Jesus and His love.
Tell me the story simply,
As to a little child;
For I am weak and weary,
And helpless and defiled.

(Refrain)
Tell me the old, old story;
Tell me the old, old story,
Tell me the old, old story,
Of Jesus and His love.

Kate Hankey

Family Tradition

> "I commend you because you remember me in everything and maintain the traditions just as I handed them on to you."
>
> 1 Corinthians 11:2

A FAMILY TRADITION is a way families can share information, values, beliefs, or customs with one another. This sharing can be by word, action, behaviors, etc., and the sharing occurs with some repetition. The repetition may be daily as mealtime prayers, weekly as church attendance, family fun night, or family devotionals, monthly as birthday celebrations, or annually as holiday meals and gatherings. Family traditions are valuable because they unite people and bring continuity and a sense of belonging and stability. The world moves fast and is sometimes difficult to navigate. We each need a sense of belonging that is created by tradition, history, and a future. These elements create a basis upon which we can depend and find security. Work to create and maintain traditions, and actively speak of family history to help provide and strengthen this center.

Traditions are important to the family and should support your family's values and beliefs; however, they do not need to be expensive. These practices will vary from family to family, and that is not important, but enjoying some family traditions will be a blessing. Examples of traditions might include:

FAMILY TRADITION

- Physical expressions of love - hugs and holding hands to pray, a pat on the back as one passes by, etc. Each of these gestures can develop into a valuable tradition.
- Shared family time – movie night, game night, dinner conversation themes, family meetings to discuss calendars, concerns, joys, sing and/or laugh together. Develop a schedule and plan for these happenings so the family members can look forward to this shared time together.
- Spiritual heritage - attend church together each week, pray before meals, utilize family devotions. Demonstrate how faith molds your life choices and your character. Faith practices provide a strong tradition.
- Holiday celebrations – Days that have significance for your family, marked by faith or culture, should be celebrated. Christmas and Easter are among such days for the Christian faith. The Fourth of July and Thanksgiving mark days of importance for our country. If appropriate for your family, celebrate and create a tradition.

As a family grows and changes, it is essential to talk about family traditions and continue to uphold traditions and establish new ones. Established and practiced habits build memories, love, and affection. So, make traditions a priority for your family.

Some Traditions Need to be Broken

*"Beloved, I pray that all may go well with you
and that you may be in good health,
just as it is well with your soul."*

3 John 1:2

LIVING UNDER ONE roof with others is complicated. Even in strong, healthy families, members have shortcomings. Any family member may create brokenness or heartache, but it is exceedingly hurtful when parents are self-serving, angry, out-of-control, bitter, hostile, or self-destructive. In these situations, the family suffers. For the heartaches and broken dreams, there is great sadness.

Family members may pass qualities on for generations. Both good and bad attributes exist, and when practiced over time, they become habits. Within our families, sometimes our shortcomings are passed on rather than our virtues. For a variety of reasons, some choose to work against one another instead of uplifting each other. This tragedy creates tremendous sorrow. When families carry this burden, it is necessary to seek God and find resources that give support, healing and forgiveness.

SOME TRADITIONS NEED TO BE BROKEN

Practice makes behaviors become patterns. Break the pattern! If that is what's needed, break the pattern! Resist those bad habits. It is not easy to break a habit, but God is there to help and give you the courage and strength needed. With God by your side, a future of greater peace and joy will return to your life.

God offers hope. He will support and comfort you and others in the process of healing and allow you to create new memories and traditions. Together, with the help of our Lord, you can embrace the hope of a bright future and a joyful and healthy family!

"For surely I know the plans I have for you, says the Lord, plans for your welfare and not for harm, to give you a future with hope." Jeremiah 29:11

"Let the wise also hear and gain in learning, and the discerning acquire skill." Proverbs 1:5

FOLLOWING CHRIST

Softly and Tenderly Jesus Is Calling

Softly and tenderly Jesus is calling,
Calling for you and for me;
See, on the portals he's waiting and watching,
Watching for you and for me.

(Refrain)
Come home, come home;
You who are weary come home;
Earnestly, tenderly, Jesus is calling,
Calling, O sinner, come home!

Why should we tarry when Jesus is pleading,
Pleading for you and for me?
Why should we linger and heed not his mercies,
Mercies for you and for me?

O for the wonderful love he has promised,
Promised for you and for me!
Though we have sinned, he has mercy and pardon,
Pardon for you and for me.

Will L. Thompson

Families Grow and Change

> "May the Lord make you increase and abound in love
> for one another and for all,
> just as we abound in love for you."
> 1 Thessalonians 3:12

AS ONES' FAMILY grows and members marry, each new spouse brought into the family opens a new world of interests and opportunities while sharing values and ideals. Lives change when another family is brought into the extended family relations. If and when they choose to have children, the heritages of the two families will blend.

Family heritage, careers, stories, etc., are essential to the family. When you marry, you must realize that you do not just marry a spouse, but also a family. Each family has traditions and a heritage that will blend into a new family structure. This new family will create traditions that will be passed to the future generations of your family, your children's children, and beyond. These traditions are strong influences as they impact one's sense of identity and belonging.

Marriage changes families, but life brings other family changes that may be less joyful and create tremendous stress. Death, divorce, remarriage, in-laws, etc., can cause families to go through unwanted challenges and new beginnings. Change may be difficult but necessary. Honor your unique circumstances and your new family and strive for happiness and unity. Make sure your actions create acceptance for these new families made of loving, wonderful and unique people. Make room for them and reach out in kindness and love. Bonding isn't instant. It is a process of giving, but the result is worth the effort. A new dynamic is developing in a relationship of acceptance and love.

An actual and hard fact of life is that you cannot control other people. It is appropriate that you may invite or try to influence others, but they may not respond. Unfortunately, people sometimes attempt to manipulate or coerce. Realize you cannot make another person do anything, whatever tactic is utilized. If both parties in the situation are not interested in developing a healthy relationship, it may not happen, and you must accept that fact and prayerfully move forward. You can only control yourself and your response. Matthew records Jesus' advice to the disciples as they prepared to go and tell others the message of Christ. "If anyone will not welcome you or listen to your words, shake off the dust from your feet as you leave that house" (Matthew 10:14). As a follower of Christ, you recognize time on earth is short and precious. If someone is not interested in your skills and talents, move on and offer your gifts to those who care. No need to argue or have hard feelings. Just try to keep the door open and pray for healing.

Build your family heritage on godly principles of love, strength, caring, integrity, and sharing. A spiritual legacy is the greatest gift you can give your children and their families. However, memories of time shared in personal interests, community activities, church involvement, and shared time with family, even including shared chores are influential in creating a family that brings a sense of belonging and joy but is also pleasing to God.

Praying Together

> "Rejoice always, pray without ceasing,
> give thanks in all circumstances;
> for this is the will of God in Christ Jesus for you."
> 1 Thessalonians 5:16-18

PRAYER IS ESSENTIAL to your faith. It is our means of talking to God, and when practiced daily, prayer will encourage and strengthen your walk with Christ. Reverend Bob Casady offers insight into prayer. A synopsis of his sermon follows:[67]

A willingness to share with others can expand this gift of worship and prayer. In the Bible, the Book of Acts, the majority of the prayer passages involve people praying together. They pray during a personal crisis, for enemies, for healing, for people entering (hospitality) or leaving their company (good-byes), and for leadership. Their prayer is lifted knowing that there is someone listening, guiding, hearing, caring, and responding to their concerns. They expect God to answer, and he does!

Sharing time in prayer requires a mutual trust between the individuals. This trust will allow openness and sharing of your innermost thoughts and being. All individuals present should understand and respect the privacy of the moment and not judge. During a shared prayer, each individual would pray for the joys or concerns in their hearts, knowing the prayer is lovingly offered to God, who delivers guidance, comfort, and power. The closing of a shared prayer often includes a quiet time to think and listen to what God might be saying or doing.

Praying with others, maybe a dear friend, a brother or sister, a spouse, etc., can be a powerful experience. So, pray that you may find a prayer partner and know the joy of having an open and trusting heart for another human being who can share God's joy with you!

"Therefore, confess your sins to one another, and pray for one another, so that you may be healed." James 5:16

Keep on the Sunny Side

There's a dark and a troubled side of life;
There's a bright and a sunny side, too;
Tho' we meet with the darkness and strife
The sunny side we also may view.

Refrain:
Keep on the sunny side,
Always on the sunny side,
Keep on the sunny side of life,
It will help us every day,
It will brighten all the way,
If we keep on the sunny side of life.

Tho' the storm in its fury breaks today,
Crushing hope that we cherished so dear;
Storm and cloud will in time pass away,
And the sun again will shine bright and clear.

Let us greet with a song of hope each day,
Tho' the moments be cloudy or fair;
Let us trust in our Savior always,
Who keepeth everyone in His care.

Ada Blenkhorn

Related Scriptures

"God is love. Whoever lives in love lives in God, and God in him."
1 John 4:16

"Love one another as I have loved you." John 13:34

"Children, let us love, not in word or speech, but in truth and action."
1 John 3:18

"Above all, maintain constant love for one another for love covers a multitude of sins." 1 Peter 4:8

"Whoever does not love does not know God, for God is love."
1 John 4:8

"And now faith, hope, and love abide, these three, and the greatest of these is love." 1 Corinthians 13:13

"Above all, clothe yourselves with love, which binds everything together in perfect harmony." Colossians 3:14

"Love must be completely sincere. Hate what is evil, hold onto what is good. Love one another warmly as Christian brothers, and be eager to show respect for one another." Romans 12:9-10

"God proves his love for us in that while we still were sinners Christ died for us." Romans 5:8

"Let all that you do be done in love." 1 Corinthians 16:14

"This is my commandment, that you love one another as I have loved you." John 15:12

"They who have my commandments and keep them are those who love me; and those who love me will be loved by my Father, and I will love them and reveal myself to them." John 14:21

"This is the boldness we have in him, that if we ask anything according to his will, he hears us. And if we know that he hears us in whatever we ask, we know that we have obtained the requests made of him." 1 John 5:14-15

Afterword

> "The Lord bless you and keep you;
> The Lord make His face shine upon you,
> and be gracious to you;
> the Lord lift up his countenance upon you,
> and give you peace."
> Numbers 6:24-26

> "Every good and perfect gift comes from the Father."
> James 1:17

TO BE A faithful follower of Christ, you must understand the doctrine of your faith, what you profess to believe. A Christian believes in the Triune God – the Father, the Son, and the Holy Spirit. God created the heavens and the earth and it was perfect until sin entered. Sin is not a result of your opinion, your intention, how you feel or what you think; sin is determined by whether or not the action or deed is in agreement with the Word of God. God did not cause sin, nor did he bring it into existence. The devil tempted Eve in the Garden of Eden, and sin entered our world. We are not unlike Eve. We are sinful beings and are easily tempted to sin. God's love and compassion for humans is the reason he sent his Son, Jesus, to die on the cross to forgive our sins. Three days later, Jesus entered into heaven promising that we may join him. The grace of God allows each of us to receive

AFTERWORD

the gift of salvation through Christ Jesus. Although we are worthy of eternal death, Christ offers us eternal life. Mark has written in his book, chapter 16:16, a reminder as to how we receive this gift, "The one who believes and is baptized will be saved." The Holy Spirit is also an essential part of the Trinity of God. The Holy Spirit guides our comprehension and gives enlightenment and counsel throughout our earthly journey.

When this basic understanding is established, and you choose to believe the Word of God is true, you are a child of God, a follower of Christ. Because of your appreciation and love for the Lord, prayerfully you make efforts to continue to grow and learn about God's guiding principles and commands, striving to interweave God's will into all aspects of your life. You honestly recognize yourself as a sinner in need of repentance and ask for God's forgiveness. As a follower of Christ, you are blessed by God's guidance and wisdom as he offers inner peace, hope, joy, security, and love.

The scripture below, Matthew 28:19-20, is Jesus' message to his disciples at their last meeting together. This passage, known as the Great Commission, is also recorded in Mark 16:15-16.

> "All authority in heaven and on earth has been given to me.
> Go therefore and make disciples of all nations,
> baptizing them in the name of the Father
> and of the Son and of the Holy Spirit,
> and teaching them to obey everything
> that I have commanded you.
> And remember, I am with you always, to the end of the age."
> Matthew 28:19-20

This passage shares Jesus' innermost thoughts as he prepares to leave the disciples and face his own death on the cross. His message entrusts his followers with a task. Jesus tells the disciples to go share with others the message of salvation and teach them God's commandments. As a follower of Christ, that is exactly what God wants of you.

You may wonder how all this translates to your life. To begin, you must acknowledge the majesty of God, he is in control. You must also recognize that your actions, words and deeds will draw others to the goodness of your Lord, and with his grace, cause them to seek Him. It is essential that you continue to learn about Jesus' teachings and strive to be obedient to them in your everyday life. Your daily habits, character traits, and relationships are each areas in which you may show love and honor to God. Seek God and prayerfully live your life as of a Child of God.

> "You shall love the Lord your God with all your heart,
> and with all your soul, and with all your might.
> Keep these words
> that I am commanding you today in your heart.
> Recite them to your children
> and talk about them when you are at home
> and when you are away,
> when you lie down and when you rise.
> Bind them as a sign on your hand,
> fix them as an emblem on your forehead,
> and write them on the doorposts of your house
> and on your gates."
>
> Deuteronomy 6:5-9

The message shared in Deuteronomy 6:5-9 clearly identifies how you can show others you are a follower of Christ. In all life's experiences follow God's example, and share God's love. That is what God wants you to do for him and others. Always remember, you are not alone. God is with you always through his gift of the Holy Spirit.

AFTERWORD

> "What does the Lord your God require of you?
> Only to fear the Lord your God, to walk in all his ways,
> to love him, to serve the Lord your God with all your heart
> and with all your soul,
> and to keep the commandment of the Lord your God
> and his decrees that I am commanding you today,
> for your own well-being."
>
> Deuteronomy 10: 12-13

God has a plan for your life and he wants only what is best for you! Trust God to guide your journey and to give you strength for the trials that come. Your walk on earth is for a short time, you do not belong here. Live this earthly life for the Lord and the everlasting rewards Christ offers will be yours to enjoy today. Live life God's way!

> "Do not let your heart be troubled.
> Believe in God, believe also in me.
> In my Father's house there are many dwelling places.
> If it were not so, would I have told you
> that I go to prepare a place for you?
> And if I go and prepare a place for you,
> I will come again and will take you to myself,
> so that where I am, there you may be also.
> And you know the way to the place where I am going."
>
> John 14:1-4

> "The grace of the Lord Jesus Christ
> the love of God,
> and the communion of the Holy Spirit
> be with all of you."
>
> 2 Corinthians 13:13

Bibliography

Unless otherwise noted, Scripture quotations are from *The Holy Bible, New Revised Standard Version*. Copyright Graded Press 1990. Nashville, Tennessee: Thomas Nelson Publishers, 1990.

Scripture quotations noted GNB are from the *Good News Bible, Today's English Version*. Copyright American Bible Society 1966, 1971, 1976. New York, New York: American Bible Society, 1976.

Scripture quotations noted MSG are from the Peterson, Eugene H. *The Message//Remix*. Copyright Eugene H. Peterson 2003, 2006. Colorado, Colorado: NavPress, 2003.

Scripture quotations noted NASB are from the *New American Standard Bible*. Copyright The Lockman Foundation 1960, 1962, 1963, 1968, 1971, 1972, 1973, 1975, 1977. East Brunswick, New Jersey: World Home Bible League, 1986.

Barclay, William. *The Acts of the Apostles: The New Daily Study Bible*. 3d Ed. Louisville, Kentucky: Westminster John Knox Press, 2003.

BIBLIOGRAPHY

Barclay, William. *The Gospel of John: Volume 1*. Revised Ed. Philadelphia, Pennsylvania: Westminster Press, 1975.

Barclay, William. *The Gospel of John: Volume 2*. Philadelphia, Pennsylvania: Westminster Press, 1956.

Barclay, William. *The Gospel of Luke*. Louisville, Kentucky: Westminster Press, 2001.

Barclay, William. *The Gospel of Matthew: Volume 1*. Revised Ed. Louisville, Kentucky: Westminster John Knox Press, 1975.

Barclay, William. The Letters of James and Peter. Louisville, Kentucky: Westminster John Knox Press. 2003.

Barclay, William. *The Letter to the Romans: The New Daily Study Bible. 3d Ed*. Louisville, Kentucky: Westminster John Knox Press, 2002.

Casady, Robert. *Lessons From the Mountain*. Schweitzer United Methodist Church, Springfield, Missouri; 2008.

Casady, Robert. *Prayer*. Schweitzer United Methodist Church, Springfield, Missouri; 2008.

Filson, Floyd V. *The Layman's Bible Commentary: The Gospel According to John Volume 19*. Richmond, Virginia: John Knox Press, 1963.

Frazer, Sarah. *6 Ways the Holy Spirit Prays for You*. https://www.crosswalk.com/faith/prayer/ways-the-holy-spirit-prays-for-you.html; 4/23/20.

Furtick, Steven. *Crash The Chatterbox*. Colorado Springs, Colorado: Multnomah Books, 2014.

Graham, Billy. *Answers.* https://billygraham.org/answer/gods-gift-of-salvation-is-free/; 4/22/2020.

Hoft, Jessica R., Educator in gifted education program, Columbia, South Carolina.

How Is Salvation A Gift From God? https://www.compellingtruth.org/salvation-gift.html; 4/22/2020.

How to Identify and Effectively Use Your Spiritual Gifts. https://www.crosswalk.com/faith/spiritual-life/how-to-identify-and-effectively-use-your-spiritual-gifts.html; 4/13/2020.

Jenkins, Jerry B. *Twelve Things I Want My Kids To Remember Forever.* Chicago, Illinois: Moody Press, 1991.

Kalenga, Erick. *Following the Path of Discipleship Means Losing Yourself in Christ.* https://starexponent.com/news/following-the-path-of-discipleship-means-losing-yourself-in-christ/article-64cd0541-523d-538d-91f7-9c65355b08c3.html; 9/2/2021.

Koehler, Edward W. A. *A Summary of Christian Doctrine.* St. Louis, Missouri: Concordia Publishing House; 1952.

Leeds, Lilo and Gerard. *Wonderful Marriage.* Great Neck, New York: Luma Press, 2005.

Locklear, Herbert. *The Names of Jesus.* http://www.tentmaker.org/lists/names.html; 12/11/2008.

Luther's Small Catechism with Explanation. St. Louis, Missouri: Concordia Publishing House, 1986.

BIBLIOGRAPHY

Lyons, Eddie. *David and Jonathan*. High Street Church, Springfield, Missouri; November 7, 2021.

Lyons, Eddie. *David and Goliath*. High Street Church, Springfield, Missouri; October 31, 2021.

Miller, Donald G. *The Layman's Bible Commentary: The Gospel According to Luke*. Volume 18. Richmond, Virginia: John Knox Press, 1959.

Moore, Marilyn. Retired educator, Springfield, MO.

Newport, John P. *Layman's Library of Christian Doctrine*, Nashville, Tennessee: Broadman Press, 1984.

Shook, Jerry & Chris. *One Month To Live: Thirty Days To A No-Regrets Life*. Colorado Springs, Colorado: Waterbrook Press, 2008.

Smalley, Erin. *Are You Planning For A Marriage Or Just A Wedding?* https://www.focusonthefamily.com/marriage/are-you-planning-for-a-marriage-or-just-a-wedding/; 4/10/2020.

Van Buren, Abigail. *Adopt Healthy Habits During The New Year*. URL http://www.phillipscollection.org.

Young, Wm. Paul. *The Shack*. Newbury Park, California: Windblown Media, 2007.

Endnotes

1 Kalenga, 1.
2 Newport, 7.
3 Koehler, 14.
4 Young, 98.
5 *Luther's Small Catechism with Explanation,* 13-15.
6 Koehler, 14.
7 Ibid., 14
8 Barclay, *The Gospel of John: Vol. 1, Revised Ed.*, 52.
9 Barclay, *The Gospel of John: Vol. 1, Revised Ed.*, 49.
10 Barclay, *The Gospel of John: Vol. 2,* 151.
11 Filson, 30.
12 Barclay, *The Gospel of John: Vol. 1, Revised Ed.*, 47.
13 Graham, 1.
14 *How is Salvation A Gift From God?* 2.
15 Barclay, *The Gospel of John: Vol. 1, Revised Ed.*, 171.
16 Barclay, *The Acts of the Apostles: The New Daily Study Bible, 3d Ed.*, 210.
17 Ibid., 21.
18 Frazer, 2-3.
19 Ibid., 1.
20 Barclay, *The Acts of the Apostles: The New Daily Study Bible, 3d Ed.,* 21.
21 Koehler, 313.
22 Barclay, *The Letter to the Romans: The New Study Bible. 3d Ed.*, 117.
23 Ibid., 138.
24 Ibid., 23-24.
25 Koehler, 78.
26 Barclay, *The Letter to the Romans: The New Daily Study Bible, 3d Ed.*, 80.
27 Koehler, 285.
28 Ibid., 288.
29 Barclay, *The Gospel of Luke: The New Daily Study Bible,* 232.
30 Barclay, *The Gospel of Luke: The New Daily Study Bible,* 234.
31 Hoft, 2020.
32 Ibid., 2020.
33 Barclay, Gospel of John, Vol. 2, 206-209.
34 Young, 143.

ENDNOTES

35 Young, 97.
36 Casady, *Lessons From the Mountain*, 3/22/2008.
37 Ibid, 3/22/2008.
38 Ibid., 3/29/2008.
39 Koehler, 172.
40 Koehler, 173.
41 Barclay, *The Gospel of Luke*, 144.
42 Barclay, *The Gospel of Matthew: Volume 1*, 397.
43 Barclay, *The Letter to the Romans: The New Daily Study Bible*, 3d Ed., 172.
44 Furtick, 137.
45 Ibid, 162.
46 Barclay, *The Gospel of John: Vol. 1*, 240.
47 Shook, 202.
48 Barclay, *The Letters of James and Peter*, 109-112.
49 Barclay, *The Gospel of John: Volume 2*, 126.
50 Young, 140.
51 Ibid, 227-228.
52 Furtick, 1.
53 Ibid., 107.
54 Ibid., 121.
55 Van Buren, 4C.
56 Jenkins, 49.
57 Ibid., 55.
58 Barclay, *The Letter to the Romans: The New Daily Study Bible, 3d Ed.*, 85.
59 Lyons, *David & Jonathan*, 11/7/2021.
60 Smally, E., 3-5.
61 Leeds, 12.
62 Leeds, 102-116.
63 Lyons, *David & Goliath*, 10/31/2021.
64 Shook, 65.
65 Leeds, 54-65.
66 Ibid., 65.
67 Casady, *Prayer*. 4/6/2008.

Index of Hymns

Abide With Me   334
Amazing Grace   253
Blessed Assurance   108
Beneath the Cross of Jesus   33
Christ Jesus Hath the Power   38
Come Holy Spirit, Heavenly Dove   74
Count Your Blessings   195
Day by Day   160
Fairest Lord Jesus   96
God Be With You   273
God is the Fountain   339
Going with Jesus, Walking Together   152
Great is Thy Faithfulness   137
Have You Counted the Cost   82
Have Thine Own Way Lord   317
He Leadeth Me   69
His Eye Is On the Sparrow   149
I Can't Feel at Home Anymore   78
I Need Thee Every Hour   250
I Surrender All   256
I Will Sing the Wondrous Story   101
It Is Well With My Soul   193
I'd Rather Have Jesus   241
I'm in the Lord's Army   222

INDEX OF HYMNS

Jesus Loves Me   45
Jesus Our Brother, Kind and Good   28
Joyful, Joyful, We Adore Thee   58
Just a Closer Walk with Thee   290
Just As I Am   90
Keep on the Sunny Side   370
Leaning on the Everlasting Arms   166
Low In the Grave He Lay   65
Now the Day is Over   280
O Holy Night   25
O Jesus, I Have Promised   227
Onward Christian Soldiers   183
Praise God from Whom All Blessing Flow   203
Praise Him! Praise Him!   116
Softly and Tenderly Jesus Is Calling   365
Stand Up, Stand Up for Jesus   163
Standing on the Promises   12
Sweet Hour of Prayer   49
Tell Me the Old, Old Story   359
Tell Me the Story of Jesus   356
The Church's One Foundation   114
The Old Rugged Cross   61
The Whole Armor of God   206
This is My Father's World   199
This Little Light of Mine   195
Thy Word, Almighty God   7
'Tis So Sweet To Trust in Jesus   171
To God Be the Glory   85
Trust and Obey   157
Turn Your Eyes upon Jesus   43
What a Friend We Have In Jesus   233
What Wondrous Love is This   128
Whispering Hope   133
Wonderful Words of Life   343

About the Author

The most valued and treasured responsibilities I have held through life are being a wife, a mother, and a grandmother. I am blessed to be married to a God-fearing, supportive, and delightfully kind man, Doug Bloch. Additionally, it has been an honor being the mother to my children, Julianna and Andrew, and my son-in-law, Justin. Together, we enjoy a wide circle of family and friends who have brought great joy to our lives and for whom we are most grateful. We strive to honor God by enjoying music, entertaining, dancing, traveling (especially to visit grandchildren), gardening, cooking, and teaching friends to play bridge. Jan and Doug live in Springfield, Missouri.

My birth family provided me with a spiritual heritage of love for God, family, and creation. In addition, they reinforced the importance of

ABOUT THE AUTHOR

compassion, integrity, persistence, and hard-work. We attended the Lutheran Church, where I was baptized and confirmed. I cannot remember a time when I did not love the Lord. However, through the years, I have grown and discovered a deeper understanding of how the Lord's love for me impacts my life. My family life is blessed with joyful times and happy memories. There have, however, been many challenges. Through each of the trials, it is apparent that the Lord was in the details as he provided sustenance, comfort, and strength. As God promises, I believe he has used our misfortunes and tribulations to strengthen our faith and to further His kingdom.

Professionally, I received a bachelor of fine arts degree in Vocational Education with an emphasis in family living and child development from Missouri State University (MSU). I earned a master's degree from Drury University in Springfield, Missouri, and later a specialist degree from MSU, both in educational administration. My career began in public education as a Family and Consumer Science teacher. Later, I was allowed to serve as an administrator in programs with children from kindergarten to 12th grade. My vocation involved working closely with students, parents and faculty, businesses, and the community.

Upon retirement in 2005, besides spending time with my family, three areas have filled my life and time. First, I taught at the Ozark Technical Community College's Middle College, which serves high school students whose life circumstances make its flexible, non-traditional environment more suitable to their needs. Second, in 2005, I worked with Marie Hewlett, a dear friend in Christ and a professional colleague, to organize and implement a Bible Study for working women called "God's Lunch Bunch." This group met weekly, served lunch during the noon hour, and before the restrictions of the Covid pandemic, had a regular attendance of approximately 50 each week. This group still exists today, fifteen plus years later. Third, my husband Doug and I perform as vocalists and instrumentalists in a family-friendly, fun-filled, acoustic gospel music band called The

Bridgetones. The Bridgetones play at various venues including, community fairs and festivals, special-occasion parties, church socials, retirement communities, and assisted living homes.

In the future, I will continue to strive to serve my God each day and eagerly await the joys and challenges that He has in store. When I meet my Lord at heaven's gates, I pray He will say, "Well done, good and faithful servant."

Printed in the USA
CPSIA information can be obtained at www.ICGtesting.com
CBHW071753300524
9301CB00002B/2